flavors

paul gayler

flavors

photography georgia glynn smith

kyle books

This edition published in 2005 by Kyle Books
An imprint of Kyle Cathie Limited
general.enquiries@kyle-cathie.com
www.kylecathie.com

Distributed by National Book Network
4501 Forbes Blvd., Suite 200
Lanham, MD 20706
Phone: (301) 459 3366 Fax: (301) 429 5746

ISBN 1-904920-14-4

First published in 2002 as *Flavors of the World* by Kyle Cathie Ltd.

Project Editor: Sheila Davies
Editors: Jane Middleton and Morag Lyall
Editorial Assistant: Sarah Epton
Designer: Paul Welti
Photographer: Georgia Glynn Smith
Production: Lorraine Baird and Sha Huxtable

The Library of Congress Cataloguing-in-Publication Data is available on file.

Printed and bound in Singapore by Star Standard

Acknowledgements

To my wife, Anita, and family, without whose support of my endless ambitions and culinary journeys, I might have never have traveled this road.

To Georgia Glynn Smith and Linda Tubby, photographer and food stylist, a talented and formidable team, who were a great delight to work with. To Penny Markham, for locating superb props.

To Jane Middleton and Morag Lyall who, between them, skillfully shaped this book into what it is. To Paul Welti for his inspired design.

To Lara Mand-King, her endless hours of typing and re-typing of the recipes made the foundation of this book possible.

To my Sous-Chefs and all my team at The Lanesborough in London, for always enthusiastically endorsing our kitchens on a daily basis.

To Mr. Geoffrey Gelardi, for his support at all times.

To Fiona and Linda, my agents at Limelight, there for me as always.

A special tribute: to Kyle, Sheila, and all at Kyle Cathie who, once again, have guided me in producing another book. I deeply value their support, enthusiasm, and, more importantly, their friendship. Without them, I could not have begun to bring this entire project together. A big thank you.

Contents

introduction

Flavorings are not the mainstay of our diet, yet imagine how dull food would be without their bright accents. Pungent or delicate, fiery or cooling, they stimulate the appetite, transforming what we eat from mere fodder to something that delights all the senses.

Flavor has been defined as "the blend of taste and smell sensation experienced when food and drink are placed in the mouth" (*International Dictionary of Food and Cooking* by Charles Sinclair). Where flavorings are concerned, this link between taste and aroma is the key to their allure. It is often their smell that draws you to them in the first place, and then makes the food appetizing. Think of ginger, a gnarled and knobbly root whose unglamorous appearance provides no clue to its power. Yet crush it roughly and you are instantly hit by a waft of warm spice, giving you a foretaste of its flavor and offering a world of opportunity, from spicy Indian dals and Chinese stir-fries to rich, sticky gingerbreads.

Over the last twenty years, our love of flavors has become global in its scope, so it's no surprise to see Lemongrass listed next to Mint in this book, or Tamarind next to Salt. Several stints working in the Far East have given me a real passion for flavorings such as lemongrass, ginger, holy basil, cumin, coriander, and chile. These tastes define their native cuisines but I believe they also have a role to play in Western cooking—for example, adding lemongrass to an Italian panna cotta (see page 19). Purists may disapprove, but spices have been imported from the East for centuries, and using them to give vibrancy and excitement to our cooking can be seen as following an honorable tradition.

Herbs and spices are not the only flavorings, of course. When deciding what to include in this book, I couldn't possibly leave out chocolate, coffee, honey, olives, and that overwhelmingly popular condiment, balsamic vinegar. The latter stopped being an exclusively Italian flavoring years ago, and it seems our love affair with it is not over yet. It has undoubtedly been overused but I still think it is one of the great flavors of the world. Like many flavorings, part of the appeal of balsamic vinegar is its versatility: it is just as successful in icecream or sprinkled over strawberries as it is when used in a salad dressing or with meat or fish.

New flavors come into vogue all the time, and two recent ones that spring to mind are lavender and coffee. Lavender has been used in French cuisine for centuries, in both savory and sweet dishes, but it is now being taken up by chefs in the UK and elsewhere. I have always been intrigued by the culinary telepathy that seems to operate between chefs, which means that associated ideas and flavors will suddenly start to crop up in unconnected places. Just recently I have been experimenting with coffee in savory dishes, resulting in my Veal Fillet with Mocha Porcini Sauce (see page 157), among others. On a short break in Paris, I went to the Crillon for lunch, where I was astonished to see that the chef, Dominique Bouchet, had included chicken cooked in coffee butter on the menu.

Now that almost all foods are available all year round, flavorings can act as a gentle reminder of the seasons. Cooling mint and basil add freshness to summer dishes, while cumin and coriander, mustard and cinnamon give a warm glow on winter days. Others have year-round appeal. Rosemary, for example, is wonderful tossed on a summer barbecue to flavor grilled meats or fish, and also makes a superb addition to a hearty

cold-weather dish such as Baked Onions (see page 49).

Using flavorings that are appropriate to the season is reminiscent of the time when they played an important role in peasant cuisine. Fresh herbs and dried spices were an economical way of livening up humble staples such as pasta (for example, chile in the Italian dish, Pasta Arrabbiatta) and lentils (black pepper in the Indian soup, Rasam—see page 94). Some herbs, spices, and flavorings are associated with luxury—think of saffron, vanilla, and balsamic vinegar—but even these need not be expensive, as just a small quantity will leave its unique stamp on a dish.

Each flavoring in this book really deserves an entire book to itself, and there simply hasn't been space for all the recipes I would have liked to include. But for every flavoring I have given a list of complementary flavors, which I hope will inspire you to come up with your own ideas for using them. Remember that flavorings should enhance food rather than overpower it, and try not to mix too many together, otherwise it confuses the palate. If in any doubt, think about the country the flavoring comes from and combine it with ones from the same area.

I hope you will enjoy the recipes in this book and be inspired to create your own world of flavors. One final tip: herbs, spices, and other flavorings should be as fresh as possible, otherwise they lose their potency and their magical ability to transform a dish. Use fresh herbs and on ingredients such as mustards and vinegars, jot down the date you bought them so you can keep an eye on their age, and buy dried spices in small quantities as you need them.

ALL RECIPES SERVE 4 UNLESS OTHERWISE STATED.

coriander *Coriandrum sativum*

Coriander leaves, known as Chinese parsley in the East and cilantro in the West, are grown from the coriander seed and are related to both parsley and carrots. Coriander is now one of the most popular and commonly used herbs worldwide. Today it is prevalent in the most fashionable cuisines in the world, such as North African, Greek, Middle Eastern, Indian, Thai, Malaysian, Chinese, Mexican, and American; in fact in most of the "hotter" food regions of the world.

recipes

The Chinese have been using cilantro since 5000 B.C., and it is frequently mentioned in the Bible, so its popularity soon spread far and wide. History tells us that cilantro (*Coriandrum sativum*) is indigenous to southern Europe, where it was used for medicinal, as well as culinary, purposes for 5,000 years. It was the Romans who first introduced it to Britain in the form of fresh leaves.

DESCRIPTION

Opinions are divided as to the taste of its leaves: some say it's soapy, others that it has strong elements of cut wet grass, forest humus, and wild mushrooms such as chanterelles. For me, the taste is grassy and a bit oily, with an aftertaste that combines bitter and sweet to leave a faint lemon flavor on the tongue. But I do agree that the scent and flavor of coriander leaves (cilantro) are curiously hard to pin down. The name coriander derives from the Greek word *koris*, meaning insect or bug, and it has been said that the plant smells like a bed-bug, which I find hard to imagine.

Whatever side of the fence you are on, I personally believe it is a wonderful herb that I could not live without. I find it a breath of fresh air, packed with flavor. If you haven't tasted it yet, try it. I assure you it will soon become a passion.

Cilantro leads an exciting dual life as both a herb and a spice. It is an annual (and occasionally a perennial) herb, which grows up to 8 to 10 inches high and has many branches. Its fragrant leaves and wispy stems give cilantro a delicate look. The plant bears flowers which mature into seeds, which are picked when ripe. If you are ever lucky enough to eat them green and fresh, you are in for a real treat—an experience I had in Spain in one of the world's greatest restaurants, El Raco de Con Farbas (St. Celoni), near Barcelona. More commonly, however, the seeds are dried and used with other spices in many preparations, such as sauces and marinades. The seeds are used both whole and ground. I love the herb and the spice (they have very different tastes) but, for me, the leaves have the most magical properties.

BUYING AND STORING

Whenever I purchase cilantro in supermarkets, I find the small packages are never large enough so I find it is better and infinitely cheaper to buy it in bunches from Asian stores. When bought like this you have an added bonus: the plant's roots are still attached. These not only prolong the life of the herb, but have a wonderful strong flavor and are used in some recipes such as in spicy pastas, sauces, and Indian-style breads.

If you need to keep cilantro for longer than one day, I find it is better to stand the plant in a jar of water, enclose the whole bunch in a plastic bag, and set it in the fridge. This year I will attempt to grow cilantro in my own garden, as I use it so frequently. It is a hardy plant, easy to grow in warmish climates where an early spring sowing is possible.

For cooking, good-quality seeds can either be bought whole, or ground. Since ground coriander

quickly loses its flavor, it is best to grind your own seeds, which is easily done using a mortar and pestle or a spice or coffee grinder. The whole seeds will keep almost indefinitely.

CULINARY USES

Cilantro is used extensively in Mexican, Indian, and Thai cooking. The herb's peppery, slightly coarse, lemon-anise flavor, when added to hot dishes especially, provides a cooling balance to other ingredients such as chiles. It also makes a great partner to lemongrass, coconut milk (which, along with chile, creates the quintessential "Thai" taste), cumin, and tamarind.

Cilantro also has a great affinity with tomatoes, garlic, lemons, and limes. I love it chopped or whole, added to soups and salads, and made into power-packed chile sauces to go with fried eggs (see page 11). When cooked, it loses some of its harshness, and imparts a deeper flavor rather than a sharp accent. For greatest effect in cooked dishes, it is best thrown in at the very last moment.

In Indian cooking, cilantro is usually chopped up and used as a garnish on curries and raitas (yogurt-based salad dips). In Mexican cooking, the leaves are generally used in soups, salsas, and marinades where the flavors are allowed to infuse and develop. Cilantro roots, which have a concentrated and intense flavor, are often used in Thai cooking. Gai Yang (grilled chicken with cilantro sauce), for example, uses the leaves, stalk, and roots. Cilantro also plays an important role in Thai salads (such as Gado gado, a vegetable salad with peanut sauce) and is added to curry pastes and breads.

Cilantro seeds, which are often lightly roasted first to enhance their flavor, are used in minced meat dishes such as Middle Eastern koftas, Mexican enchiladas, English black puddings (blood sausage), and sausages such as Italian mortadella. They are also added to cakes, gingerbreads, and chutneys. Finely-ground cilantro is a key ingredient in spice mixes such as garam masala (with cloves, cinnamon, cardamon, and black pepper), with cumin in chermoula, with garlic in taklia, and with chiles in salsas and zoug.

The French use it in sauces such as antiboise (with olive oil, garlic, and tomatoes) which is served with fish.

OTHER USES

Like most herbs, cilantro has reputed medical properties and Chinese doctors have long considered its seed a powerful remedy for flatulence, arthritis, chest infections, and for general well-being.

complementary flavors

COCONUT MILK

SPICES (ESPECIALLY GINGER AND CINNAMON)

YOGURT

FRUIT (FIGS, NECTARINES, LEMONS, LIMES, MANGOES, AND GREEN MANGOES)

VEGETABLES (TOMATOES, CUCUMBER, ONIONS, AND GARLIC)

CHICKEN

FISH AND SHELLFISH

beet, tomato, and cilantro salad with labna

14 oz. new-season baby beets
7 oz. (1 1/4 cups) red cherry tomatoes, cut in half
4 oz. (2/3 cup) yellow cherry tomatoes, cut in half
Juice of 1/2 lemon
6 tablespoons virgin olive oil
1/2 teaspoon cilantro seeds, lightly cracked in a mortar and pestle
Cayenne pepper
4 oz. (2 1/2 cups) fresh cilantro, leaves only
20 small balls of labna cheese
Salt

Place the beets in a pan, cover with cold water, and bring to a boil. Reduce the heat to a simmer and cook until they are just tender (alternatively, you could steam them). Drain well and peel. Cut the beets into halves or quarters, so they are approximately the same size as the tomatoes. Place the beets and tomatoes in a large bowl and add the lemon juice, olive oil, and cilantro seeds. Season with salt and a little cayenne, and toss the whole lot together. Finally toss in the fresh cilantro leaves, then serve, topped with the balls of labna cheese.

Paul's Tip Labna is a strained yogurt cheese, available from Middle Eastern food stores and some supermarkets. It is easy to make at home: simply strain some thick, whole-milk yogurt through a piece of cheesecloth over a period of two days to drain off the whey, leaving you with a firm yogurt cheese. Roll into small balls between your hands.

aztec eggs

This hearty dish is served with a green salsa made from cilantro, green chiles, and tomatillos. Tomatillos are a vital ingredient in many Mexican dishes, particularly sauces and salads. They are related to the cape gooseberry (physallis), and are not green tomatoes, as is often believed. However, if you cannot find fresh tomatillos (canned ones aren't suitable for this recipe), green tomatoes make an acceptable substitute.

Oil for frying
9 oz. (1 1/2–2 cups) cooked new potatoes, peeled and sliced 1/2-inch thick
3 oz. (1/2 cup) chorizo, cut into 1/4-inch cubes
4 corn tortillas
4 organic or cage-free eggs
Salt and freshly ground black pepper

FOR THE GREEN SALSA:

6 oz. (about 6 medium) tomatillos (or green tomatoes)
2 green chiles
1 garlic clove, chopped
1/4 cup chopped cilantro

First make the salsa. If using tomatillos, remove the husks first, then place all the ingredients in a food processor or blender and blitz to a coarse purée. Season with salt and pepper, transfer to a bowl, and set aside.

Heat some oil in a frying pan, add the potatoes, and cook until golden on both sides. Add the chorizo and cook for 2 minutes. Season to taste, remove from the pan, and keep warm.

Wipe out the frying pan, add some more oil, and fry each tortilla until lightly golden and slightly puffed. Remove from the pan and keep warm. Finally fry the eggs, adding more oil to the pan if necessary, and season them with salt and pepper.

To serve, put a tortilla on each serving plate and top with the potato and chorizo mixture. Place a fried egg on each pile, spoon the green salsa on top, and serve immediately.

fava beans with pancetta and cilantro

Fava beans are a much underrated vegetable, to my mind. In France they are partnered with savory, in Italy with mint, and in Portugal with cilantro. If I had to make a choice, I think the cilantro just gets it—particularly when combined with salty pancetta, as in this recipe. These beans make a wonderful accompaniment to chicken or fish.

4 1/2 lbs. (5–6 cups shelled beans) fava beans (unshelled weight)
3 oz. (1/3–1/2 cup) piece of smoked pancetta, cut into small dice
1 onion, finely chopped
1 bunch of cilantro, chopped
Salt and freshly ground black pepper

Shell the fava beans and cook them in a pan of boiling salted water for 4–5 minutes, until just tender. Drain well, refresh in cold water, then drain again and peel off the thin skins. Set aside.

Heat a heavy frying pan over high heat. Add the pancetta and fry until it is golden brown and has released its fat. Remove from the pan with a slotted spoon and set aside. Add the onion to the fat in the pan, reduce the heat, and cook until it is tender but not colored. Return the beans and pancetta to the pan, season to taste, then toss it with the chopped cilantro and serve.

cilantro-marinated sardines with coconut milk

This is one of my favorite appetizers. It is so simple to prepare, but has an amazing flavor and freshness. Make sure that your sardines are very fresh or the result will not be as good. If you prefer, fresh tuna (sliced very thinly) could replace the sardines in this Asian-inspired dish.

10 very fresh medium-sized sardines, filleted
Leaves from 1 large bunch of cilantro
14 oz. can of unsweetened coconut cream
Juice of 4 limes
1 small red chile, seeded and finely chopped
2 tablespoons virgin olive oil
A pinch of cayenne pepper
5 oz. green beans
Salt and freshly ground black pepper
Lime wedges, for serving

Rinse the sardine fillets under cold running water to clean them thoroughly, then pat dry with a cloth. Layer the fillets in a bowl with the cilantro leaves in between each layer, reserving some cilantro for garnish.

In another bowl, whisk together the coconut cream, lime juice, chile, and olive oil. Season with salt, pepper, and cayenne, then pour this mixture over the sardines and let it marinate in the fridge for 6 hours.

Cook the green beans in boiling salted water until just tender, then drain well and adjust the seasoning. Divide between 4 serving plates. Arrange the sardine fillets on top, pour some of the marinading juice over them and garnish with lime wedges and the remaining cilantro leaves. Serve chilled.

cilantro-lime broiled figs

You may be amazed by this recipe—broiled figs in a vibrant green, spicy syrup that really adds zip to the fruit. A good dollop of icecream is all that is needed to complete an unusual dessert that never fails to impress.

1 bunch of cilantro
Juice from a 2-inch piece of fresh ginger root
Juice and grated zest of 2 limes
1/2 pint (1 1/4 cups) Sauternes (or other sweet wine)
1/4 pint (2/3 cup) glucose syrup (if unavailable, use corn syrup)
4 green cardamom pods, split
12 ripe purple figs
1 1/2 teaspoons vanilla sugar (see page 143)

Separate the cilantro leaves from the stalks. Put the stalks in a pan along with the ginger juice, lime juice and zest, wine, glucose syrup, and cardamom pods, and bring gently to a boil. Reduce the heat and simmer for 5 minutes. Add the whole figs and poach gently for 3 minutes, then remove from the heat and let cool.

Remove the figs from the syrup and set aside. Return the syrup to the heat and simmer until it begins to thicken. Meanwhile, blanch the cilantro leaves in a large pan of boiling water for a few seconds, then drain well and refresh in ice water. Drain again and pat dry. Add the cilantro leaves to the hot syrup and leave for 2–3 minutes. Pour the mixture into a blender and blitz until smooth. Strain and let cool, then chill.

Cut the figs lengthwise in half and place on a baking tray. Sprinkle with the vanilla sugar and place under a hot broiler for 2–3 minutes, until caramelized. Arrange the figs on serving plates, drizzle the syrup over them, and serve.

lemongrass *Cymbopogon citratus*

This is grown in tropical Asia, but has spread to Africa and America and can, in fact, be grown successfully anywhere with a temperate climate. It is said that Queen Victoria regularly enjoyed lemongrass tea during her reign.

recipes

DESCRIPTION

Growing in tall bunches of leaves on a 3-foot perennial, greenish plant, lemongrass (*Cymbopogon citratus*) is a grass-like herb with a refreshing citrus tang and flavor, with gingerish overtones.

Similar to scallions in appearance, it is generally used as a seasoning and aromatic in southern Asia, although nowadays it is one Asian flavor that crosses over comfortably with Western-style dishes.

BUYING AND STORING

When buying lemongrass, look for firm, smooth stems and green leaves without any brown edges. Lemongrass loses its flavor within a few days of being picked, so buy it as fresh as possible and use it up quickly. Having said this, it will keep for a couple of weeks, if wrapped in paper in the fridge. Ensure, however, that it is securely covered, as its smell can permeate other foods.

PREPARATION

To prepare lemongrass, first discard the tough upper end of the stalk and use only the bottom 5–6 inches. Lemongrass can be used in a number of ways. Trimmed with a knife, the stems make a flavorful and strong skewer for broiling fish, meat, and fruit. When adding to soups and other dishes as a flavoring, the stalk should be coarsely cut into pieces and then bruised (by bashing them with the back of a knife or a pestle, like the Thais do). This helps to release the inner oils and lemony flavor. The pieces, which will be quite tough, should be removed before serving. Another way to use lemongrass is to strip away all the hard outer layers and slice the tender inner core, very finely, into rings. These can be added to all sorts of dishes, from salads to stir-fries.

Dried lemongrass is available, as is a variety in a water solution in a jar; I find both rather flavorless so unless you can get the real thing, I suggest you leave it out. Occasionally, I resort to using a little finely grated lemon zest, simply soaked in water for 2 hours before using (1 tablespoon is roughly equal to 1 fresh lemongrass stalk) as a substitute. This won't, however, achieve the unique flavor of lemongrass.

CULINARY USES

Lemongrass, with its distinctive citrus and ginger notes, is a key ingredient in Thai cooking and is often used as a flavoring for seafood. In traditional Thai and Vietnamese cooking, the stems are used whole and also roughly cut to flavor soups, curries, and stews, while the tender inner parts are used in Asian spice pastes. I find that, when chopped very finely, they equally give a wonderful twist to Western-style dressings and salads.

As a delicate flavoring in a soup (try my Lemongrass and Crab Broth, page 16), sautéed with wild mushrooms, or used in a set custard with coconut milk, lemongrass always gives an intriguingly different flavor note.

OTHER USES

Lemongrass tea is said to be good for stimulating appetite and, as a mild diruretic, helps to clear the skin. The essential oil is used in aromatherapy to treat stress-related conditions, as it has a sedative effect, and can also serve as an insect repellent.

complementary flavors

- GARLIC
- SHALLOTS
- CHILES
- FRESH CILANTRO
- SHELLFISH (ESPECIALLY SHRIMP, LOBSTER, AND CRAB)
- MEAT (ESPECIALLY PORK)
- COCONUT MILK

lemongrass and crab broth

1¼ pints (3½ cups) well-flavored fish broth (or chicken broth)
14 oz. can of chopped tomatoes
2 teaspoons grated fresh ginger root (or galangal)
4 lemongrass stalks, white part only, cut in half lengthwise
2 kaffir lime leaves
4 oz. Chinese vermicelli rice noodles
1 teaspoon brown sugar
1 garlic clove, crushed
1½ teaspoons *nam pla* (Thai fish sauce)
1 lb. fresh white crabmeat
4 scallions, finely shredded
A handful of baby spinach leaves (optional)
8 Thai basil leaves, torn into small pieces
Salt and freshly ground black pepper

Put the broth in a saucepan along with the tomatoes, ginger, lemongrass, and lime leaves, and bring to a boil. Reduce the heat and simmer for 8–10 minutes, then remove and discard the lemongrass. Add the noodles, sugar, and garlic and simmer for 3–4 minutes.

Stir in the fish sauce, crabmeat, scallions, and spinach, if using, and heat through for 2 minutes. Season to taste, sprinkle the Thai basil over it and serve immediately.

wok-fried fungi with lemongrass

2 tablespoons sesame oil
2 tablespoons unsalted butter
1 garlic clove, crushed
2 shallots, finely chopped
1¼ lbs. mixed mushrooms (such as oysters, shiitake, trompettes, and girolles), cut into thick pieces
2 lemongrass stalks, outer layers removed, tender inner core very finely chopped
A handful of cilantro leaves
1 tablespoon soy sauce
Salt and freshly ground black pepper

Heat a wok until almost smoking, add the sesame oil and butter, then add the garlic and shallots and cook for 30 seconds. Throw in the wild mushrooms and stir-fry for 2 minutes. Add the lemongrass, cilantro leaves, and soy sauce and toss well. Season to taste and serve immediately.

lemongrass soy chicken skewers

4 skinless, boneless chicken breasts, cut into 1-inch cubes
8 lemongrass stalks, outer layers removed

FOR THE MARINADE:

1 tablespoon honey or maple syrup
4 garlic cloves, crushed
1-inch piece of fresh ginger root, finely chopped
2 green chiles, finely chopped
Juice of 2 limes

Grated zest of 1 lime
1/4 cup rice wine vinegar
2 tablespoons sweet chili sauce
1/4 cup dark soy sauce, plus extra for serving
A pinch of turmeric

Place all the marinade ingredients in a bowl and mix together well. Add the chicken, then cover and let it marinate in the fridge for at least 8 hours—preferably 2 days, for the best flavor.

Remove the chicken cubes from the marinade and thread them onto the 8 lemongrass stalks. Heat a barbecue, ideally, or a ridged grill pan until smoking. Add the skewers and cook for 8–10 minutes, turning them regularly and brushing liberally with the marinade. Serve hot from the grill, with some extra soy sauce for dipping.

lemongrass, coconut, and vanilla panna cotta

1 vanilla pod
2 lemongrass stalks, outer layers removed
12 fl oz. heavy cream
1/4 pint unsweetened coconut milk
1 1/2 oz. superfine sugar
1 1/2 gelatin leaves
Assortment of exotic fruits (such as mango, papaya, lychee, and dragonfruit), peeled and diced, for serving

FOR THE PASSIONFRUIT-CHILI SYRUP:
2 passionfruit, cut in half
3 1/2 fl oz. sugar syrup (see page 153)
Juice and grated zest of 1/2 a lime
1/8 teaspoon seeded and finely diced red chile

Cut the vanilla pod in half lengthwise and scrape out the seeds with the tip of a sharp knife. Bruise the lemongrass (see page 14) and shred it finely. Heat the cream, coconut milk, vanilla seeds, lemongrass, and sugar in a pan but do not let it boil. Meanwhile, cover the gelatin leaves with cold water for 5 minutes, then squeeze out the excess water. Remove the cream mixture from the heat, add the softened gelatin, and stir until dissolved. Let cool, stirring occasionally, then strain into individual tumbler-style glasses, and place in the fridge overnight.

For the passionfruit-chili syrup, scrape the juice and seeds from the passionfruit into a small pan, add the broth syrup, and heat gently. Leave for 10–15 minutes to infuse, then strain. Add the lime juice and zest, and the diced chile and let cool.

Arrange the exotic fruits on top of the panna cotta, pour over a little of the chili syrup, and serve.

lychee and lemongrass sorbet

I think lychees are one of those exotic fruits that were made to be canned. They work much better than fresh in this particular sorbet.

2 tablespoons superfine sugar
1 tablespoon finely grated fresh ginger root
4 lemongrass stalks, outer layers removed, tender inner core very finely chopped
1 lb 14 oz. (5-6 cups) canned lychees in syrup
2 tablespoons white rum

Place the sugar, ginger, and lemongrass in a pan with 3 1/2 fl oz. water. Bring to a boil and simmer for 5 minutes, until the sugar has dissolved. Remove from the heat and let cool.

Drain the lychees, reserving 2/3 cup of their syrup. Purée the lychees in a blender, then add the reserved lychee syrup and the lemongrass syrup and blitz to a smooth purée. Strain through a fine mesh strainer into a bowl and stir in the rum. Pour into an icecream machine and freeze according to the manufacturer's instructions. Or if you don't have an icecream machine, refer to the tip on page 180.

lavender *Lavandula angustifolia & L. latifolia*

Lavender has been valued for centuries, not just for its sweet-smelling freshness and use as a beauty fragrance, but as a culinary herb with medicinal qualities.

The French have long admired lavender; Provence in spring presents the glorious sight of field after field of mauve lavender and the air is heavy with the scent of the flowers in full bloom. A sensory experience I will never forget.

recipes

OLIVE OIL AND LAVENDER-SCENTED GUINEA FOWL (PAGE 22)

TWICE-COOKED DUCK WITH LAVENDER HONEY (PAGE 23)

APRICOT AND LAVENDER MARMALADE (PAGE 23)

PEAR BEIGNETS DUSTED WITH LAVENDER SUGAR (PAGE 24)

STUFFED APPLES WITH RHUBARB CRUMBLE AND LAVENDER (PAGE 24)

SEE ALSO:

LAVENDER HONEY AND SAUTERNES LACQUERED NECTARINES (PAGE 162)

DESCRIPTION

Lavender is a perennial plant that may reach between 1 and 3 feet tall. There are three main varieties, although these in turn have up to thirty other varieties. The color of the flowers varies depending on the type, with spikes usually appearing in early summer. Only the English (*Lavandula angustifolia*) and French (*L. latifolia*) versions are suitable for cooking. French lavender, which has smaller spikes, is more akin to rosemary and it is without doubt the best one for culinary use. English lavender, or "true lavender" as it is more commonly known in Britain, is to this day generally used in aromatic bath oils. It is very fragrant and ideal for perfumes. Both English and French lavender are, incidentally, native to the Mediterranean.

BUYING/SELECTING

Nowadays, although lavender is still somewhat hard to obtain, there is a move among chefs to make more use of it. Chefs like myself, in an effort to create new dishes and flavor combinations, buy lavender from flower markets and growers, so if you take the trouble, it is available.

When buying lavender, however, it is important to buy it untreated with pesticides or fragrance enhancers, which not only affect its gentle natural aroma but could upset your digestion. If you are unsure if it has been treated or not, wash it thoroughly.

There is no doubt in my mind that lavender is in for a major comeback over the next few years. It has a unique flavor, but it must be fresh. On no account be tempted to use sachets or potpourri bags with their chemically intensified aroma, making them inedible. Ideally, pick your own lavender in the wild or from the garden.

PREPARATION AND STORING

To prepare lavender, simply pick off the little flowers from the stems and use as directed by the recipe.

When recipes call for dried flowers, simply place the flowers on a baking sheet and dry in a preheated very slow oven (about 120°F) for 1 hour.

Alternatively, for those in a hurry, you can place the flowers between a brown paper bag and microwave for 1 minute. The paper will absorb the moisture.

Lavender should be stored in an airtight container, in the fridge.

CULINARY USES

In Provence, lavender is used to make wonderful honey but is also used in sauces, to flavor delicate crème brûlées, to sweeten fruit tarts and as an interesting flavor for a sauce with roast duck (page 23).

Elsewhere in Europe, especially the Mediterranean, lavender also has a place in cooking. The Moroccans, for example, use dried lavender with salt and spices to flavor broiled meats; in fact, I have an old recipe for ras el hanout in my possession which contains lavender.

If you browse through old English recipes, you will discover that lavender was used extensively in

complementary flavors

SOFT CHEESES (ESPECIALLY RICOTTA AND MASCARPONE)

ROSEMARY

MEAT (ESPECIALLY LAMB, CHICKEN, AND DUCK)

DRIED FRUIT (IN PRESERVES)

HONEY

DAIRY PRODUCTS (EGGS, CUSTARD, AND CREAMS)

NUTS (ESPECIALLY WALNUTS)

cooking; its intense yet gentle sweetness valued in puddings and in candied fruits.

Cooking with lavender opens up a great range of interesting uses. I like to use it to flavor milk puddings, custards, butters, mousses, sauces, and icecreams. I have also used lavender successfully in a stuffing for roasted fowl; or added to salads as you would other flowers.

Some of my recipes call for **Lavender pollen**, which is the name given to ground lavender flowers. To make, simply dry the flowers (as described under "preparation"), then place in a mortar or blender and blitz to a fine powder. Use this to flavor all sorts of dishes: for instance, add to pasta with chopped parsley and walnuts, or to ricotta with lemon and lime zest and cream to make a wonderful mousse.

For **Lavender sugar**, to sprinkle over fruit tarts, to use in jam-making, or to coat crisply fried fruit beignets, simply place the lavender flowers in a jar of superfine sugar and leave for 2 weeks before using. Generally, 1 part lavender to 10 parts sugar is a good guide.

Dried lavender flowers make a wonderful garnish for desserts and pastries. Either crystallize them in sugar, or cook them in caramel before crumbling into small pieces as lavender praline.

Lavender praline

½ cup superfine sugar
1 oz. fresh lavender flower only

Place the sugar and lavender in a pan and melt over a medium heat until brown and caramelized. Pour on to a greaseproof tray, and let cool. Pound to a fine powder or blitz in a blender. Makes a great topping for icecreams and mousses.

OTHER USES

Lavender has a number of uses, but it has long been recognized for its sedating effect on the nervous system—which is why Queen Elizabeth I drank lavender-infused water daily as a relief for her well-documented migraines and other ailments. She also had her breakfast conserves flavored with lavender. The Elizabethans considered it an aromatic stimulant and it was used to revive ladies after fainting. The oil is very versatile and is often used in skin care, to ease and treat acne, insect bites, and diaper rash.

olive oil and lavender-scented guinea fowl

With lavender's closeness in taste to rosemary, it makes perfect sense to use it as you would rosemary with roast poultry. The people of southern France have long used lavender with chicken and duck. Always look for untreated lavender, free of additives and other harmful properties.

1/2 cup (1 stick) unsalted butter
1 lemon
1 tablespoon chopped summer savory
1 tablespoon lavender pollen (see page 21)
3 1/2 4 lbs. guinea fowl
3 1/2 fl oz. (1/2 cup) olive oil
1/4 pint (2/3 cup) Sauternes (or another sweet white wine)
1/2 pint (1 1/4 cups) well-flavored chicken broth
Salt and freshly ground black pepper

FOR THE VEGETABLES:
14 oz. (about 15 tiny ones) baby new potatoes, scrubbed
1 eggplant, cut into 1-inch dice
1 red pepper, cut into quarters
1 fennel bulb, cut into wedges
8 garlic cloves, unpeeled

In a bowl, beat the butter to soften it slightly, then grate in the zest from the lemon and add the chopped savory and lavender pollen. Mix well and season with salt and pepper. Season the guinea fowl all over with salt and pepper. Carefully lift the skin of the breast and push the flavored butter underneath so it sits on top of the breasts. Place in the fridge to firm up for 1 hour.

Preheat the oven to 400°F. Place the guinea fowl in a large flameproof roasting pan. Cut the lemon in half and rub it all over the fowl, squeezing the juice over it. Pour the olive oil over the bird, then place in the oven and roast for 30 minutes. Remove from the oven, add the potatoes, and return to the oven until they are tender and golden. Add the remaining vegetables and cook until lightly caramelized.

Transfer the guinea fowl and vegetables to a serving dish and keep warm. Place the roasting pan on the stove over medium-high heat, add the sweet white wine, and bring to a boil, stirring to scrape up any residue from the bottom of the pan. Add the broth, return to a boil, and simmer until the sauce has reduced enough to coat the back of a spoon. Adjust the seasoning, then pour the sauce over the guinea fowl and serve surrounded by the roasted vegetables.

twice-cooked duck with lavender honey

If you have any reservations about using lavender in cooking, do me one favour and try this roasted duck dish. I promise you it will open your eyes to its possibilities. The sauce has a wonderfully rich flavor that acts as a superb foil for the duck—go on, give it a try!

4 teaspoons fresh lavender flowers
1 tablespoon thyme leaves
1/4 teaspoon black peppercorns
2 teaspoons coarse salt
1 x 5 lb. duck, with all giblets removed, but the liver set aside for later
3 fl oz. (1/3 cup) red wine vinegar
1 pint (2 1/2 cups) duck broth (or chicken broth)
1/4 pint (2/3 cup) red wine
2 tablespoons lavender honey
2 tablespoons vegetable oil
4 slices of baguette, toasted (1/2-inch thick)
Salt and freshly ground black pepper

Preheat the oven to 400°F. Place half the fresh lavender flowers in a mortar (or spice grinder), add the thyme, peppercorns, and salt and grind to a powder. With a knife, lightly score the duck breasts in a criss-cross pattern, ensuring you don't cut through the breasts. Rub the surface and outside of the duck with half the ground spice mixture. Place the duck in a flameproof roasting pan and roast for 1 3/4 hours.

Remove from the oven, transfer the duck to a plate and keep warm. Pour off excess fat from the pan and place it on the stove over a high heat. Pour in the red wine vinegar and bring to a boil, stirring to loosen any residue from the bottom of the pan. Pour in the broth and red wine and return to a boil. Place the duck back in the pan and brush half the lavender honey over it. Return to the oven and cook, basting the duck once or twice with the pan juices, brushing it with the remaining honey and sprinkling the remaining spice mixture over it. After about 15 minutes the duck should be beautifully caramelized. Remove it from the flameproof roasting pan and keep warm. Put the roasting pan back on the stove and simmer the cooking liquid until it is thick enough to coat the back of a spoon. Strain through a fine mesh strainer, then taste and adjust the seasoning. Keep warm.

Sauté the duck liver in the vegetable oil for 3–4 minutes. Remove and mash in a bowl along with a little salt and pepper, then spread it over the 4 toasted baguette slices. Cut the duck into 8 pieces and arrange in a serving dish. Pour the sauce over the duck and garnish with the liver toasts.

apricot and lavender marmalade

This marmalade makes a great breakfast treat, spread thickly on buttered country toast or brioche. If, like me, you don't worry too much about the calories, top it with a dollop of crème fraîche or sour cream. Close your eyes and you could be in Provence.

MAKES ABOUT 3 LBS.

2 1/4 lbs. apricots
2 1/4 lbs. (5 cups) superfine sugar
Juice of 1/2 lemon
1/2 cup lavender honey
2 tablespoons dried lavender flowers

Cut the apricots in half and pit them. Combine the apricots, sugar, and lemon juice in a boiling-water canner or large, heavy pot. Let macerate for 3–4 hours at room temperature.

Place the pot on the heat, add the honey and dried lavender, and bring to a boil over high heat, stirring often. Reduce the heat and cook for 40 to 45 minutes, scraping the bottom of the pot with a wooden spoon occasionally so the mixture doesn't burn.

To test if the marmalade has reached setting point (220°F on a sugar thermometer), put a teaspoonful of it on a cold saucer, leave it for a minute or two, then push it with your finger—if it wrinkles, the marmalade is ready. Remove from the heat and let it stand for 10 minutes. Pour into sterilized jars (see below) and seal.

Paul's Tip To sterilize jars, wash them thoroughly in hot soapy water, then rinse well and place on a baking tray. Dry in an oven preheated to 275°F.

pear beignets dusted with lavender sugar

Lavender sugar has a wonderful perfume that can pervade a room. It is best made in advance, for it just gets better as time goes by. Be sure to make plenty, as it is also good sprinkled on fruit tarts and other sweet confections.

4 ripe pears
Oil for deep-frying

FOR THE LAVENDER SUGAR:

5 tablespoons superfine sugar
1 1/2 teaspoons dried lavender flowers

FOR THE BATTER:

6 oz. all-purpose flour
1 egg
2 egg yolks
2 tablespoons olive oil
4 teaspoons superfine sugar
A pinch of salt
1/2 pint (1 1/4 cups) whole milk

To make the lavender sugar, mix the superfine sugar and lavender flowers together, place in a sealed jar, and leave for up to 2 weeks, ideally, although it's fine to use it right away, if necessary.

For the batter, whisk all the ingredients together, holding back half the milk. When smooth, whisk in the remaining milk. Strain through a fine mesh strainer and let it to rest for 30 minutes before using.

Peel the pears, remove the core, and cut them into thick slices or wedges. Heat the oil to 325°F in a deep-fat fryer or a large, deep pot. Dip the pears into the batter and fry them in the hot oil until golden and crisp. Drain on paper towels and place in a serving dish. Sprinkle liberally with the lavender sugar and serve immediately.

Paul's Tip If you don't have a thermometer, test the oil temperature by adding a cube of day-old bread to the pan; if it browns in 30 seconds, the oil is hot enough.

stuffed apples with rhubarb crumble and lavender

Here is a sexy preparation for our much-loved apple crumble, served in a baked apple. The crumble mixture includes dried lavender, which gives it an unusual fragrant taste.

1 1/4 lbs. (5 cups) rhubarb, chopped
Juice and grated zest of 1 orange
1/3 cup raw (or brown) sugar
1 teaspoon ground cinnamon
4 Russet or Golden Delicious apples

FOR THE CRUMBLE TOPPING:

5 oz. (1 1/4 cups) all-purpose flour
1 teaspoon baking powder
3 oz. (1/3 cup) raw (or brown) sugar
1 teaspoon lavender pollen (see page 21)
3 oz. (3/4 cup) blanched almonds, chopped (optional)
1/3 cup (3/4 stick) unsalted butter, diced
1 teaspoon lavender flowers, for decorating

Put the rhubarb, orange juice and zest, sugar, and cinnamon in a pot and bring to a boil. Cover and simmer for 8–10 minutes, then cool slightly.

Cut the tops off the apples, about 3/4-inches from the top, and with a small teaspoon, carefully scoop out the core and seeds. Fill the apples with the rhubarb mixture.

Preheat the oven to 350°F. For the topping, sift the flour and baking powder into a bowl and stir in the sugar, lavender pollen, and almonds, if using. Rub the butter into the flour mixture until it resembles bread crumbs. Sprinkle the crumble mixture over the apples, pressing down lightly to form a crust.

Place the apples in a buttered ovenproof dish and bake for 35–40 minutes, until they are tender and the crumble is golden and crisp. Decorate with the lavender flowers and serve with lots of cream or good old custard.

mint *Mentha*

If there is an easier herb to grow than mint, I have yet to come across it! So many mint lovers who grow the herb are at pains to control its rapid expansion and prevent it from completely crowding out other plants. A tip I have learned over the years for restricting mint growth is to plant it in a separate garden bed or container, placed above ground.

Few things smell as much like summer as freshly snipped mint from the garden. I know I'm one chef who couldn't live without its freshness in the kitchen.

recipes

DESCRIPTION

There are around thirty species of mint (genus *Mentha*), apart from the common garden mint; among them the widely available spearmint, so commonly confused with the common mint, and peppermint. Nowadays other unusual varieties are propagated, too, hybrids such as apple, lemon, pineapple, bergamot, and, if you really have an open mind, varieties of lavender, ginger, and even chocolate! As yet I have only seen them in America, but I'm sure they will spread far and wide eventually. All mint varieties are perennials, and all have invasive roots and a tendency to take over. The common, or garden, mint originated in Greece.

BUYING, STORING, AND PREPARATION

Although dried mint is available, I never use it. Always choose bright green leaves with no bruising or wilting, and a strong aroma. Fresh leaves can be kept for a couple of days in the refrigerator, or in a glass of water with their stems immersed.

Remove the leaves from the stems before using.

CULINARY USES

Mint is primarily used for flavorings and garnishes. Garden mint is used in both sweet and savory dishes, to decorate desserts, or is added (chopped or whole) to salads. With its rounded green and sweet-smelling leaves, it is the type most frequently used in the kitchen. Generally it is also the variety preferred in Mediterranean and Middle Eastern countries, as in the classic Middle Eastern cracked wheat salad, Tabouleh, in which mint is used as a primary ingredient (or why not try my Fruit Tabouleh, see page 32). In Greece, mint is often used to flavor dolmas (stuffed vine leaves) and in stuffed vegetables.

Mint is added to yogurt-based dips in a number of countries, for example, in the Greek tzatziki, in some Indian raitas, and in the Turkish haydari (it is also added to a abdug, a rejuvenating yogurt drink). Mint jelly or sauce served with roast lamb is, of course, a British classic. One of my favorite ways of using mint is to flavor boiled, freshly dug potatoes. It also works very well with tender new carrots or peas.

Spearmint, a close relation, is suitable for use in most recipes in place of garden mint. A native of the Mediterranean, it has long, light-green, narrow leaves with serrated edges and a distinctive fresh flavor.

Peppermint is used in preparing desserts, and forms the basis of crème de menthe liqueur. It is delicious when added to chilled long drinks, sherberts, punches, and tea.

Another variety of mint that I very much favor is Vietnamese mint, or "Hot" mint, which is in fact not a mint at all. It has a hot, slightly spicy, acidic

complementary flavors

GREEN VEGETABLES (ESPECIALLY PEAS, FAVA BEANS, FENNEL AND ARTICHOKES)

FRUIT (ALL HARD FRUITS, ESPECIALLY WATERMELON)

SOFT FRUITS (PEACHES, STRAWBERRIES AND RASPBERRIES)

MILK PRODUCTS (CREAM, EGGS AND YOGURT)

MEAT (ESPECIALLY LAMB)

CHEESE (FETA AND RICOTTA)

flavor, much admired in the Far East. I use it in salads, Asian marinades, in Vietnamese spring rolls, and it's great in soup. It is hard to find but well worth shopping around for.

IDEAS WITH MINT

- Infuse it in olive oil for salad dressings (Substitute mint for the basil in the recipe on page 35).
- Add leaves to sweet syrup when poaching fruits.
- Use small mint leaves to decorate desserts.
- Add chopped leaves to thick yogurt and serve with broiled lamb and fish.
- Steep the leaves for a mint tea, served hot or chilled in summer.

OTHER USES

Apart from mint's superb culinary attributes, it is much favored for its medicinal qualities, especially peppermint, which is said to aid digestion, cure hiccups, clear the mind, and treat the common cold. It is also used for making a soothing and relaxing tea to calm weary travelers, as for example the iced mint tea served in Middle Eastern and Mediterranean countries as a sign of hospitality. All mint contains a volatile oil called menthol which gives it its characteristic cool, clean feeling, but peppermint has the highest concentration of it—which is why it's such a popular flavorant in chewing gums and toothpastes.

roman-style artichokes

For centuries the Italians have had a love and admiration for artichokes. However some of us find their preparation a little too laborious, but with practice it does get easier. Choose firm artichokes for the job; the baby ones are very tender and delicious.

20 baby artichokes
6 tablespoons olive oil
1 garlic clove, crushed
1 teaspoon dried chili flakes
6 fl oz. (3/4 cup) dry white wine
1 good bunch of mint, roughly chopped
Grated zest of 1 lemon
Coarse salt and freshly ground black pepper

Preheat the oven to 300°F. Trim the leaves from the artichokes and cut 1/4 inch off the top of each one, but leave the stalks intact. Place in a bowl of water acidulated with a little lemon juice as you go.

Heat the oil in a flameproof casserole dish, add the garlic and chili flakes and cook for 2 minutes. Add the artichokes, pour in the wine, then cover with a lid or foil and place in the oven to braise for 15–20 minutes, until the artichokes are tender.

Stir in the chopped mint and lemon zest, season to taste, and serve. It can be served at room temperature, if you prefer.

minted chicken and eggplant salad

Pick up a food magazine anywhere in the world and I bet you will find a recipe for an Asian-style salad within. Fish and meat in fragrant Asian dressings really hit the spot. Here is my version, using Vietnamese mint as a prime ingredient. I find it best served at room temperature.

Sesame oil
4 skinless, boneless chicken breasts
1 eggplant, cut into slices 1/2-inch thick
2 tablespoons brown sugar
1 tablespoon *nam pla* (Thai fish sauce)
1 garlic clove, crushed
2 green chiles, thinly sliced
Juice of 4 limes
1 lemongrass stalk, outer layers removed, tender inner core very finely chopped
1 onion, thinly sliced
2 shallots, chopped
2 oz. Vietnamese mint leaves
1/4 cup roasted peanuts, chopped
Salt and freshly ground black pepper

Heat a ridged grill pan, brush it with a little sesame oil, then season the chicken breasts and place on the grill. Cook for 5-6 minutes on each side, until lightly charred and cooked through. Brush the eggplant slices with sesame oil, place on the grill, and cook until lightly charred, turning them regularly and brushing with a little more oil if necessary.

Meanwhile, place the sugar in a bowl, add the fish sauce, garlic, chiles, and lime juice, and mix well. Stir in the lemongrass, onion, and shallots.

Remove the chicken and eggplant from the grill and let cool, then shred the chicken and cut the eggplant into small pieces. Add to the bowl, toss well, cover with plastic wrap and let marinate at room temperature for 1 hour.

Add the mint leaves, and serve in a deep bowl, sprinkled with the peanuts.

linguine with pumpkin seed-mint sauce and feta cheese

Pumkin seeds are full of flavor and very nutritious. You should certainly find them in health food stores but they are generally becoming more available everywhere. They give a wonderful nuttiness to the sauce in this unusual pasta dish.

9 oz. (2–3 cups) pumpkin flesh, cut into 1/2-inch dice
1/4 cup olive oil
1 lb. linguine
4 oz. (1 cup) feta cheese, crumbled
Salt and freshly ground black pepper
Shavings of Parmesan cheese (or freshly grated Parmesan), for serving

FOR THE PUMPKIN SEED-MINT SAUCE:
5 oz. (1 cup) pumpkin seeds
2 oz. (2–3 handfuls) mint leaves
3 garlic cloves, chopped
A pinch of ground cumin
1/4 teaspoon dried chili flakes
About 1/4 pint (2/3 cup) virgin olive oil

Preheat the oven to 350°F. For the pumpkin seed-mint sauce, spread the pumpkin seeds out on a baking sheet and roast in the oven for 10 minutes, until fragrant. Let cool, then place in a blender or food processor, along with the mint, garlic, cumin, and chili flakes. Blitz to a fine paste and then, with the motor running, slowly pour in enough olive oil to give a smooth, slightly runny sauce. Season to taste and set aside.

Place the pumpkin cubes on a baking sheet, toss with the olive oil and some salt and pepper, and bake for 10–15 minutes, until tender and lightly browned. Meanwhile, cook the pasta in a large pot of boiling salted water until al dente.

Drain the pasta, toss it with the sauce, and adjust the seasoning. Top with the roasted pumpkin cubes and feta cheese, sprinkle some Parmesan shavings over it, and serve immediately.

sweet and sour zucchinis

Zucchinis, to my mind, do not have a great flavor. They can be rather bland and watery and I think they generally need something of a helping hand. This sweet and sour dish is best made with very young, tender zucchinis, but if you can't get them, simply replace with thickly sliced larger ones. Serve at room temperature for the best results.

2 tablespoons virgin olive oil
1 lb. baby zucchinis, trimmed
1 small garlic clove, thinly sliced
1 tablespoon raisins
1 teaspoon sugar
8 mint leaves, roughly chopped
3 tablespoons white wine vinegar
2 tablespoons pine nuts, toasted

Heat the oil in a large frying pan, add the zucchinis, and fry until they are beautifully golden and almost tender. Add the garlic and raisins and cook for 2 minutes. Sprinkle the sugar and mint over them and toss together so that the zucchinis become lightly caramelized. Pour in the vinegar and toss again for 30 seconds. Remove from the heat and let cool before serving, scattered with the pine nuts.

seafood with fennel and mint

Visit any Italian coastal town and you will find a similar dish to this one, comprising fresh local seafood in a dressing of good olive oil and lemon juice. The addition of mint gives an unusual twist and complements the seafood beautifully, especially when you leave it overnight for the flavors to develop. On no account overcook the fish or it will become chewy and inedible.

18 oz. fresh mussels
1 onion, roughly chopped
Stalks from the mint leaves for the marinade
1/2 cup dry white wine
12 oz. monkfish (angler fish) fillet, cut into 1-inch dice
8 oz. (1 cup) squid, cut into rings
16 uncooked tiger shrimp, de-veined (see page 119)
8 fresh scallops, cut horizontally in half
1 fennel bulb, very thinly sliced with a large peeler or knife
Salt and freshly ground black pepper

FOR THE MARINADE:

Juice of 2 lemons
1/2 cup virgin olive oil
2 garlic cloves, crushed
2 tablespoons chopped mint
Fronds from the fennel

Clean the mussels under cold running water and pull out the beards. Discard any open mussels that don't close when tapped on the counter. Place the mussels in a pot, add the onion and mint stalks, then pour in the white wine and 2/3 cup of water. Place on a high heat, cover, and steam for 3–4 minutes, until the mussels open. Drain in a colander, placed over a bowl to catch the liquid. Strain it through a fine mesh strainer back into the pot.

Season the remaining fish and shellfish and cook in the mussel liquid—first cook the monkfish for 3–4 minutes, then add the squid, shrimp, and scallops, and cook for a minute longer. Transfer the fish and shellfish to a clean bowl and set aside, also setting aside the cooking liquor. Remove the mussels from their shells and add them to the bowl.

Make the marinade by whisking all the ingredients together. Mix in the cooking liquor from the seafood. Add the shredded fennel to the seafood, then pour the dressing over it and mix well. Cover and let it marinate in the fridge overnight, turning the mixture occasionally.

Serve with lots of crusty farmhouse bread.

fruit tabbouleh

Tabbouleh is traditionally a cracked wheat (bulgur) salad from the Middle East, made with lots of garlic and parsley. I sometimes prepare it using couscous instead. This fruit variation is very light and fresh, and makes a simple addition to a barbecue dessert table.

1/3 cup superfine sugar
1 vanilla bean
1 cup couscous
2 cups strawberries, cut in half
1 cup raspberries
1 cup blackberries
1 ripe pear, peeled, cored, and cut into wedges
1 ripe nectarine, pitted, and cut into wedges
1 banana, peeled and thickly sliced
Leaves from 1 good bunch of mint

Place the sugar in a pan along with 2 1/2 cups of water and bring slowly to a boil. Meanwhile, slit the vanilla bean open lengthwise and scrape out the seeds with the tip of a sharp knife. Add the vanilla bean and seeds to the pan, and simmer for 5 minutes.

Place the couscous in a bowl. Remove the vanilla bean from the sugar syrup and pour the syrup over the couscous. Cover with a lid or plastic wrap and let it steam for 5 minutes. Uncover and fluff up the couscous with a fork, then cover and let it steam again for 2–3 minutes. Fluff up with a fork again and let cool, uncovered.

Add all the fruit to the couscous and mix together carefully. Stir in the mint leaves and mix again. Chill for 30 minutes before serving.

gin, tonic, and mint sorbet with pineapple carpaccio

One of my favorite tipples before dinner (or at any time, if I am truthful!) is a good old G&T. In the summer, I like it with extra lemon and a sprig of mint, which funnily enough led me to think about a sorbet on the same lines. I tried it and here it is, served with thin slices of ripe pineapple.

1 cup superfine sugar
1 good bunch of mint
1½ cups tonic water
½ cup dry gin
Juice of 6 lemons
Grated zest of 1 lemon
1 ripe medium-sized pineapple, peel removed, thinly sliced

Place the sugar in a pan along with 9 fl oz. water and bring to a boil slowly, to avoid the sugar crystallizing. Remove from the heat and let cool, then add most of the mint (reserve a few leaves for decoration), and blitz in a blender. Strain and chill.

Combine the tonic water, gin, lemon juice, and zest with the mint syrup. Pour into an icecream machine and freeze according to the manufacturer's instructions. (See page 180 if you don't have a machine).

Arrange the slices of pineapple on 4 serving plates, top with a scoop of the sorbet, and decorate with the reserved mint.

mint turkish delight

I have always enjoyed Turkish delight, even as a child, especially when it is enveloped in a thin coating of chocolate and highly perfumed with rosewater. Well, this recipe uses mint as the main flavor. It is very simple to prepare and you and your guests will love it.

2⅓ cups superfine sugar
1 large bunch of mint
½ teaspoon lemon juice
¾ cup cornstarch
½ teaspoon cream of tartar
A drop of green food coloring
Confectioners' sugar for dusting

Lightly oil an 8-inch baking tin, line it with plastic wrap, then lightly oil the plastic wrap.

Place the sugar in a pan along with the mint, lemon juice, and 1 cup of water, and bring to a boil slowly, to avoid the sugar crystallizing. Leave over a low heat to infuse for 10 minutes, then remove from the heat and strain out the mint. Return the syrup to the pan and cook over a high heat until it reaches 240°F on a sugar thermometer (soft-ball stage). Remove from the heat.

In a separate pan, blend the cornstarch and cream of tartar with 1 cup of water. Bring to a boil, whisking constantly, until thick. Gradually pour the hot mint syrup on to the cornstarch mixture, then reduce the heat and simmer for 40 minutes, until translucent. Stir in the green food coloring (taking great care not to add too much), then pour into the oiled pan and let it cool. Cut into cubes and dust very generously with confectioners' sugar before serving.

basil *Ocimum*

For me, basil conjures up the real essence and flavor of summer. And who would believe that basil, a herb I love to use at any opportunity, would have such a long and interesting history? Basil is native to India, Asia, and the Mediterranean, and Hindus used to wash their dead in basil water and place a leaf of holy basil on the deceased's chest before burial to ward off evil spirits. So highly do Hindus still regard basil that they regularly grow the plant beside their temples.

recipes

In Italy, basil holds many connotations, too; for instance, a pot of fresh basil placed on a woman's windowsill to this day extends an invitation to visit her. Perhaps it has a lot to answer for in establishing the country's romantic image!

DESCRIPTION

There are believed to be over 100 varieties of basil, ranging from the ornamental to the fragrant varieties that we love to use in cooking.

Most basils are annuals and grow into bushy plants up to a foot high. The most commonly used variety for cooking is sweet basil (*Ocimum basilicum*) which has oval, shiny green, buttery soft leaves. Other commonly used varieties include anise basil, lemon basil, the gingery flavored purple or opal basil, lettuce leaf basil, and Thai basil (otherwise known as holy basil). Less common varieties include a Mexican one called cinnamon basil, which is unfortunately not available in this country, but is great used in marinades and spicy dishes. Thai basil (*O. sanctum*), which must be cooked in order to release its flavor, has a stronger and more intense flavor than sweet basil and is good in Asian-style curries, and delicious added to spicy soups and stir-fries.

When people are asked to describe the taste of basil, opinions differ: some claim overtones of sweet licorice, others cloves; some say spicy, others sweet. You may be surprised to know that in fact, basil is a member of the mint family.

GROWING/BUYING, STORING, AND PREPARATION

As hardy as basil looks, it can be difficult to grow. I personally have not had much success in my own herb patch. It likes sunshine and shade, plenty of water but not too much, and, more importantly, temperatures above 60°F. Luckily we now have access to basil throughout the year, coming from all over the world.

When purchasing basil, always look for stumpy, shiny, bright green leaves and not those that are limp or blackened in appearance. Only buy it when required (it doesn't keep very well unless you buy a rooted plant), and pick as needed. I find the best way to keep it is to wrap the leaves in a damp cloth and store in the fridge.

Great care is needed when using sweet basil, as the leaves are fragile and bruise easily. When using it in dishes, crush in a mortar and pestle or simply chop the leaves. For salads I prefer to tear the leaves into small pieces.

CULINARY USES

Basil is one of the most popular herbs worldwide, typically playing a supporting role in dishes, such as a pesto stirred into a light vegetable soup (Soupe au Pistou, see page 36), or added to sauces, eggs, fish, and meat dishes. Where, for example, would the Italians be without the fragrance of basil in many of their staple sauces and pasta dishes, or the Thais without holy basil in their curries and noodle dishes?

Fresh basil leaves make a very effective and aromatic garnish, and are wonderful added to salads—try a mixture of sweet and purple basil. Basil, as the Italians show, marries particularly well with tomatoes, both cooked and raw.

Basil intensifies with cooking, so start with small amounts and remember that overcooking can spoil its flavor. For a fresher taste, I find it is better to add more towards the end of the cooking time.

IDEAS WITH BASIL

- Use plenty with olive oil to marinate goat cheese or mozzarella.
- Basil butter (see below) is superb on broiled fish or vegetables.

Basil butter

1 cup (2 sticks) butter
1/4 cup chopped basil
1 teaspoon lemon juice

Soften the butter with a wooden spoon. Add the basil and lemon juice. Shape into a bonbon or sausage in wax paper and refrigerate. Slice when needed.

- Pesto or basil oil (see below), added to the same amount of basic vinaigrette makes a delicious dressing for salads.

Basil oil

4 oz. (about 8 handfuls) basil leaves
1 cup virgin olive oil

Blanch the basil leaves in boiling water for 10 seconds, drain, and refresh in iced water. Remove, squeeze dry, and blitz in a blender with the olive oil until smooth. Let it settle overnight. Strain through cheesecloth, and use as required. Any leftover basil oil should be stored in the refrigerator.

- Use the larger leaves to wrap around shrimp or asparagus, just before steaming.
- Add to sweet syrup to make a delicious poaching liquid for fruits such as peaches, strawberries, and rhubarb.
- Dip basil leaves in melted chocolate to make an interesting and attractive decoration for desserts.

complementary flavors

SOFT CHEESES (RICOTTA, FETA, MOZZARELLA, AND GOAT CHEESE)

PARMESAN CHEESE

VEGETABLES (ESPECIALLY FENNEL, ROASTED PEPPERS, AND TOMATOES)

GARLIC

OLIVE OIL

ORANGES AND LEMONS

MEAT (ESPECIALLY LAMB)

FISH AND SHELLFISH (ESPECIALLY SEA BASS, SALMON, MULLET, SCALLOPS, AND MUSSELS)

COCONUT MILK AND GINGER (FOR THAI BASIL)

soupe au pistou

This simple, fragrant vegetable soup is synonymous with the South of France, but its distinctive flavor can only be achieved with good fresh tomatoes and lots of fresh pistou—a basil paste similar to pesto—added at the last moment. In France, the pistou would be made with a mortar and pestle but a blender or food processor is fine, too.

1 leek, white part only
1 potato
1 onion
1 celery stalk
1 zucchini
2 carrots
10 green beans
6 ripe plum tomatoes, skinned, and seeded
2 tablespoons olive oil
1/4 teaspoon thyme leaves
1 small bay leaf
4 cups well-flavored chicken broth (or vegetable broth)
Salt and freshly ground black pepper

FOR THE PISTOU:

3 1/2 oz. (7 handfuls) basil leaves
3 garlic cloves, roughly chopped
1 tablespoon pine nuts
2 tablespoons Parmesan cheese, freshly grated (optional)
About 1/2 cup virgin olive oil

Cut all the vegetables into 1/4-inch dice. Heat the olive oil in a large pot, add all the vegetables except the tomatoes, then add 3 tablespoons of water and cover with a lid. Let it cook gently until the water has evaporated, but don't let the vegetables brown. Add the thyme and bay leaf and pour in the broth. Return to a boil, reduce the heat to a simmer, and cook for 20–25 minutes, until the vegetables are tender.

Meanwhile, prepare the pistou. Put all the ingredients except the oil in a food processor or blender and blitz to a paste. Slowly add the oil, while the motor is still running, until the pistou has a smooth, slightly runny texture. Season to taste.

Add the pistou to the soup, followed by the diced tomatoes, and stir thoroughly; do not let it boil again. Season and serve.

summer vegetable salad

A wonderful crisp summer salad. Be sure to use prime-quality vegetables and serve them warm, which really brings out the flavor.

12 oz. (12–15 spears) asparagus, trimmed
12 oz. baby carrots, trimmed
8 baby zucchinis, trimmed
8 oz. sugar snap peas, trimmed
8 oz. baby leeks, trimmed
3 tablespoons balsamic vinegar
1/4 cup extra virgin olive oil
1/4 chopped basil (a mixture of purple and green looks good)
2 tablespoons white wine vinegar
4 organic or cage-free eggs
2 tablespoons pine nuts, toasted
Salt and freshly ground black pepper

Bring a large pot of salted water to a boil, add the asparagus, and simmer for 3–4 minutes, until tender. Remove with a slotted spoon and place in a large bowl of iced water (this helps preserve the color). Drain immediately and set aside.

Return the water to a boil and cook the other vegetables in it until just tender, and then plunge them into iced water as well. When all the vegetables are cooked, mix them together in a large bowl and set aside.

For the dressing, put 3 tablespoons of the balsamic vinegar in a bowl, add some salt and pepper, then beat in the olive oil and basil. Set aside.

Bring a large pot of water to a boil, add the white wine vinegar, then reduce the heat and poach the eggs in it. Meanwhile, warm the vegetables in a little boiling water for 1 minute, or place in a microwave for 30 seconds.

Arrange the drained vegetables on 4 serving plates, spoon the basil dressing over them and sprinkle the pine nuts on top. Place a poached egg on the side of each salad and serve immediately.

goat cheese and basil mousse with basil and almond sauce

The recent popularity of goat cheese is quite astonishing. In this recipe, pureéing it with basil and roasted garlic to make a mousse, then topping it with a basil and almond sauce makes a great dish. A tomato and olive salad and some toasted bread rubbed with garlic and olive oil goes well with it.

2 garlic cloves, unpeeled
1 tablespoon olive oil
12 large basil leaves
1/4 cup light cream
7 oz. soft goat cheese
1/4 cup heavy cream
A little cayenne pepper
2 gelatin leaves (if unavailable, use 1/2-package granulated)
Salt and freshly ground black pepper

FOR THE BASIL AND ALMOND SAUCE:
1/3 cup ground almonds
6 basil leaves
1/2 small garlic clove, crushed
1/2 cup virgin olive oil

Preheat the oven to 350°F. Put the garlic cloves in a small dish, pour the oil over them, and roast for 20 minutes, until tender and brown. Let cool, then pop the garlic from its skin.

Blanch the basil leaves for the mousse in boiling water for 30 seconds, then drain and refresh in iced water. Drain again and dry well. Place in a food processor or blender along with the garlic and light cream, and blend until smooth. Pour into a bowl, add the goat cheese and heavy cream, and mix well. Season with cayenne, salt, and pepper.

Cover the gelatin leaves with cold water and let soak for 5 minutes. Drain and squeeze out excess water, then place in a small saucepan with 2 tablespoons of water. Heat gently to dissolve, without letting the water boil. Stir the dissolved gelatin into the mousse mixture. Pour into 4 ramekins, or small coffee cups, and place in the fridge for about 4 hours, until set.

Meanwhile, make the sauce. Put the ground almonds, basil, and garlic in a food processor or blender and gradually pour in the olive oil, blitzing it to a coarse purée, pesto style.

To serve, dip each ramekin into a little hot water, run a knife around the edge, and turn out onto a serving plate. Top each mousse with a spoonful of the sauce.

spaghetti with lobster, basil, and tomatoes

Lobster is expensive, I know, but when you're looking for something light, tasty, and simple yet special, this dish fits the bill. A taste of summer, if ever there was one. It is also good served cold as part of a barbecue buffet.

2 lb. lobster, cooked
1/2 cup lobster oil (see Tip below), made with the lobster shell
1 lb. (1 1/2–2 cups) firm plum tomatoes, skinned, seeded, and cut into 1/4-inch dice
1 garlic clove, crushed
Juice of 1/2 lemon
16 large basil leaves
1 lb. spaghetti
Salt and freshly ground black pepper
Freshly grated Parmesan cheese, for serving

Remove the lobster meat from the claws and body, cut it into chunks, and set aside. Use the shell to make the lobster oil.

The following day, place the tomatoes, garlic, lemon juice, and lobster oil in a bowl. Tear half the basil into small pieces and add to the bowl, then add the lobster chunks and season to taste. Let it marinate at room temperature for up to 1 hour.

Cook the spaghetti in plenty of boiling salted water until al dente. Drain in a colander and return to the pot. Add the lobster and marinade and toss together. Place in a serving bowl and sprinkle the Parmesan and the remaining torn basil leaves over it.

Paul's Tip To make lobster oil, crush the lobster shells into small pieces using a rolling pin and fry in 2 tablespoons oil for 10–15 minutes. Add a handful of a chopped garlic, onion, celery, and carrot mixture, plus a bay leaf and a few tarragon stalks. Pour in 2/3 cup dry white wine and simmer for 15 minutes. Reduce the heat, add 2 1/2 cups vegetable oil and simmer for 30 minutes. Remove from the heat, cover, and leave overnight (do not refrigerate). Strain through cheesecloth and store in the fridge.

oven-glazed mozzarella cakes with eggplant and basil

his colorful dish with its robust flavors makes a great first course or vegetarian dish.

2/3 cup olive oil
2 garlic cloves, crushed
2 beefsteak tomatoes, peeled, seeded, and chopped
1/2 cup pistou (see page 36)
2 eggplants, cut into slices 1/2-inch thick
1 buffalo mozzarella cheese, cut into 8 slices
2/3 cup heavy cream
1 egg yolk, beaten
2 tablespoons freshly grated Parmesan cheese
Salt and freshly ground black pepper

FOR THE MOZZARELLA CAKES:

2 1/4 cups whole milk
1/4 cup (1/2 stick) unsalted butter, diced
2 1/4 cups chickpea flour (gram flour)
1 buffalo mozzarella cheese, grated
1 teaspoon salt
1 teaspoon sugar
1 large egg yolk
3 tablespoons olive oil

First make the mozzarella cakes. Put the milk and butter in a pan and bring to a boil. Combine the flour with the grated mozzarella, salt, and sugar, and rain this mixture into the hot milk. Stir until well combined. Reduce the heat and cook for 4–5 minutes, until the mixture leaves the sides of the pan clean. Beat in the egg yolk thoroughly, then let cool. Roll the mixture into eight 2-inch balls and flatten them slightly.

Preheat the oven to 350°F. Heat the olive oil in a large frying pan, add the mozzarella cakes and fry for 5–6 minutes on each side, until golden. Keep warm.

Heat 4 tablespoons of the olive oil in a pan and add the garlic, tomatoes, and half the pistou. Reduce the heat and cook until the the mixture is concentrated. Season to taste.

Heat the remaining oil in a frying pan and fry the eggplant slices for 4–5 minutes on each side, until golden. Remove and drain on paper towels. Lay 8 slices in an oiled gratin dish and top each with a mozzarella cake, a slice of mozzarella, some tomato sauce, another slice of eggplant, and more tomato sauce. Pour a little pistou over each stack. Mix the cream with the egg yolk, Parmesan, and the remaining pistou and pour it over each stack. Bake for about 20 minutes, until golden and glazed.

red mullet with orange and basil stuffing

Red mullet is a firm-fleshed fish from the Mediterranean. The orange stuffing keeps it wonderfully moist during cooking. If the thought of boning the fish is daunting, ask the person at the fish counter to do it for you.

12 oz. red mullet, cleaned
1/4 cup olive oil
Salt and freshly ground black pepper

FOR THE STUFFING:

3 oz. (about 6 handfuls) basil leaves
2 garlic cloves, crushed
1/4 cup pine nuts
1/4 cup freshly grated Parmesan cheese
Grated zest of 1 orange
1/2 cup virgin olive oil
3 cups fresh white breadcrumbs

To make the stuffing, place the basil, garlic, pine nuts, Parmesan, and orange zest in a blender or food processor and slowly add the oil, with the motor running, to give a smooth purée. Add the bread crumbs and blitz for 10 seconds.

Preheat the oven to 400°F. Using a sharp knife, cut each red mullet down the backbone, then snip the bone with scissors behind the head and the tail. Remove the bone, keeping the head and tail intact, and take out the pinbones. Open the vent and fill with the stuffing. Lightly tie the fish with string to secure the filling.

Butter 4 pieces of foil, approximately 15 inches square. Place the red mullet on top, spoon the olive oil over it, and season. Lift up the sides of the foil and twist to seal. Bake for 15–20 minutes, depending on the size of the fish.

Serve at the table, opening the packages in front of your guests to let the smell of basil pervade the room.

lamb cutlets with basil and parmesan crust

The beauty of this crust is that it can be made well in advance and used as needed. It has a fantastic flavor and is so versatile it could be used on most meats, especially chicken and beef, or as a topping for fish.

Grilled vegetables, such as eggplants, zucchinis, and peppers, make an ideal accompaniment to this summery dish.

1/4 cup olive oil
8 lamb cutlets
Salt and freshly ground black pepper

FOR THE BASIL AND PARMESAN CRUST:

3 1/2 oz. (about 7 handfuls) basil leaves
3 1/2 oz. softened unsalted butter
5 oz. (3 cups) fresh white breadcrumbs
3 oz. (1 1/4 cups) freshly grated Parmesan cheese
2 oz. (1/2 cup) shredded Gruyère cheese
1 garlic clove, crushed
1/4 cup pine nuts, toasted

FOR THE SAUCE:

1/4 cup (1/2 stick) unsalted butter
1 shallot, finely chopped
4 tomatoes, peeled, seeded, and finely chopped
1/3 cup dry white wine
1 1/4 cups lamb broth (or other meat broth)
10 basil leaves, chopped

For the basil and Parmesan crust, place the basil leaves in a food processor along with the butter and a little seasoning and blitz until smooth. Add the remaining ingredients and blend until smooth again. Transfer the mixture to a piece of foil and wrap into a bonbon shape. Place in the freezer until needed.

For the sauce, heat 2 teaspoons of the butter in a pan, add the shallot, and cook for a few minutes, until soft but not colored. Add the tomatoes and cook for 5 minutes, then add the white wine and boil for 5 minutes. Pour in the broth and simmer until the sauce has reduced by half its volume. Stir in the basil. Dice the remaining butter, whisk it into the sauce, then season to taste and keep warm.

Heat the olive oil in a large, heavy frying pan until very hot, season the lamb cutlets, and fry for 2–3 minutes on each side, until golden on the outside but still pink inside. Remove from the heat and keep warm.

Preheat the broiler to its highest setting. Remove the crust from the freezer, cut it into fairly thick slices, and place them between 2 sheets of plastic wrap. Roll out to about 1/8-inch thick. Cut out 8 circles of crust and place one on top of each lamb cutlet. Put the cutlets on a baking tray and place under the broiler until golden and crisp. Serve with basil sauce.

monkfish curry with green mango and thai basil

With its firm-textured flesh, monkfish is the ideal choice for this fragrant Asian curry. If kaffir lime leaves are not available, replace them with a bay leaf and 1/2 teaspoon of grated lime zest.

2 tablespoons vegetable oil
2 tablespoons green curry paste
1 lb. monkfish fillet, cut into large cubes
1 lemongrass stalk, hard outer layers removed, tender inner core chopped
1 1/4 cups coconut milk
4 kaffir lime leaves
1 teaspoon ground turmeric
1 teaspoon ground cilantro
1 eggplant, cut into large batons
2 tablespoons *nam pla* (Thai fish sauce)
3 green chiles, finely sliced
1/2 green, unripe mango, peeled, pitted, thinly sliced
10 Thai basil leaves, roughly chopped

Heat the oil in a large heavy frying pan, add the curry paste, and fry until it bubbles and becomes fragrant. Add the monkfish and lemongrass and cook over a gentle heat for about 2 minutes. Stir in the coconut milk, kaffir lime leaves, turmeric, and cilantro, and bring to a boil. Add the eggplant and fish sauce and cook over a gentle heat for about 5 minutes, until the fish is cooked. Finally stir in the green chiles and the mango. Serve immediately, sprinkled with the basil.

rosemary *Rosmarinus officinalis*

"Parsley, sage, rosemary, and thyme" goes the song that so many of us remember from our childhood, but it is rosemary that, during my long career as a chef, has given me the most pleasure from a culinary standpoint. It was the herb I was most familiar and comfortable with and I love its needlelike texture and its aromatic and intense flavor.

recipes

Rosemary was originally cultivated in the Mediterranean, where it remains a principal component of *herbes de Provence*, and is widely used in dishes of the region. Rosemary (*Rosmarinus officinalis*) was introduced to Britain during the eleventh century, where it was commonly believed to encourage merriment. During medieval times it was associated with love and remembrance. Romans placed branches of it in the hands of the dead, and in many older church graveyards, rosemary can be seen planted next to gravestones.

DESCRIPTION

Rosemary is an evergreen perennial, intensely flavorful and aromatic. The shrub can grow up to 5 feet in height and has narrow, spiky hard leaves. Rosemary enjoys sun and, because it is hardy, can withstand the wind and salt of coastal regions. It is easy to grow in containers.

BUYING AND STORING

Only buy fresh, firm-looking rosemary. It will keep well in the fridge (or frozen in the freezer) but I find it best kept in a dry, cool place. Of course it is ideal to grow your own so you can pick and use it fresh. Strip the leaves from their woody sprigs before using.

CULINARY USES

People began cooking with rosemary during the Middle Ages. These days it is a particular favorite in Britain, France, and Italy where it is used in all sorts of savoury and sweet dishes. In southern France, rosemary is added to the coals of a barbecue to grill fish and meat.

Rosemary can be used whole or finely chopped, which helps to release its aroma. Use it whole to flavor roast meats, marinades, and infusions during cooking. Flavor your oils and vinegars with a rosemary branch and blend it, chopped finely, with butter and lemon juice for a lovely herbal butter. A sprig of rosemary can also be added to *bouquet garni* (along with sage, thyme, parsley, and a bay leaf).

I like to use it to flavor sauces, stews and soups, and I always use it in one form or another with lamb, especially simply roasted (added to garlic it makes a lovely crusty topping). Use fresh rosemary in conjunction with garlic and anchovy, which really brings out the flavors. It is also, to my mind, surprisingly good in sweet dishes, made into syrup and added chopped into shortbread.

Rosemary flowers are very pretty and fragrant and are wonderful included in summer salads, or as a decoration for desserts.

In the following section you will see just how versatile rosemary is, from forming a base for a rabbit stew to using its fresh stems as ideal skewers for grilling scallops. And whatever you do, try to use it with chocolate (see page 176)—for me an unexpected marriage made in heaven!

OTHER USES

Rosemary has special medicinal properties which aid digestion and liver complaints. In Provence, it is regularly made into a herbal tea to encourage a healthy complexion. This tea is also said to be

complementary flavors

GARLIC

MEAT (CHICKEN, LAMB, PORK, AND BEEF)

VEGETABLES (ESPECIALLY MUSHROOMS, BUTTERNUT SQUASH, ONIONS, AND POTATOES)

FRUITS (ESPECIALLY APPLES, ORANGES, APRICOTS, AND PEARS)

SOFT FRUITS (ESPECIALLY STRAWBERRIES AND APRICOTS)

LAVENDER

CHOCOLATE

good for clearing headaches. The aromatic branches are sometimes thrown into fires to scent rooms—and are added to barbecues to flavor whatever is grilling. In medieval times, rosemary was thought to ward off evil spirits and prevent nightmares. It is a key component in many pot-pourris and the essential oil is used extensively in aromatherapy.

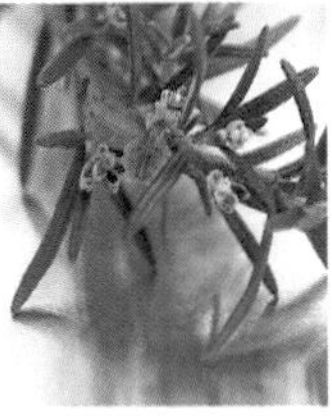

rosemary-skewered scallops with fennel and orange salsa

4 long, bushy stems of rosemary
16 large, fresh scallops
Olive oil
Salt and freshly ground black pepper

FOR THE FENNEL AND ORANGE SALSA:

6 tablespoons virgin olive oil
1 fennel bulb, fronds removed, finely chopped
2 oranges
4 plum tomatoes, finely chopped
1 garlic clove, crushed
1 tablespoon balsamic vinegar

Remove the leaves from the bottom two-thirds of each rosemary stem so that the top is still bushy but the rest can be threaded through the scallops. Carefully thread 4 scallops onto each rosemary skewer and place in the fridge until required.

For the salsa, heat half the oil in a pan, add the chopped fennel and cook for about 8–10 minutes, until golden and tender. Place in a bowl.

Segment one of the oranges by cutting away all the peel and pith, then cutting between the membranes to release the segments. Cut each segment into pieces. Add the cut-up segments to the fennel in the bowl, then add the tomatoes, garlic, balsamic vinegar, the remaining oil, and the juice from the second orange. Leave for 1 hour for the flavors to blend.

Heat a ridged grill pan until smoking and brush with olive oil. Season the skewered scallops with salt and pepper and cook for 1 minute on each side, until golden and caramelized. Place on serving plates, coat with the salsa, and grind some black pepper over them. Serve as a first course.

rosemary-braised rabbit with smoked bacon, tomato, and fava beans

1 young rabbit (about 3½ lbs.), cut up
2 tablespoons all-purpose flour
2 tablespoons olive oil
2 tablespoons unsalted butter
3 oz. (2–3 thick strips) fatty bacon
⅔ cup dry white wine
1¼ cups well-flavored meat broth
3 oz. sun-blush tomatoes (partially dried)
2 oz. shelled fresh fava beans, cooked
Salt and freshly ground black pepper

FOR THE MARINADE:

12 garlic cloves, peeled but left whole
1 small bay leaf
6 rosemary sprigs, plus extra for garnishing
2 tablespoons olive oil

Put the rabbit pieces in a dish with all the marinade ingredients. Cover and let it marinate for 24 hours.

Preheat the oven to 300°F. Remove the rabbit from the marinade and dry well, then coat it in the flour. Heat the olive oil and the butter in a large flameproof casserole dish until very hot, then season the rabbit pieces and brown them in the hot fat. Add the garlic cloves from the marinade and the smoked bacon and cook for 3–4 minutes. Drain off any excess fat, then return to the heat, pour in the white wine, and tuck in the rosemary sprigs and bay leaf from the marinade. Pour in the meat broth and bring to a boil. Reduce the heat, cover, and place in the oven. Cook for 1 hour, then add the sun-blush tomatoes, and cook for 15 minutes longer.

Remove from the oven and strain off the liquid into a saucepan. Simmer until it is thick enough to coat the back of a spoon, then stir in the fava beans and season to taste. Pour the sauce over the rabbit, garnish with a little rosemary, and serve. Creamy mashed potato, lightened with olive oil, makes a good accompaniment.

pan-fried sole with rosemary and hazelnuts

$^1/_3$ cup ($^3/_4$ stick) unsalted butter
$4^1/_2$ oz. (1 cup) hazelnuts, crushed
1 tablespoon finely chopped rosemary
2 cups fresh white bread crumbs
2 egg yolks
4 x 12–14 oz. Dover soles, cleaned
2 lemons, peel and pith removed, cut into slices

FOR THE GARNISH:
2 tablespoons olive oil
$3^1/_2$ oz. bacon lardons
11 oz. baby new potatoes, cooked, peeled, and cut into slices $^1/_2$-inch thick
12 asparagus tips, cooked

FOR THE SAUCE:
$^1/_4$ cup ($^1/_2$ stick) unsalted butter
$3^1/_2$ fl oz. veal broth (or chicken broth)
2 tablespoons lemon juice

Heat half of the butter in a frying pan, add the crushed hazelnuts, and cook, stirring constantly, over a medium heat until they turn a light golden color. Remove from the pan and let cool, then place in a blender or food processor and blitz to fine grains. Transfer to a bowl and mix in the rosemary and bread crumbs.

Beat the egg yolks until fluffy, then brush both sides of the sole with them. Coat the soles with the rosemary and hazelnut mixture, patting it on to ensure they are well covered.

For the garnish, heat the olive oil in a frying pan, add the bacon lardons, and fry until crisp. Remove from the pan and set aside. Add the sliced potatoes to the pan and fry until golden on both sides. Add the asparagus and fry with the potatoes until heated through. Return the lardons to the pan and season to taste. Put the mixture on 4 serving plates and keep warm.

Fry the fish in the remaining butter for about 4–5 minutes on each side, until golden. Place on top of the vegetables. In a small pan, heat the butter for the sauce until it is foaming and gives off a nutty aroma. Whisk in the broth and lemon juice, bring to a boil, then drizzle the sauce over the fish. Top with a slice of lemon and serve immediately.

slow-roast lamb with rosemary and anchoïade

1 x 5-lb. leg of lamb
6 anchovy fillets in oil
6 tablespoons olive oil
4 large garlic cloves, cut into thin slivers
30 rosemary sprigs
$^2/_3$ cup red wine
$^1/_2$ cup lamb broth (or other meat broth)
2 tablespoons chilled unsalted butter, chopped
Cayenne pepper
Salt and freshly ground black pepper

Preheat the oven to 400°F. With a small, sharp knife, make deep slits approximately an inch apart all over the lamb. Place the anchovies, half the olive oil, and a good pinch of salt in a blender or food processor and blitz to a smooth paste. Rub the paste into the slits and all over the lamb. Insert a sliver of garlic and a small sprig of rosemary into each slit in the meat.

Place the lamb in a flameproof roasting pan, pour the remaining olive oil over it and season lightly with cayenne, salt, and pepper. Place in the oven and roast for 20 minutes. Reduce the heat to 225°F and cook, basting occasionally with the juices, for up to 5 hours, until very tender.

Transfer the lamb to a serving dish and keep warm. Remove the excess fat from the pan juices, pour in the red wine, and add a few more rosemary sprigs. Bring to a boil, then add the broth and simmer for 5 minutes. Gradually whisk in the butter, then strain the sauce, adjust the seasoning, and serve alongside the leg of lamb.

rosemary-grilled vegetables with feta

1/2 cup olive oil
2 garlic cloves, crushed
1 bunch of rosemary, roughly chopped
12 asparagus spears
4 small zucchinis, cut in half lengthwise
8 baby eggplants, cut in half
1 red onion, cut into wedges
1 red pepper, cut into wedges
4 portobello mushrooms, thickly sliced
Salt and freshly ground black pepper

FOR THE DRESSING:

1 tablespoon balsamic vinegar
5 tablespoons olive oil
1/2 teaspoon Dijon mustard

FOR SERVING:

1 bunch of watercress
5 oz. (about 2–3 handfuls) baby spinach leaves
3/4 cup cooked chickpeas (canned are fine)
5 oz. (1 1/4 cups) feta cheese

Mix the olive oil, garlic, and rosemary together in a dish, add the vegetables, and toss well together. Let it marinate for 1 hour at room temperature.

Heat a ridged grill pan (or, better still, a barbecue), brush with a little oil, then season the vegetables and place them on the grill. Cook, turning regularly, until they are tender and slightly charred. Meanwhile, whisk all the ingredients for the dressing together and season to taste.

Put the watercress and spinach in a large, shallow dish and scatter the chickpeas on top. Top with the grilled vegetables and pour the dressing over them. Crumble the feta cheese on top and serve immediately, with lots of crusty bread.

roast butternut squash with ricotta and rosemary

2 butternut squash, peeled, seeded, and cut into large chunks
2/3 cup olive oil
3 tablespoons rosemary needles, plus a few sprigs for garnishing
2 garlic cloves, chopped
3 1/2 oz. (2 cups chopped) flat-leaf parsley
3 1/2 oz. (1/3 cup) ricotta cheese
2 oz. (1 cup) freshly grated Parmesan cheese
Salt and freshly ground black pepper

Preheat the oven to 350°F. Toss the squash with 4 tablespoons of the olive oil and place in a large baking pan. Place in the oven and roast for about 25 minutes, until tender, golden, and lightly caramelized.

Meanwhile, place the rosemary, garlic, and parsley in a blender or food processor and, with the motor running, slowly add the remaining olive oil. Season to taste.

In a small pan, warm the ricotta with a little hot water to form a paste. Add the rosemary mixture and stir until combined.

Put the roasted squash in an ovenproof serving dish and pour over the ricotta and rosemary sauce over it. Sprinkle the Parmesan on top and return to the oven for 10 minutes, until golden. Garnish with rosemary and serve.

baked onions with rosemary

4 large Spanish onions
1 pint ($2^1/_2$ cups) chicken broth (or vegetable broth)
4 branches of rosemary leaves, roughly chopped
$^1/_4$ cup virgin olive oil
$^1/_4$ cup ($^1/_2$ stick) chilled unsalted butter, chopped
Salt and freshly ground black pepper

Preheat the oven to 400°F. Peel the onions, trim the top and bottom so they will sit upright, then cut them in half horizontally. Arrange in a baking dish cut side up, pour in the broth, then scatter the chopped rosemary on top and season well. Pour the olive oil over them, place in the oven, and bake for about 50 minutes, basting the onions regularly with the broth.

Remove the onions from the oven and pour off the liquid into a pan. Bring to a boil, then remove from the heat and whisk in the butter, a little at a time. Pour the sauce back over the onions and return them to the oven for 15–20 minutes, until they have a wonderful shiny glaze and are very tender.

apple and apricot tarts with rosemary syrup

$^1/_2$ cup dried apricots
2 tablespoons apricot jam
18 oz. puff pastry dough
6 Granny Smith apples
$^1/_4$ cup ($^1/_2$ stick) unsalted butter
$^1/_2$ cup demerara (or light brown) sugar
$^1/_2$ tablespoon finely chopped rosemary, plus 4 small sprigs for decorating
$^1/_4$ cup Calvados (or other apple brandy)

Soak the dried apricots in hot water for 2 hours, until they are swollen and very soft. Drain well, then purée in a blender along with the jam until smooth. Keep chilled until ready to use.

Preheat the oven to 400°F. Roll out the pastry dough until it is $^1/_8$-inch thick and cut out four 6-inch circles. Place on a baking sheet in the fridge.

Peel the apples, cut them in half, and remove the cores. Cut each half into 4 wedges. Melt the butter in a large frying pan, add the apples, and fry for 3 minutes. Sprinkle the sugar and chopped rosemary over them, and fry for a further 2 minutes, stirring gently. By this stage, the apples should be slightly caramelized. Pour over the Calvados, then remove from the heat and let infuse. When the apples are cold, drain them well, reserving any caramelized syrup.

Arrange the apples in 4 tartlet or other molds, 4–5 inches in diameter, and top with a good spoonful of the apricot mixture and then place a pastry dough circle on top. With the back of a knife, gently ease the edge of the pastry down between the apples and the mold. Make a small hole in the center of each pastry lid to allow steam to escape.

Place the molds on a baking tray and bake for 8–9 minutes, until the crust is golden. Let them cool slightly, then turn out the tarts, upside down, onto hot plates. Spoon the reserved syrup over them, warming it first if necessary, decorate with rosemary sprigs, and serve. A dollop of yogurt goes particularly well with these tarts.

mustard *Brassica juncea, B. nigra,* and *Sinapis alba*

I think I am a little compulsive about mustard. In my kitchen at home one of my shelves is about to collapse under the strain of the weight of jars of my favorite condiment, which I add to roasts, meat pies, and fish dishes—even to beans on toast.

On my travels, I always seek out the local market to see what new mustard or condiments can be found. In Germany I have enjoyed a selection of mustards with an enormous range of specialty sausages. In Sweden I discovered a sweeter variety called Savora, served with wonderful meat and fish dishes, and in Britain, who hasn't enjoyed a dollop of mustard paste made from ground powder, served with traditional favorites such as bangers, chops, or cold meats?

recipes

MINI CRAB PIES WITH MUSTARD AND SORREL VELOUTÉ (PAGE 52)

EMMENTAL, MUSTARD, AND SAGE BEIGNETS (PAGE 53)

DEVILED LOBSTER (PAGE 53)

GLAZED BARBECUE MUSTARD SQUABS WITH SWEET POTATOES AND FENNEL (PAGE 54)

CHICKEN SCHNITZELS WITH MUSTARD, CAPERS, AND LEMON (PAGE 54)

SEE ALSO:

CAESAR STEAK SANDWICH (PAGE 111)

PORK CHOPS WITH SAGE AND CARAMELIZED GINGER APPLES (PAGE 102)

SALT-CURED SALMON (GRAVAD LAX) (PAGE 168)

PORK LOIN COOKED IN VANILLA MILK (PAGE 145)

It is unclear who first had the idea of taking mild mustard seeds and crushing them with vinegar to use as a condiment or remedy. In England, where the name of mustard comes from the Latin meaning "burning must", the seeds were mixed with "must" or unfermented grape juice.

The Chinese were already using mustard some 3,000 years ago in its whole form. In the first century A.D. the Roman writer, Pliny the Elder, proclaimed in his *Natural History* that mustard's pungent flavor burned like fire. In medieval Europe, mustard was one of the few spices ordinary people could afford to use to flavor their bland monotonous dishes.

DESCRIPTION

Mustard, a member of the Cruciferae family, is a herbaceous annual which can grow to 3 feet in height. The plants bear clusters of bright yellow flowers, which in turn yield the fruit pods that contain the mustard seeds. These pods need to be harvested just before they are fully ripe and the pods burst. There are about forty varieties throughout the world, three of which are grown for their seeds:

White mustard (*Brassica alba*), beige-colored seeds, mild in flavor. This is the most common variety and is used to make American and English mustard, condiments, and for pickling.

Brown or Chinese mustard (*Brassica juncea*), dark brown seeds, used for making strong mustards and added to curry powders and pastes. The seeds are small and not as pungent as the black variety. The leaves (mustard greens) have a peppery flavor and are widely used in Chinese cooking.

Black mustard (*Brassica nigra*), seeds are smaller and more pungent than the white variety. They are used in strong and aromatic mustards such as Meaux, Djion, Bordeaux, and German.

To make mustard, the seeds are slightly crushed to crack the outer husk (for coarse-grain mustard, the husks remain untouched), then soaked in brandy vinegar, water, and salt for several hours, before being weighed, then mixed with spices and ground. The mustard is then matured for several hours in wooden vats, during which time it loses its initial bitter flavor. Finally, citric acid is added and (sometimes) a little turmeric to produce the strong yellow color.

Blended mustards fall into two categories: smooth and coarse. They can be flavored with herbs, chiles, green peppercorns, or soft berry fruits, especially black currant, and alcohol (such as Champagne). They can be mild or fiery, aromatic or pungent. Originally, when mustard was prepared at home, the seeds would be pounded in a mortar and blended with honey and vinegar.

DIJON MUSTARD By the fourteenth century, Dijon in France was firmly established as a mustard-producing center. Today, much of the world's mustard emanates from Dijon, the capital of Burgundy. Dijon mustard, made with black and brown seeds, is pale, smooth, and clean-tasting. Dijon-style mustard can be made legally anywhere on the globe, as the ingredients are not found locally. In fact, the provinces of Saskatchewan, Alberta, and Manitoba in Canada provide most of the seeds for the mustard industry in Dijon, the firm of Caveda supplying 90 percent of the total.

COARSE-GRAIN MUSTARD Coarse-grain or seed mustard is made by leaving the seed husks on, and can vary in flavor from mild to very hot. It has a lot more texture than the smooth Dijon varieties. The most famous is Moutarde de Meaux, which is stored in small earthenware pots.

CULINARY USES

Taillevent, the celebrity French chef and author, used mustard in his seasonings and sauces and even created a recipe for mustard soup. In dishes calling for a lot of mustard, and a little added punch, I usually use my favorite Dijon variety. Coarse-grain mustard is wonderful in sauces, vinegars, or dressings, or as an accompaniment to cold meats. It is also great added to creamy mashed potatoes. I rub the grains over the skin of pork before roasting and use them in marinades. Mustard and bread crumbs make a delicious crust for lamb, pork, and chicken; The Italian fruit relish, Mostarda di Frutta, is the most famous "sweet" use of mustard.

Mustard can be kept in the cupboard in a cool place, and should always be added to dishes at the end of cooking, otherwise it loses character. Never boil a sauce once mustard has been added, or it will taste bitter.

Apart from prepared mustard, the seeds are used in their own right. White seeds are used as a pickling spice, while the brown are an important flavoring in south Indian cuisines where they are ground to form the base of sauces for fish. Seeds are also used for flavoring butter (tadka) and are added to the Bengali spice mixes, panch phoron and sambal pods. Indian chefs fry black seeds with other seasonings such as cumin in a hot dry pan until they pop. This "tempering" brings out their nutty flavor before adding them to dishes.

Mustard sprouts, grown from white and brown seeds, add a spark of flavor to sandwiches and salads and can act as a substitute for alfafa sprouts.

Mustard must be used with care, as its true purpose is not to dominate, but to provide subtle background flavors, to add depth and intensity.

OTHER USES

Pliny noted some forty remedies that mustard could cure, including arthritis and loss of appetite, and that it was used in the treatment of wounds. Black mustard was once used for poultices, and mustard plasters are still in use today. Warmed mustard oil is an excellent treatment for easing arthritic pain, and in India it is rubbed into the scalp to promote hair growth. Pythagoras believed that mustard improved the memory.

complementary flavors

- MILK- AND CREAM-BASED SAUCES
- PEPPERCORNS
- VEGETABLES (ESPECIALLY LEEKS, ONIONS, AND POTATOES)
- HARD CHEESES (EMMENTAL, GRUYÈRE, AND CHEDDAR)
- OTHER CONDIMENTS (CAPERS AND GHERKINS)
- HONEY
- HAM AND PORK
- SALMON

mini crab pies with mustard and sorrel velouté

These delicious mini pies are basically a fishcake mix baked in crisp puff pastry. The slightly sour mustard sauce acts as a perfect foil to the sweet crabmeat. They make a great dinner party hors d'oeuvre.

2 tablespoons unsalted butter
1 onion, finely chopped
1 small leek, finely chopped
1 cup freshly flaked crabmeat
Juice and grated zest of 1/2 lemon
1 tablespoon Dijon mustard
1 egg yolk
1 tablespoon crème fraîche (or sour cream)
2 cups fresh white breadcrumbs
1/2 tablespoon chopped fresh tarragon
A dash of Tabasco sauce
9 oz. dough puff pastry
Beaten egg, for glazing
Salt and freshly ground black pepper

FOR THE SAUCE:

1 cup fish broth
1/2 cup dry white wine
2 shallots, finely chopped
1/2 cup heavy cream
Juice of 1/4 lemon
1/2 teaspoon Dijon mustard
A handful of sorrel leaves

Heat the butter in a pan, add the onion and leek, and cook gently until tender. Let cool, then place in a bowl and add the crabmeat, lemon juice and zest, mustard, egg yolk and crème fraîche. Stir in the bread crumbs and tarragon, and season with the Tabasco and some salt and pepper.

Preheat the oven to 400°F. Roll out the pastry dough and cut out circles with a 3-inch cutter to line 8 greased muffin cups, reserving another 8 pastry circles for the lids. Divide the crab mixture among the dough-lined muffin cups, brush the dough edges with beaten egg, and top with the pastry dough lids. Brush each pie with a little more egg glaze, then make 2 small holes in the lid to let the steam escape. Bake for 10–12 minutes, until puffed and golden.

For the sauce, put the fish broth, wine, and shallots in a pan and boil over high heat until it becomes reduced and syrupy in consistency. Add the cream and boil again until the sauce is thick enough to coat the back of a spoon. Strain through a strainer into a clean pan, add the lemon juice and mustard, and then drop the sorrel into the sauce. Cook for 30 seconds more, then adjust the seasoning to taste and serve with the mini crab pies.

emmental, mustard, and sage beignets

These crisp little fritters are nice served with a tomato sauce or tomato salad. Smaller ones make great nibbles or canapés.

MAKES 32

1 lb. Emmental cheese
1 tablespoon Dijon mustard
8 sheets of brek pastry dough, cut into 4 sections
1/4 cup (1/2 stick) unsalted butter, melted
32 small sage leaves
Vegetable oil for deep-frying

FOR THE BATTER:

1 1/2 teaspoons fresh yeast
1/2 cup warm milk
a scant cup cornstarch
Salt and freshly ground black pepper

Cut the Emmental into 32 sticks, about 2 1/2 inches x 1 inch each, and brush them with the mustard. Lay out the brek pastry dough and brush liberally with melted butter. Put a piece of cheese on top of each piece of dough and then roll in the ends of the pastry and roll it up like an egg roll. Brush the outside liberally with butter. Put a sage leaf on top of each one, pressing it down lightly so it sticks. Place in the fridge for 1 hour.

To make the batter, place the yeast in a bowl, pour in 2 tablespoons of the warm milk and leave for 1 minute. Mix in the cornstarch and then stir in the remaining milk to give a smooth batter. Season to taste.

Heat the oil to 350°F in a deep-fat fryer or a large, deep pot. (Make sure you test the temperature of the oil with a cube of day-old bread before using; if it is hot enough, the bread will brown in 30 seconds.) Drop the sage-covered cheese rolls into the batter, then into the hot oil and cook for 2 minutes, until golden brown and crisp. Drain on paper towels to remove excess oil, then serve immediately.

deviled lobster

If the idea of cooking live lobsters doesn't appeal, ask the person at your fish counter to get you cooked fresh ones, not frozen; as the freshness of the succulent, sweet lobster meat is paramount for this dish.

4 x 1 1/2 lbs. live Scottish or Canadian lobsters
1 tablespoon Dijon mustard
1/2 cup (1 stick) unsalted butter, melted
1 garlic clove, crushed
3 tablespoons chopped flat-leaf parsley
2 tablespoons brandy
1 tablespoon Worcestershire sauce
Juice of 1 lemon
2 3/4 cups fresh white bread crumbs (allowed to dry out)
Salt and freshly ground black pepper

In the largest pot you have, plunge the lobsters head first into plenty of boiling water, return quickly to a boil, and cook for 5 minutes (it may be necessary to cook them one at a time unless you have a very large pot). Transfer the lobsters to a sink of cold water to refresh them until cold.

Remove the claws and crack them to remove the meat. Place it in a bowl. Cut the lobsters in half lengthwise, reserving the shells, and remove and discard the intestines and the sacs near the head. Take out the meat, cut it into 3/4-inch pieces and add to the bowl. Add the tomalley (a greenish substance) and any coral to the bowl, too. Mix in the mustard, half the melted butter, the garlic, parsley, brandy, and Worcestershire sauce. Season with salt and pepper and stir in the lemon juice and bread crumbs.

Preheat the oven to 375°F. Season the 8 lobster halves and place them on a baking tray. Fill them with the lobster mixture, packing it firmly into the cavities. Drizzle the remaining melted butter over the lobsters and place in the oven for 5–6 minutes, until heated through and wonderfully golden and crispy on top.

Serve with more melted butter, if you like, and a great big mixed salad.

glazed barbecue mustard squabs with sweet potatoes and fennel

4 x 1 lb. squab pigeons
1 teaspoon ground cumin
1/4 cup Dijon mustard
1/4 cup olive oil, plus extra for serving
1/4 cup Madeira wine
1 tablespoon roughly chopped rosemary
1 tablespoon thyme leaves
1 tablespoon chopped parsley
1 teaspoon black peppercorns
1/2 teaspoon mustard seeds
2 tablespoons honey
2 tablespoons unsalted butter
Salt
Lemon wedges, for serving

FOR THE SWEET POTATOES AND FENNEL:

1 1/4 lbs. orange-fleshed sweet potatoes, peeled and cut into chunks
1 large fennel bulb, cut into wedges
1/4 cup olive oil
2 garlic cloves, crushed
1 tablespoon chopped rosemary

To prepare the squabs, cut out the backbone with kitchen scissors. Break down the wishbone using your hand, turn each bird cut-side down, and flatten it by pressing down with the heel of your hand. Turn it over and remove all the ribcage bones.

Season the squabs with salt and the cumin, then brush with half the Dijon mustard. Place in a dish, pour the olive oil and Madeira over them, and sprinkle the herbs on top. Cover with foil and leave in the refrigerator to marinate for 24 hours, turning occasionally.

Preheat the oven to 400°F. Toss the sweet potatoes and fennel with the oil, garlic, and rosemary, transfer to a flameproof roasting pan, and roast for about 30 minutes, until golden and tender.

Meanwhile, make the glaze. Roughly crack the peppercorns and mustard seeds in a mortar and pestle, then put them in a pan with the remaining mustard and the honey. Bring to a boil, add the butter, and remove from the heat. Heat a barbecue or a ridged grill pan. Remove the squabs from the marinade and place on the barbecue or grill pan. Cook for 4–5 minutes on each side, basting occasionally with the mustard glaze.

To serve, place the sweet potatoes and fennel on serving plates, top with the squabs, then drizzle a little olive oil over them and garnish with lemon wedges.

Paul's Tip The mustard glaze can be used on other grilled meats and fish, with excellent results.

chicken schnitzels with mustard, capers, and lemon

4 boneless, skinless chicken breasts
1 large tablespoon Dijon mustard
3 tablespoons honey
Juice and grated zest of 1 lemon
1/4 cup all-purpose flour
2 eggs, beaten
3 cups fresh white bread crumbs
2 tablespoons olive oil
1/4 cup (1/2 stick) unsalted butter
2 tablespoons superfine capers, drained and rinsed
1 tablespoon chopped parsley
2 lemons, peel and pith removed, cut into slices
Salt and freshly ground black pepper

Place the chicken breasts between 2 sheets of plastic wrap and, with a meat mallet or rolling pin, bash them out into escalopes about 1/2-inch thick.

Mix the mustard, honey, and lemon zest together in a bowl and then brush the mixture liberally all over the chicken. Season with salt and pepper. To make the schnitzels, dip the chicken in the flour to coat it, then in the beaten egg, and finally dredge it in the bread crumbs.

Heat the oil in a large frying pan, add the schnitzels, and fry for about 2–3 minutes per side, until golden and cooked through. Add the butter to the pan and, when it begins to foam, add the capers, parsley, and lemon juice. Spoon this mixture over the schnitzels, then transfer to 4 warm serving plates. Garnish with the lemon slices and serve immediately.

cinnamon *Cinnamomum verum*

True cinnamon and its less refined cousin, cassia (*Cinnamomum cassia*), are two of the earliest spices to have been traded between ancient civilizations. References to it are found in the Old Testament in early rituals, while the ancient Egyptians used it for embalming their pharaohs. Roman Emperor Nero reportedly burned his pregnant wife on a cinnamon pyre as a gesture of remorse after murdering her.

recipes

True cinnamon is indigenous to Sri Lanka, although it is also grown in India, Indonesia, and the Seychelles. The Portuguese colonized Sri Lanka (then called Ceylon) for its cinnamon until they were driven out by the Dutch in 1636. The Dutch later controlled prices worldwide by limiting its supply.

DESCRIPTION

Cinnamon is an evergreen tree (*Cinnamomum verum*) of the laurel family. Sri Lanka is the largest and considered to be the best producer of cinnamon in the world, exporting up to 10,000 tons a year. The spice we use in cooking is the dried inner bark from the branches of the cinnamon tree. This tree can grow as tall as 30 to 40 feet high in the wild, but is cropped when cultivated to 8 feet to aid harvesting and to keep the bark both thin and tender.

Harvesting is carried out twice a year, following the rainy seasons in late spring/early summer, and then again in the late fall, when the trees' aromatic oils are at their peak. The finest bark comes from the center of the plant. The outer bark is carefully scraped away, the paper-thin inner bark is peeled off and rolls naturally into quills as it dries. The rolled quills are eventually tied into large bundles for shipping.

Cinnamon and cassia are very similar, but are different in flavor and in form. Whereas the true cinnamon is rolled, cassia comes as a flat bark which is stronger and sometimes bitter—an inferior relative.

BUYING AND STORING

When buying cinnamon, ensure that quills are long and whole, not chipped. Store in a dry, dark place, wrapped in brown paper. Although good-quality ground cinnamon is readily available, it is easy to grind your own in a spice grinder or blender (some cheaper, ready-ground brands can be lackluster). Only buy a little at a time, when needed, as it quickly loses its fragrance and the color fades with age.

CULINARY USES

From a culinary standpoint, cinnamon has a special, somewhat seductive, fragrance and a comforting taste. It flavors sweet and savory dishes worldwide. In the Far East it is regularly used in rice dishes, especially Malaysian; it is an ingredient in Asian curries, and forms an essential part of garam masala along with cloves, cilantro, cardamom, and black pepper.

The Persians created wonderful ingredient dishes with cinnamon, dusted it onto soups, and used it to flavor salads and stews. Along with raisins and toasted almonds, it is also used to flavor Persian rice dishes, and is an important ingredient in the spice mix, advieh. In Spain, it is a much-loved commodity which can be traced back to the Moorish occupation. The Spanish add it to pork dishes and dust it over custard desserts.

The Moroccans, whose cuisine I adore, use it in slowly braized stews, tagines, and salads. It is an important spice in many Moroccan blends of ras el hanout and forms the main flavor in the classic B'stulla, a savory yet delicate cinnamon-flavored pie of pigeon with almonds, eggs, and saffron.

In Europe and Britain, the spice is enjoyed in baked goods, bread, apple pies, strudels, and as a flavoring in fruit compôtes. It is especially good with pears, plums, apples, and in the old recipes for mulled wine. In cooking it can be used whole or freshly ground. I particularly like to use it to flavor milk puddings and custards. It also makes a great icecream and is wonderful combined with chocolate in a mousse or sauce. Cinnamon is a spice I could certainly not do without in my kitchen. It is delicate yet intense, as homey as it is comforting, and for me conjures up many happy memories of freshly baked apple pies.

OTHER USES

Cinnamon was prized by ancient physicians for its anti-fungal and anti-bacterial properties and was used in religious ceremonies. Nowadays it is thought to soothe rheumatic pains and its oil is used in the perfume industry.

complementary flavors

- MEAT (ESPECIALLY LAMB, CHICKEN, AND OTHER WHITE MEATS)
- DAIRY PRODUCTS (EGGS, CUSTARDS, ICECREAM, AND YOGURT)
- CHOCOLATE
- NUTS
- HONEY
- SAFFRON
- RICE
- COUSCOUS
- FRUIT (PEARS, PLUMS, APPLES, ORANGES, CHERRIES, AND APRICOTS)

cinnamon quails

The quails are braized in cinnamon-scented broth, then a little sumac is sprinkled on top before serving. Sumac is the crushed dried berries of the sumac bush and has a pleasant sour lemon flavor. It can be found in Middle Eastern grocery stores.

2 tablespoons unsalted butter
4 tablespoons vegetable oil
1 lb. small shallots, peeled but left whole
1/3 cup raisins
1 tablespoon best-quality ground cinnamon
3 cups well-flavored chicken broth
8 oven-ready quails
3/4 cup pine nuts, toasted
1/2 teaspoon sumac
Salt and freshly ground black pepper

Heat the butter and 1 tablespoon of the oil in a saucepan, add the shallots, and fry for 2–3 minutes, until golden all over. Add the raisins and cinnamon and cook gently for 5 minutes. Pour in the chicken broth, bring to a boil, and simmer for 15–20 minutes.

Heat the remaining oil in a large heavy pan until very hot. Season the quails and brown them all over in the hot oil. Add the chicken broth, shallots, and raisins, and bring to a boil. Reduce the heat and simmer for 15 minutes, turning the quails occasionally; the sauce should have reduced a little.

Put the quails in a serving dish, pour the sauce over them, and sprinkle the pine nuts and sumac on top. Serve immediately.

lamb tagine with prunes and cinnamon

This recipe uses all the wonderful flavors of Morocco. The lamb is slow-cooked with ginger and saffron and sweetened with cinnamon, one of Morocco's most popular spices.

1/4 cup vegetable oil
1 3/4 lbs. boned leg of lamb, cut into 1-inch cubes
2 onions, thinly sliced
2 garlic cloves, crushed
1 tablespoon best-quality ground cinnamon
1-inch piece of fresh ginger root, finely chopped
1/4 teaspoon saffron strands
4 cups lamb broth (or water)
1/4 cup honey
5 oz. (1-1 1/4 cups) whole blanched almonds
6 oz. (1-1 1/4 cups) prunes, pitted
2 teaspoons sesame seeds, toasted
Salt and freshly ground black pepper

In a tagine or large heavy pan, heat the oil until smoking. Add the lamb and fry until golden brown all over (do this in batches if necessary). Add the onions and garlic and cook for 10 minutes, until golden. Sprinkle half the cinnamon over it and mix well with the meat. Add the ginger and saffron, cover with the lamb broth or water, and bring to a boil. Reduce the heat, cover and cook gently for 1 hour or until the lamb is very tender.

Meanwhile, in a separate pan, heat the honey with the remaining cinnamon. Add the almonds and prunes and cook gently for 2 minutes, until they are glazed.

When the meat is cooked, adjust the seasoning, scatter the cinnamon-glazed prunes and nuts over it, sprinkle over the sesame seeds on top, and serve.

date and blood orange salad

A fragrant Moroccan-style salad, highly spiced with *ras el hanout*, a North African spice mix. *Ras el hanout* is made up of some 30 different spices, including dried roses, cardamom, turmeric, and cloves. Look for it in Middle Eastern stores and some specialty food stores. Serve this salad as a refreshing side dish.

Juice of 1 lime and 2 lemons
Grated zest of 1/2 lime and 1 lemon
About 3/4 teaspoon ground cinnamon
1 teaspoon orange flower water
2 tablespoons superfine sugar
4 blood oranges, peeled and thickly sliced
12 fresh dates, cut in half, pitted, and cut into strips
A pinch of *ras el hanout*

Put the lime and lemon juice and zest in a bowl, add a pinch of the cinnamon, plus the orange flower water and sugar, and mix well. Leave for 1 hour at room temperature. Place in a pan and boil for 5 minutes to form a light syrup. Remove from the heat and let cool, then chill.

Place the orange slices and dates in a bowl and pour the chilled syrup over them. Sprinkle the *ras el hanout* on top, then sprinkle over the remaining cinnamon to taste, and serve.

caramelized cinnamon cassata

Cassata is an iced Sicilian dessert usually made with sponge cake or amaretti cookies. Here I serve these with the dessert rather than using it in the recipe.

SERVES 8

1/2 cup superfine sugar
2 tablespoons freshly ground cinnamon
1 1/4 cups whole milk
1 1/4 cups heavy cream
8 egg yolks
1/2 teaspoon vanilla extract
1/2 cup mixed almonds, walnuts, and hazelnuts, lightly toasted and roughly chopped
1/3 cup mixed candied peel (citrons), finely chopped
1/2 teaspoon grated lemon zest
1/2 cup sweet marsala wine

FOR SERVING:
Chocolate sauce (see page 180), lightly flavored with marsala wine
Amaretti cookies

Put the sugar and cinnamon in a small, heavy pan and heat gently until melted. Raise the heat and cook, without stirring, until it becomes a dark amber colored caramel.

Meanwhile, heat the milk and cream almost to boiling point. When the caramel is ready, whisk it into the cream mixture (take great care; it is best to cover both hands with a cloth as the hot caramel will splatter). Set aside.

In a bowl, whisk the egg yolks and vanilla extract together. Carefully pour in the caramel cream mixture, whisking all the time, then return the mixture to a clean pan and cook, stirring, over a low heat until it has thickened enough to coat the back of the spoon (do not let it boil or it will curdle). Remove from the heat and let cool completely. When cool, churn in an icecream machine for 20 minutes until just beginning to set, adding the toasted nuts, candied peel, lemon zest, and marsala just before the end of the churning process. Line the bottom of a 2 1/2-pint pudding mold or 8-inch springform cake pan with waxed paper, fill with the cassata mixture, and freeze until needed.

To serve, dip the pudding mold or cake pan into hot water and then run a hot knife around the edge. Turn out the cassata onto a plate and cut into wedges. Serve with the chocolate sauce and some amaretti cookies.

slow-baked tamarillos in cinnamon-wine sauce

This very easy dish is an ideal winter dessert, particularly as tamarillos are now available in most large supermarkets and many produce markets. If you can't find them, however, plums make a good alternative. It's wonderful served with vanilla icecream.

3 cups Cabernet Sauvignon (or other full-bodied red wine)
2/3 cup soft brown sugar
1 vanilla bean, slit open lengthwise
2 cinnamon sticks
1 clove
8 ripe tamarillos, cut in half

Preheat the oven to 300°F. Put the wine, sugar, vanilla bean, cinnamon sticks, and clove in a saucepan, bring to simmering point, and leave on a low heat for 10 minutes to infuse.

Arrange the tamarillo halves in a single layer in a shallow ovenproof dish or pan, about 10 inches long. Pour the spiced wine syrup over them, place in the oven, and bake for 40–45 minutes, until the tamarillos are tender, spooning the juices over them a couple of times during baking.

Remove the tamarillos from the dish and keep warm. Strain the sauce through a strainer. It should be syrupy and thick; if it is not, pour it into a pan and simmer until it has reduced and thickened enough to coat the back of a spoon. Serve the warm tamarillos coated with the sauce.

cinnamon snow eggs with chocolate-cinnamon custard

Snow eggs, also called floating islands, are a classic dessert of which there are many variations. This version includes cinnamon, whose delicate flavor is highly compatible with both eggs and chocolate. It's a marriage made in heaven.

SERVES 6

6 egg whites
A tiny pinch of salt
3/4 cup superfine sugar, mixed with 1 teaspoon best-quality ground cinnamon
2 tablespoons unsalted butter, melted

FOR THE CUSTARD:

1 1/4 cups heavy cream
2/3 cup whole milk
1 teaspoon best-quality ground cinnamon
1/4 cup superfine sugar
4 egg yolks
2 oz. good-quality milk chocolate, grated or broken into pieces
1/2 cup dark rum

FOR THE CARAMELIZED HAZELNUTS:

1/4 cup superfine sugar
1/2 cup hazelnuts

Preheat the oven to 250°F. Put the egg whites and salt in a large, clean bowl and beat until they form peaks (you can use an electric beater for this). Gradually mix in the cinnamon sugar and continue beating until the meringue is stiff.

Lightly grease 6 large dariole molds or custard cups (about 3/4-1 cup in capacity) with the butter, then fill with the meringue and level off the tops. Tap the molds on a flat surface to ensure there are no air pockets. Place on a baking tray and bake for 10 minutes at 200°F, or until just set. Remove from the oven and let cool.

For the custard, put the cream, milk, ground cinnamon, and half the sugar in a saucepan and bring to a boil. Meanwhile, place the egg yolks and remaining sugar in a bowl and whisk together until pale and creamy. Gradually pour the cinnamon cream on to the egg yolks, whisking constantly. Return the mixture to the saucepan and cook, stirring, until it has thickened enough to coat the back of the spoon (do not let it boil or it will curdle). Remove from the heat, stir in the chocolate, and leave it until it melts. Strain the custard into a bowl and let it cool, then stir in the rum.

For the caramelized hazelnuts, put the sugar in a small, heavy pan and heat gently until melted. Raise the heat and cook, without stirring, until it becomes a golden amber color. Add the nuts, stir well, then pour out onto an oiled baking tray. Let cool and set, then chop into pieces.

To serve, run a knife around the snow eggs and turn them out onto 6 serving plates. Pour the custard around them and sprinkle the caramelized hazelnuts on top.

cinnamon milk fritters with hot cherries

3 cups whole milk
1 teaspoon vanilla extract
1 tablespoon best-quality ground cinnamon
4 egg yolks
1 1/4 cups superfine sugar
Grated zest of 1 lemon
A heaped cup all-purpose flour
2 egg whites
2 cups fresh white bread crumbs
Vegetable oil for deep-frying
1/4 cup cinnamon sugar (see Tip opposite)

FOR THE CHERRIES:

1 lb. morello cherries (or other fresh cherries), pitted

3/4 cup preserving sugar (with pectin)
1/3 cup kirsch

Put the milk, vanilla extract, and cinnamon in a saucepan and bring gently to a boil. Meanwhile, beat the egg yolks and sugar together in a bowl until blended, then add the lemon zest and sift in the flour, stirring well. Whisk a boiled milk slowly into the egg mixture, then return to the pan and cook over medium heat until the custard becomes smooth and thick. Raise the heat to bring it to a boil, then pour into a shallow dish in a layer about 1-inch thick. Let cool, then transfer to the fridge until set firm.

Meanwhile, prepare the cherries. Put them in a bowl, along with the sugar and kirsch, and mix well. Let marinate for 2 hours, during which time they will release their juices. Strain off the juice into a saucepan and simmer until it forms a syrup. Add the cherries and keep warm while you cook the fritters.

To finish the fritters, cut the well-chilled mixture into 3-inch squares. Lightly beat the egg whites in one bowl and put the bread crumbs in another. Dip the custard squares in the egg whites, then dredge them in the bread crumbs, coating them well all over.

Heat the vegetable oil to 325°F in a deep-fat fryer or large, deep pot. To test the temperature of the oil, drop in a cube of day-old bread, it should brown in 30 seconds. Fry the fritters a few at a time, until golden and crisp. Remove with a slotted spoon and place in a dish lined with paper towels. Dust with the cinnamon sugar and serve with the hot cherries.

Paul's Tip To make cinnamon sugar, mix 1/2 cup superfine sugar with 1 teaspoon of best-quality ground cinnamon and store in an airtight jar.

breakfast brûlée

At the Lanesborough we have, I like to think, a breakfast menu capable of brightening the most jaded palate, ready for the day ahead. A popular dish is this breakfast brûlée, prepared like the classic creme brûlée but with oatmeal. Try it for breakfast or brunch, topped with some seasonal berries or fruit compôte.

1/2 pint whole milk
A pinch of salt
1 cinnamon stick
4 tablespoons superfine sugar
1/2 cup old-fashioned oats
6 egg yolks
1 1/4 cups heavy cream
1/4 cup demerara (or light brown) sugar

Bring the milk, salt, cinnamon stick, and half the sugar to a boil. Remove from the heat and let it infuse for 2–3 minutes, then remove the cinnamon stick. Return the pan to the heat and rain in the oats, stirring constantly. Reduce the heat and simmer for 2–3 minutes, then let cool.

In another bowl, whisk the egg yolks with the remaining sugar until the sugar has dissolved. Add the heavy cream and the cooked oatmeal, and mix well.

Preheat the oven to 275°F. Divide the oatmeal custard between 4 shallow gratin dishes, each 1 cup in capacity. Place the dishes in a flameproof roasting pan, then place the pan in the oven. Pour enough cold water into the pan to come about halfway up the sides of the dishes and bake for 30–35 minutes, until set. Let cool for 2 minutes, then sprinkle the brown sugar evenly over the surface of each custard. Use a blowtorch to caramelize the tops, holding it at an angle (the flame should barely touch the surface). Alternatively, caramelize the sugar under a very hot broiler.

Serve immediately.

saffron *Crocus sativus*

Sources differ greatly as to the number of crocus blossoms (*Crocus sativus*) needed to produce 1 lb. of fresh saffron, but estimates range from 400,000 to 750,000—which undoubtedly explains why it is the world's most expensive spice, if not ingredient. It is even more expensive than silver, per gram.

recipes

Saffron originated in Persia. It was carried from there to Kashmir, and has been used in Hindu rituals for centuries. Ancient Greeks and Romans later used it as a cosmetic and to dye and scent their bathing water. Emperor Nero ordered that the streets of Rome be doused with saffron oil before he entered astride his horse (could this be the predecessor of today's red carpet ritual, I wonder?). Saffron was a symbol of power, wealth, and refinement across Europe until the fall of the Roman Empire, when its use declined tremendously. Throughout its history, the spice has been used to gild all manner of pastries, meat, and seafood dishes.

Arab merchants introduced saffron to Spain in the eighth century and today it is the principal producer, along with India, South America, and some smaller producers, such as Italy. The best saffron comes from the La Mancha region of Spain.

DESCRIPTION

Saffron is contained in the stigmas of the saffron crocus, a perennial bulb that flowers for two weeks in the late fall. Harvesting, an emormously painstaking and labor-intensive task, is carried out at dawn, before the flowers wilt in the heat of the sun. The ankle-high purple flowers are collected by hand and from each small flower are picked the three tiny red strands which are then dried in mesh strainers over the embers of a fire—a procedure which greatly enhances the flavor, and gives a slightly toasted taste.

BUYING AND STORING

You can buy saffron in two forms, as threads (or hebras), or as a powder. In good-quality saffron, the threads should be a fiery reddish brown, wire-like in appearance. The powder comes in small sachets, generally enough for a single use, and is far cheaper and more generally available. However, as a powder it is much harder to detect its quality or pureness; most is adulterated with marigold or safflower (known as bastard saffron) which, while similar in appearance and lending the same beautiful color to food, has nowhere near the same flavor.

Do not be fooled or tempted to buy cheaper, easily available varieties—especially when on vacation in Spain or other Mediterranean countries. During a recent vacation in Marrakesh I saw mounds of saffron-colored spices which, while visually appealing, was in fact turmeric (or Indian saffron). It is not the same thing at all, so beware, and remember that price is the definitive guide to the real thing.

Store saffron in a cool dry place, away from light (which can bleach it to a faded yellow) in an airtight jar to keep its fragrance. It may also be well wrapped in plastic wrap and kept in the freezer.

CULINARY USES

Traditionally used in Europe in such dishes as French Bouillabaisse and other fish soups, it is more commonly used to flavor dishes such as the Spanish Paella and Italian Risotto a la Milanese. In Morocco, India, and throughout the Middle East (but particularly in Iran), saffron is used for flavoring and color rice dishes. In Iran and India, it is also used in puddings, breads, and cakes for religious celebrations.

complementary flavors

- RICE
- FISH (ESPECIALLY SEA BASS, TURBOT, AND HALIBUT)
- SHELLFISH
- MEAT (ESPECIALLY CHICKEN AND VEAL)
- TOMATOES
- BASIL
- CHOCOLATE
- VANILLA
- DAIRY PRODUCTS (CREAM, CUSTARD, YOGURT, EGGS)
- SPICES (SMOKED PAPRIKA AND CINNAMON)

Saffron not only adds a wonderful magical quality to savory dishes, but it is also used in desserts, transforming milky custard, brûlées, and icecreams, or in sweet syrup to poach fruits. The northern Indians use it for flavoring sweet rice dishes such as Pirni, and add it to drinks. Even the simplest dish is transformed with a little pinch of saffron; it gives a vibrant yellow-gold color and a honey-like musty flavor. I love adding saffron to creamy mashed potatoes or infusing it into mayonnaise for fish.

When using saffron, I prefer to use fresh saffron stigma every time, rather than the powder. Having said this, the powder does have its uses in dishes where the spice can be added at any stage of the cooking process. I prefer to use the powder in cakes.

Fresh stigmas must be heat-activated before using, or their impact will be disappointing. As a rule, saffron is added to hot liquids such as broths, syrup, and sauces to extract its natural coloring and fragrance. I generally rub the stigmas between my fingers prior to adding them to the liquid, and then steep them for 20–30 minutes to really liberate the flavors and aromas. Some purists suggest steeping saffron in water (or broth or wine, depending on the recipe) for 4 hours to get the best from it.

One last word on saffron: follow the recipes carefully. Very little is needed to flavor a dish, and too much, although it might give a wonderful color, can leave an unpleasant taste. Never be tempted to add more than a recipe calls for.

OTHER USES

Rich in carotenoid, a light yellow to deep red pigment, saffron was used in ancient times as a dye for fabrics. Nero had filaments of the spice sown onto his pillows believing it to be a remedy for insomnia. It was also thought to be an aphrodisiac and was prescribed for fevers and urinary disorders.

andalusian fish soup with saffron aïoli

1/2 cup olive oil
1 onion, finely chopped
2 garlic cloves, crushed
1/2 teaspoon dried chili flakes
1 small bay leaf
1/2 teaspoon ground cumin
1 teaspoon grated orange zest
A good pinch of saffron strands
4 cups fish broth
12 oz. mixed shellfish (such as mussels and clams)
3 slices of white bread
1 teaspoon tomato paste
1 teaspoon smoked paprika
1 lb. mixed fish fillets (such as monkfish, snapper and cod), cut into 1-inch pieces
Salt and freshly ground black pepper

FOR THE AÏOLI:
1 garlic clove, chopped
A good pinch of saffron strands
1 tablespoon lemon juice
2/3 cup good-quality mayonnaise

Heat half the oil in a large pan, add the onion, and cook for about 8 minutes, until tender. Add the garlic, chili flakes, bay leaf, cumin, orange zest, and saffron. Pour in the fish broth, bring to a boil, and simmer for 10–15 minutes.

Meanwhile, clean the mussels and clams under cold running water and pull out the beards from the mussels. Discard any open mussels or clams that don't close when tapped hard on the counter.

Soak the bread in a little water, squeeze it dry, then place in a blender, with the tomato paste, smoked paprika, and the remaining oil. Blend to a paste and add to the soup. Carefully add the fish to the soup and simmer gently for 5 minutes. Add the shellfish and cook for 3–4 minutes, until the shells open. Season to taste and keep warm.

To make the aïoli, crush the garlic and saffron in a mortar along with the lemon juice and then stir into the mayonnaise.

Divide the fish and shellfish between 4 serving bowls and pour the broth over them. Serve with the aïoli, plus some good crusty bread to mop up the juices.

persian scrambled eggs

1/4 teaspoon saffron strands
1/4 cup (1/2 stick) unsalted butter
6 tablespoons heavy cream
1/4 teaspoon ground cumin
8 large organic or cage-free eggs
1/2 tablespoon chopped cilantro
1 tablespoon chopped mint
1 small green chile, seeded and finely chopped
Salt and freshly ground black pepper
Grilled pita bread, for serving

Place a saucepan over medium heat for 1 minute, then add the saffron strands and toast them for 10 seconds to release their delicate fragrance. Add the butter and cream and stir well. Bring slowly to a boil and add the cumin.

Lightly beat the eggs in a bowl with some salt and pepper. Pour them into the saffron cream and cook over a gentle heat until they are very softly scrambled. Fold in the herbs and green chile. Serve with freshly grilled pita bread.

lobster, saffron, and mango salad

1/2 red pepper, cut into long shreds 1/8-inch thick
1/2 green pepper, cut into long shreds 1/8-inch thick
1 mango, peeled, pitted, and cut into long shreds 1/8-inch thick
1-inch piece of fresh ginger root, finely shredded
1 1/2 lbs. live lobsters
5 oz. (2–3 cups) mixed exotic salad greens

FOR THE DRESSING:

2 tablespoons maple syrup
1 tablespoon aged balsamic vinegar
1/4 cup lime juice
6 tablespoons orange juice
1/4 cup lemon juice
1/4 teaspoon saffron strands
1/4 cup mango chutney
1 tablespoon chopped mint
1 drop of Tabasco sauce
3 tablespoons sesame oil

First make the dressing (this can be done well in advance). In a saucepan, warm together the maple syrup, balsamic vinegar, and the lime, orange, and lemon juice. Add the saffron and heat gently for 2 minutes to infuse. Remove from the heat and let cool. Place in a blender or food processor, add the mango chutney, mint, and Tabasco, and blitz until smooth. Pour into a bowl and whisk in the sesame oil. Place the shredded peppers, mango, and ginger in a bowl, pour about two-thirds of the dressing over them, and infuse for 1 hour.

Cook the lobsters (see page 53) and then let them cool in a bowl of cold water.

To serve, cut the lobster bodies and tails in half down the back and carefully remove the tail meat. Crack the claws to remove the meat in one piece. Arrange one half-tail section and claw on each serving plate. Toss the salad greens with the remaining dressing and place a small pile of greens at the head of each plate. Arrange the shredded vegetables and mango on top of the lobster and pour over them any dressing left in the bowl.

saffron brioches

MAKES 24—30

5 cups white bread flour
1 teaspoon salt
1 tablespoon sugar
1/3 cup (3/4 stick) softened unsalted butter, cut into small pieces
1 1/2 oz. fresh yeast (or 1 1/2 tablespoons dried yeast)
3 large eggs
2 good pinches saffron powder
1 egg yolk mixed with 1 tablespoon milk, for glazing

Sift the flour and salt into a warmed bowl and stir in the sugar. Make a well in the center and put the butter in it.

Blend the yeast with a quarter-cup of warm water. Put the eggs and saffron powder in a separate bowl and beat lightly. Pour into the well in the flour and add the yeast mixture. Mix to a soft dough, then knead for about 5 minutes, until smooth and elastic. Cover and leave in a warm place for about 1 1/2 hours, until doubled in size.

Punch down the risen dough and knead briefly, then roll out into a sausage shape. Divide into 24—30 pieces, about 1 1/2 inches long. Roll each piece into a ball and place them on greased baking sheets, ensuring they are at least 2 inches apart. Cover the rolls with a cloth and leave in a warm place for about 30 minutes, until risen and puffy.

Preheat the oven to 425°F. Brush the rolls with the egg glaze and bake for 10—12 minutes, until golden. Remove from the oven and transfer to a wire rack to cool.

saffron pavlova with lime curd

SERVES 6

6 egg whites
1 cup superfine sugar
4 pinches saffron powder
1 teaspoon white wine vinegar
1 teaspoon boiling water
1/2 teaspoon vanilla extract
1 tablespoon cornstarch
Heavy cream or plain yogurt, for serving
A little blanched shredded lime zest, for decorating

FOR THE LIME CURD:
6 egg yolks
3/4 cup superfine sugar
Juice and grated zest 6 large limes (you will need 3/4 cup juice)
A pinch of salt
1/2 cup (1 stick) chilled unsalted butter, chopped

Preheat the oven to 250°F. Put the egg whites and sugar in a clean, dry bowl and beat until they form stiff peaks. Mix the saffron powder with the vinegar and boiling water, then beat it into the beaten whites, along with the vanilla extract. Finally fold in the cornstarch.

Line 2 baking sheets with parchment paper and spread the meringue mixture on it in 6 mounded circles (alternatively, pipe the mixture into 6 nests, using a pastry bag with a plain nozzle). Bake for 50–60 minutes, until they are crisp but still pale on the outside and have a soft marshmallow center. Store in an airtight container until needed.

For the lime curd, beat the egg yolks and sugar together until thick and creamy, then add the lime juice and zest. Place in a heavy pan and cook, stirring, over low heat until the mixture thickens a little. Add the salt and immediately remove from the heat. Whisk in the chilled chopped butter and let cool. Cover and keep in the fridge until needed.

To serve, top each saffron pavlova with a good dollop of lime curd and then pour some cream or yogurt over them, and decorate with a little blanched lime zest.

cumin *Cuminum cyminum*

Suited to most cuisines of the world, cumin is an essential spice. Native to Egypt, it has been used by the Egyptians for over 5,000 years.

recipes

TOMATO, CUMIN, AND POMEGRANATE SOUP (PAGE 72)

CUMIN SWORDFISH SOUVLAKI (PAGE 72)

ROASTED BABY CARROTS WITH CUMIN (PAGE 74)

PORK ADOBO (PAGE 75)

CUMIN SHORTBREAD (PAGE 75)

SEE ALSO:

SPICE-GRILLED PUMPKIN SALAD (PAGE 116)

ASIAN-STYLE DIRTY RICE (PAGE 119)

COFFEE-ROASTED SPARE RIBS (PAGE 156)

SPICY GARLIC AND TOMATO RELISH (PAGE 112)

STEAMED MUSSELS WITH SPICY GREMOLATA (PAGE 101)

GLAZED BARBECUE MUSTARD SQUABS WITH SWEET POTATOES AND FENNEL (PAGE 54)

TAMARIND AND DATE CHUTNEY (PAGE 138)

DESCRIPTION

Cumin seeds are the fruit of the annual herb (*Cuminum cyminum*), a close cousin of parsley, cilantro, dill, and fennel. It is also related to caraway, and their seeds can easily be confused, so take care when labeling your spice jars.

Cumin thrives in warm weather and is now grown extensively in Iran, India, Morocco, China, and Indonesia. The seeds are oval-shaped, with deep longitudinal ridges and are between 1/8–1/4 inch long. There are three varieties of cumin. While white and brown are interchangeable, black is less common; it has more flavor, is sweeter, and is used only in specific dishes, such as in the flat breads from Turkey, Cyprus, and Lebanon. Black seeds are similar in appearance to nigella seeds, which are quite different so, again, don't get them confused.

The smell of cumin has been described as fresh, strong, and bitter. Its taste is quite pronounced, pungent, and aromatic.

BUYING, STORING, AND PREPARATION

As for all spices, buy fresh cumin in small quantities and store in a tightly sealed container in a dark, cool cupboard to retain freshness. Grind as needed or buy best-quality ground cumin.

Most of my recipes call for cumin seeds used whole. To bring out their flavor, toast the seeds lightly before adding them to recipes. To toast, simply add the seeds to a heated dry pan over medium heat and toss them around for between 30–60 seconds until they darken slightly and release their aroma.

For ground cumin tip the seeds into a mortar or spice grinder, and crush or grind. The volatile oils don't last long, so if a recipe calls for ground cumin, it is best to grind the seeds just before using.

CULINARY USES

From its origin in Egypt, cumin traveled to Asia, Iran, and India where its popularity spread quickly, and it became a standard ingredient for panch phora (a Bengali mix of five spices), garam masala, tandoori masala, and curry paste. It is also used in India to season many yogurt-based raitas and is mixed with tamarind water to create the refreshing drink, zeera pani.

In hotter countries such as Egypt, where cumin originated, the spice was used for preserving meat. North African Muslims flavor couscous and tajines with cumin, and mix it in spice blends, including *ras el hanout*. Cumin is also often sprinkled over rice and lentil dishes, rubbed into meat (especially lamb) before grilling, and used for spicing up ground meat dishes. Other Mediterranean recipes call for it to be added to marinades for olives, pickles, relishes, salads (particularly tomato), and sausages such as merguez. It is also sometimes included in hummus (the popular tangy yogurt-chickpea dip).

The Moors carried the spice to Spain where it was and still is used in stews with saffron and sweet cinnamon. It is also used to great effect in the Spanish dishes, Arroz con Pollo (chicken with rice) and Gazpacho Andulusian; and in Portuguese fish stews and with salted pork. It is thought to have then traveled to Mexico where it soon

complementary flavors

VEGETABLES (ESPECIALLY ONIONS, FENNEL, GARLIC, AND TOMATOES)

FISH

MEAT (ESPECIALLY CHICKEN, PORK, AND LAMB)

SPICES (CINNAMON, GINGER, AND SAFFRON)

YOGURT

MINT

ORANGE

became an essential component of their cuisine—just think of chili con carne, black bean soup, adobos (spicy marinades), and peccadilloes (spicy ground meat wrapped in pastry dough).

Strangely enough, in the past it was used widely in baking—especially in central Europe. During Victorian times, cumin cakes were frequently served, although the spice was considered, like many others at the time, to be an aphrodisiac. The late Elizabeth David always used to add cumin to her hot cross bun recipe.

OTHER USES

Cumin has long been recommended for its curative properties. Taken as a tea, it is said to relieve the symptoms of colds and flu. Blended with honey, it soothes sore throats. In India it is prescribed as a remedy for flatulence, indigestion, and diarrhea. Cumin is a calmative and is used, for this reason, in veterinarian medicine.

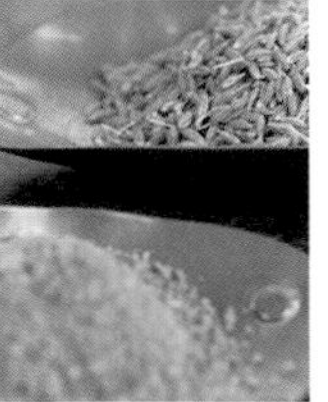

tomato, cumin, and pomegranate soup

8 garlic cloves, unpeeled
2 tablespoons olive oil
14 1/2 oz. can of chopped tomatoes
1 teaspoon cumin seeds
1 onion, chopped
1 carrot, finely chopped
1 celery stick, finely chopped
1 red pepper, finely chopped
1 sprig of thyme
A good pinch of saffron strands
1 bay leaf
1 tablespoon dried pomegranate seeds
3 cups chicken broth (or vegetable broth)
1 tablespoon pomegranate molasses
Salt and freshly ground black pepper

Preheat the oven to 350°F. Place the garlic cloves in a small dish, pour half the olive oil over them, and roast for 30–40 minutes, until they are soft and caramelized. Leave until cool enough to handle, then pop the garlic flesh out of the skin and place in a blender along with the canned tomatoes. Purée until smooth.

Heat a large saucepan until hot, add the cumin seeds and toast them for 30 seconds, to release their wonderful fragrance. Remove from the pan and set aside. Heat the remaining oil in the pan, add the onion, carrot, celery, red pepper, and thyme, and sauté until tender. Stir in the garlic and tomato purée, saffron, bay leaf, and pomegranate seeds and then the toasted cumin seeds. Add the broth, bring to a boil, then reduce the heat and simmer for 30 minutes. Stir in the pomegranate molasses, season to taste, and serve.

Paul's Tip Pomegranate molasses (sometimes labeled *dibs rumman* or *dibs rumen*) and dried pomegranate seeds are available from Middle Eastern food stores. If necessary, substitute 1 1/2 teaspoons of grenadine for the molasses in this soup.

cumin swordfish souvlaki

If ever a dish was made for a barbecue, this is it: grilled marinated swordfish wrapped in hot flatbread. When I barbecue, I usually consume two or three of these while the guests are waiting for theirs—well, the cook has to have some perks!

1 3/4 lbs. swordfish fillet, trimmed and cut into 1 1/2-inch cubes
2 tablespoons olive oil
2 tablespoons chopped parsley
1 tablespoon chopped oregano
1 teaspoon cumin seeds
A pinch of smoked paprika
2 garlic cloves, crushed
1 lemon
1 red pepper, cut into 1-inch squares
1 green pepper, cut into 1-inch squares
1 red onion, cut into small wedges

FOR SERVING:

8 flatbreads, such as lavash (or even tortillas)
1/4 cucumber, seeded and chopped
5 oz. thick, whole-milk yogurt
2 tablespoons chopped mint
2 tablespoons chopped cilantro
1 garlic clove, crushed
Salt and freshly ground black pepper

Place the swordfish cubes in a bowl, add the olive oil, parsley, oregano, cumin seeds, paprika, and garlic, and toss well together. Squeeze the lemon juice over them and let marinate for 30 minutes. Soak the wooden skewers in water to prevent them from burning.

To make the souvlaki, thread the swordfish on to 8 skewers, alternating it with the peppers and red onion, then brush with the marinade. Cook the souvlaki on a barbecue (or on a preheated ridged grill pan if cooking indoors), turning them frequently and continually basting with the marinade; they will take about 4–5 minutes.

While the swordfish is cooking, wrap the bread in foil and warm it through in a medium oven. Mix together the cucumber, yogurt, herbs, and garlic, and season to taste. Divide the mixture between the warm flatbreads, spreading it over the surface. Remove the fish from the skewers and place on the yogurt mixture, then roll up the bread into cones and serve immediately.

roasted baby carrots with cumin

2 teaspoons cumin seeds
3 tablespoons olive oil
1/2 small garlic clove, crushed
1 3/4 lbs. baby carrots, lightly scraped
2 tablespoons honey
Juice and grated zest of 1 orange
Fresh chopped mint, for garnishing (optional)

Preheat the oven to 400°F. Heat a large ovenproof frying pan over medium heat, add the cumin seeds, and toast them for 30 seconds to release their fragrance. Add the olive oil and garlic and mix well. Stir in the carrots and toss until they are sealed and lightly golden all over. Add the honey, and orange juice and zest, and stir well to combine.

Transfer to the oven and cook for 8–10 minutes, until the carrots are glazed and tender and all the liquid has evaporated. Serve immediately, sprinkled with a little mint, if you like, which goes well with the spiced carrots.

pork adobo

In 1492 the arrival of the Spanish in Cuba introduced a host of new foods to the region, from European spices and vinegar, to olive oil and wine. Adobo, made from vinegar, spices, and orange juice, has become Cuba's national marinade, used for all sorts of dishes. Black beans, spicy salsa, guacamole, and warm tortillas make great accompaniments to pork adobo.

1¾ lbs. pork blade shoulder (shoulder butt), cut into ¾-inch pieces
1 teaspoon garlic powder
Peanut or vegetable oil for frying
1¼ cups dark beer
2 onions, sliced
Salt and freshly ground black pepper

FOR THE MARINADE:

1½ teaspoons achiote seeds or paste (see Tip, above right)
1¼ cups orange juice
¾ cup white wine vinegar
2 tablespoons dried oregano
2 tablespoons cumin seeds, toasted in a dry frying pan
6 garlic cloves, chopped

To make the marinade, blitz the achiote seeds or paste, orange juice, vinegar, oregano, cumin, and garlic together in a blender or food processor and transfer to a large bowl. Season the pork pieces with salt, pepper, and the garlic powder, then add them to the marinade and leave for 1 hour.

Preheat the oven to 350°F. Heat 1 inch of the oil in a large, ovenproof and flameproof dish. Remove the pork from the marinade and brown it on all sides in the hot oil, then remove from the pan. Clean the oil from the pan and return the pork, along with the marinade, beer and onions. Season with salt and pepper. Bring to a boil, then cover, transfer to the oven and bake for 1½ hours. Remove from the oven and skim off excess fat from the surface. Remove the meat and keep warm. Put the pan back on the burner and boil until the liquid has reduced by half. Serve the pork drizzled with the cooking juices.

Paul's Tip Achiote seeds come from the annatto tree and have a brick-red color and earthy flavor. Achiote paste is also available. You should find them in some large supermarkets and in stores specializing in South American ingredients.

cumin shortbread

Mention shortbread and you immediately think of Scotland. There are many variations on these crisp, buttery cookies but this recipe using cumin might come as a surprise. When I found it in a Scottish cooking book dating back to 1840, I had to try it, and was most impressed. The shortbread is particularly good served with an orange mousse.

½ cup (1 stick) softened unsalted butter
½ cup superfine sugar
¼ teaspoon salt
2½ cups all-purpose flour
2 teaspoons freshly ground cumin
3 tablespoons finely chopped candied orange peel

Beat the butter until it is light and fluffy, then slowly beat in the sugar. Mix in the salt and flour, adding the flour in 4 batches. Add the cumin and orange peel and mix until the dough is smooth and soft.

Turn the dough onto a lightly floured work surface and roll it out into a rectangle ½-inch thick, making sure the top is flat and smooth. Cut into 1 x 2-inch sticks and, with a fork, prick each one 3 times on the diagonal. Chill for up to 2 hours.

Preheat the oven to 300°F. Place the shortbread sticks on a greased baking sheet, spacing them about an inch apart. Bake for 20 minutes, until very pale golden but not browned, then remove from the oven and transfer to a wire rack to cool. They will keep for up to 1 month if stored in an airtight container.

cardamom *Elettaria cardamomum*

Cardamom is native to the East and grows in India (the largest producer), Sri Lanka, South America, and the South Pacific. It is one of the most ancient spices in the world, as well as one of the most popular and highly valued, ranking as the third most expensive spice, behind saffron and vanilla. Sometimes called the Queen of Spices, its seeds were prized in India long before the birth of Christ.

recipes

DESCRIPTION

Cardamom (*Elettaria cardamomum*) is a member of the ginger family, a woody perennial that takes three years to produce seeds. The fruits' pods are picked just before they ripen, and are left to dry on open platforms under the hot sun, or in special drying rooms.

The seed pods are white, green, or black. The black (or brown) pods are larger than the green variety, and the white ones have been bleached. The best green cardamom comes from Kerala, in India, and sets the standard for quality and price.

Cardamom is prized for its inner brown-black seeds (the tough outer pod is inedible and generally only used for flavoring dishes such as rice, then discarded). In Western countries, cardamom, with its delicate, camphor-like flavor, is still considered fairly exotic.

There are many "false" cardamom varieties which, though related to "true" cardamom, are inferior in terms of flavor and aroma, and are marketed as cheap substitutes. False varieties include Nepal, Chinese, and Japanese cardamom.

BUYING AND STORING

I generally buy whole cardamom pods for optimum freshness and flavor. You are most likely to come across the green variety, which connoisseurs consider to be the best (the black variety tends to have a blunter, more camphorous flavor). The spice is generally available from supermarkets although I prefer to buy it from Middle Eastern or Indian food stores, which have a brisker turnover and where it is therefore more likely to be fresh. As with all spices, it is hard to know how long they have been sitting on the shelves, so I find it is best to buy small quantities and use them quickly. The pods should be plump, hard in texture, aromatic in smell, and blemish-free.

PREPARATION

The easiest way to extract the seeds is to crush the cardamom with a rolling pin, or kitchen mallet, then pick the seeds from the pods (this can be quite a tedious task, so look out for packages of seeds already removed from their pods in Indian and Pakistani food stores). If I am preparing a stew or Indian-style curry, however, I add the whole pods for flavor, but remember to remove them before serving. You can purchase a form of ground cardamom but, like many spices, its flavor is inferior to freshly ground. When a recipes calls for ground cardamom, simply pulverize the seeds in a mortar or spice grinder.

CULINARY USES

Cardamom features in many curries (such as Indian and Persian), spice mixes (like the Iranian *advieh*, or the Moroccan *ras el hanout*), and in a fiery Yemeni paste, *zoug*, which is added to soups and stews or used as a dip for bread.

It is delicious added to garam masala and to rice pilafs. Its flavor also works surprisingly well

complementary flavors

- MILK PUDDINGS, CUSTARDS, AND ICECREAMS
- GINGER
- COFFEE
- CHOCOLATE
- CITRUS FRUITS
- VANILLA
- DATES
- MEAT (ESPECIALLY LAMB AND CHICKEN)

in sweet dishes and hot drinks. All over the Middle East it is used for perfuming Arabic coffees, either alone or with other sweet spices. It adds an exquisite flavor to milky desserts, such as rice pudding and custards, and it is used to great effect in Indian-style icecream, kulfi. It is good in spicy cookies and cakes, and is a great flavoring for chocolate desserts. In Sweden, cardamom is regularly used in bread-making and baking.

OTHER USES

In India, cardamom is used not only in cooking, but as a breath freshener and digestive aid: when crushed between the teeth, a powerful lemony flavor is released, which has cleansing properties. In the past, cardamon was also used for relieving flatulence and to treat stomach disorders. It is still sometimes blended with water and used as a gargle for sore throats.

cardamom spinach purée

Serve this as a interesting side dish. It's particularly good with Middle Eastern spicy leg of lamb and roast chicken.

1 lb 10 oz. young spinach leaves
2 tablespoons unsalted butter
2 shallots, finely chopped
1 teaspoon freshly ground cardamom
1/4 teaspoon dried chili flakes
1/2 cup heavy cream
Grated zest of 1/2 lemon
3 tablespoons sliced almonds, toasted, for garnishing
Salt and freshly ground black pepper

Blanch the spinach in boiling salted water for 30 seconds, then drain in a colander and refresh under cold running water. Squeeze out the water from the spinach with your hands until it is dry, then place the spinach in a blender or food processor and blitz to a coarse purée.

Heat the butter in a saucepan, add the shallots and cook for 1 minute, until softened. Add the cardamom and chili flakes and mix well. Stir in the spinach and cream and heat gently, until they are lightly bound together. Add the lemon zest, season with salt and pepper, and serve, sprinkled with the toasted almonds.

lebanese lentil soup

1/4 cup olive oil
1 onion, finely chopped
1 garlic clove, crushed
1 cup red lentils
1 tablespoon freshly ground cardamom
1/4 teaspoon ground allspice
1/2 teaspoon grated lemon zest
4 cups beef broth
2 tablespoons unsalted butter
3 slices of white bread, crusts removed, cut into 1/4-inch pieces
2 tablespoons lemon juice
Salt and freshly ground black pepper
A few roughly crushed cardamom seeds, for garnishing

Heat half the oil in a large pan, add the onion and garlic, and cook for 2–3 minutes, until softened. Add the lentils and stir until coated in the oil. Add the cardamom, allspice and lemon zest, then pour in the broth and bring to a boil. Reduce the heat and simmer for about 30 minutes, until the lentils are very tender. Cool slightly, then blitz to a coarse-textured purée in a blender. Return to the pan, reheat gently, and season to taste.

Heat the butter in a large frying pan and fry the chopped bread in it until golden. Stir the lemon juice and the remaining oil into the soup, add the bread croûtons, then garnish with the crushed cardamom and serve immediately.

shoulder of lamb with yogurt and cardamom

This is one of the great dishes of Middle Eastern cooking. It originates from Persia and is so tender that carving is not necessary; you can simply pull the meat apart with a spoon and fork. Serve with a minted onion and tomato salad and hot grilled pita bread.

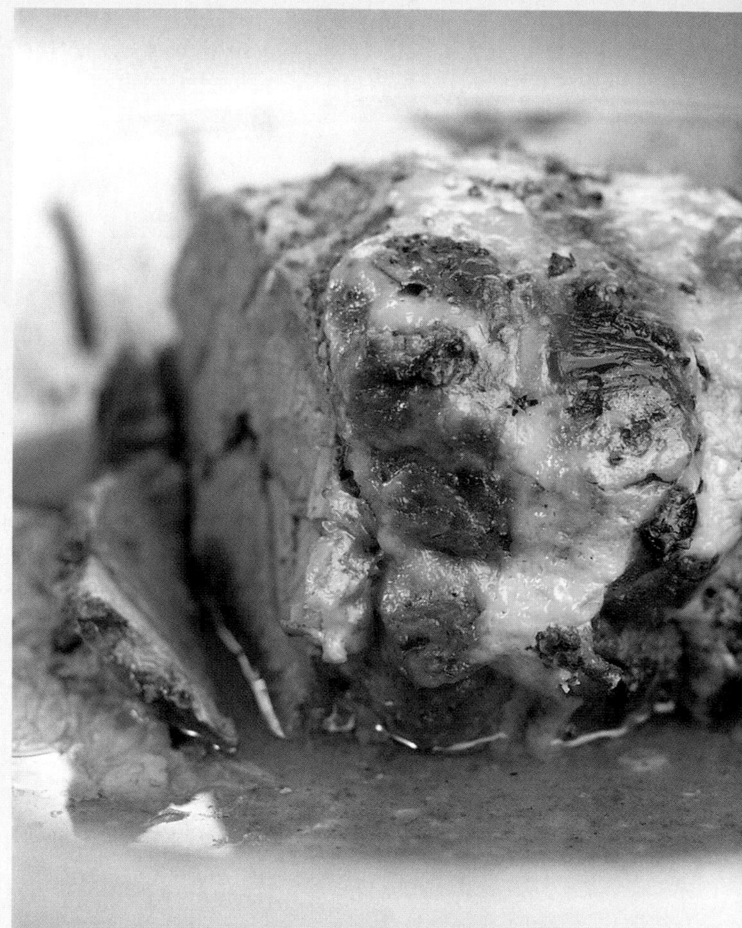

SERVES 6–8

4 lbs. shoulder of lamb, boned and rolled
4 garlic cloves, cut into slivers
1/4 cup cardamom pods
3 tablespoons olive oil
Juice and grated zest of 1 lemon
1/4 teaspoon saffron strands
2/3 cup thick, whole-milk yogurt
2 tablespoons brown sugar
Salt and freshly ground black pepper

Season the lamb with salt and pepper and make some deep cuts in it with a small, sharp knife. Insert the garlic slivers into the cuts. Lightly crush the cardamom pods and remove the seeds, then sprinkle them over the lamb and rub them in. Leave at room temperature for at least 5 hours (or overnight in the fridge).

Preheat the oven to 400°F. Heat the oil in a heavy roasting pan, add the lamb, and brown on all sides. Transfer to the oven and roast for about 20–30 minutes, until well colored. Remove from the oven and let cool slightly while you prepare the lemon yogurt coating. Reduce the oven temperature to 325°F.

Put the lemon juice and saffron in a small pan and heat gently. Let cool, then mix with the lemon zest, yogurt, and sugar. Pour half this mixture over the lamb. Return the lamb to the oven and cook, adding more lemon yogurt every 30 minutes or so, for about 2 1/2–3 hours, until the lamb is very tender and is topped with a golden yogurt crust. Let cool slightly before serving.

rhubarb and cardamom flognarde

Flognarde is a classic batter pudding from the Auvergne. To all intents and purposes, it is identical to the famous clafoutis, made in homes all over France.

1¹/4 cups superfine sugar
1³/4 lbs. rhubarb, cut into 1-inch lengths
¹/2 cup whole milk
²/3 cup whipping cream
1 teaspoon freshly ground cardamom
¹/2 vanilla bean, slit open lengthwise
4 eggs
3 tablespoons cornstarch
2 tablespoons kirsch
Confectioners' sugar for dusting

Put half the sugar in a large saucepan, add a ¹/2-cup of water, and heat gently until the sugar has dissolved. Bring to a gentle simmer, add the rhubarb, then raise the heat a little and cook for 3–4 minutes, until the rhubarb is just tender. Remove from the heat and drain, then spread the rhubarb out on a clean lint-free dishtowel to get rid of excess moisture.

Put the milk, cream, cardamom, and vanilla bean in a pan and gently bring to a boil, then remove from the heat and let infuse for 5 minutes.

Preheat the oven to 350°F. In a large bowl, whisk the eggs and the remaining sugar together until creamy. Add the cornstarch and kirsch and whisk well. Pour in the hot milk mixture through a strainer and whisk again.

Butter 4 individual gratin dishes, about a cup in capacity, and divide the rhubarb between them. Pour the cream mixture over them and bake for 15–20 minutes, until golden and slightly souffléed. Dust with confectioners' sugar and serve, with sour cream or vanilla icecream.

Paul's Tip (Right) To test if your bread is cooked, turn it out of the pan and tap the bottom with your knuckles; it should sound hollow. Alternatively, insert a toothpick in the center and check if it comes out clean.

green cardamom and apricot bread

This is a Swedish specialty, traditionally served on festive occasions. Here it is baked in loaf pans but it is more usually woven into braids.

MAKES 2 LOAVES

1 package dried yeast
2¹/4 cups whole milk
²/3 cup (1¹/4 sticks) unsalted butter, chopped
2 eggs
5 tablespoons honey
1 teaspoon freshly ground green cardamom
3 lbs 5oz. white bread flour
4 oz. (²/3 cup) dried apricots, chopped
¹/4 cup sliced almonds

Put the yeast in a bowl, add ¹/2-cup warm water, and stir until the yeast has dissolved. Set aside. Bring the milk to a boil in a pan, add the butter, and remove from the heat. Leave it until the butter has melted. Put the eggs, honey and cardamom in a large bowl and beat until well combined. Add the milk and mix again. Gradually mix in 4¹/2 cups of the flour, then let cool slightly. Add the dissolved yeast and enough of the remaining flour to make a workable, elastic dough. Turn out onto a floured surface and knead for about 10 minutes, until smooth and pliable, adding more flour if necessary. Place in a greased bowl, cover with a damp cloth and let rise in a warm place for 1 hour or until doubled in size.

Punch the dough down, turn out, and knead again for 1 minute. Return to the bowl, cover, and let rise again until doubled in size. Punch down one more time, then divide the dough in half and place in 2 greased 2 lb.-pans. Let rise again, for about 30 minutes this time. Meanwhile, preheat the oven to 375°F.

Sprinkle the loaves liberally with the apricots and almonds and bake for 25–30 minutes, until golden brown. Turn out onto a wire rack to cool.

nutmeg *Myristica fragrans*

Nutmeg was first introduced to Britain in the sixteenth century when the British invaded the Molucca Islands (formerly known as the Spice Islands). Soon after, they carried nutmeg to the East Indies and the Caribbean. Up until that time, the spice had (almost exclusively) been grown on two small islands. In fact, the Dutch, who controlled the islands before the British (but after the Arabs and Portuguese!), did everything in their power to restrict the cultivation of nutmeg, in order to control its supply and prices.

recipes

Once out, however, it rapidly became very popular, perhaps due to the fact that it was thought to have magical properties, and to be an aphrodisiac; even a small amount combined with alcohol is said to heighten the alcohol's narcotic effect. Nutmeg is now very successfully grown in the West Indies and Granada—which has adopted the name "the nutmeg island."

DESCRIPTION

Nutmeg grows like fruit on an evergreen tree (*Myristica fragrans*) that is usually 30–40 feet tall with dark leaves, the fruit resembling apricots in appearance. When the fruit is ripe, it bursts open and cracks, revealing a bright red outer husk called mace (which is also edible and used in ground form) enveloping the hard, brown kernel which is the nutmeg.

Nutmeg and mace are similar in aroma and taste, although mace is said to be more refined and cleaner in taste—a matter of opinion in my view. Both have a rich, fresh, and warm taste, and are hugely aromatic, sweetish in nutmeg, while mace is a little more bitter. Nutmeg and mace are not interchangeable in recipes, however. It is the myristicin in the nut's oil that is responsible for its narcotic effect, its toxicity in high doses, and probably also for its "magical" reputation.

BUYING AND STORING

Although ground nutmeg is readily available, the flavor of the freshly grated whole spice is far superior. Pre-ground nutmeg quickly loses its aroma and flavor, so whenever possible use whole nutmeg. Small, handy nutmeg graters are stocked by most kitchen stores and supermarkets. Be sure to refrigerate any surplus grated nutmeg in an airtight container, but as a general rule, only grate as much as needed for a particular recipe.

CULINARY USES

Nutmeg has a strong, peculiar but delightfully sweet and nutty fragrance, and adds a slightly bitter, warm aroma to food. There is nothing quite like a little freshly grated nutmeg to liven up a dish. Among its supporters are the Indians who use it especially in Moghul dishes and for spicing meats, rice dishes, and desserts. In southern Asia it is used for making jellies and jam. The Arabs enjoy it in long, slow-braised lamb stews and the Dutch use it as a standard seasoning in many traditional dishes, from mashed potato to fruit puddings and breads.

In Italy, they have long enjoyed nutmeg in savory dishes with vegetables, in their mortadella sausages, and as a seasoning for pasta. In Britain and France, a basic white sauce, or spinach cooked in butter, would not be complete without a fresh grating of nutmeg. Britain's Queen Victoria was reported to have been very partial to its use in a special royal household recipe for sweet mincemeat prepared at Christmas-time. It became popular throughout Britain as a flavoring in pies and cakes, to liven up potted fish and the Scottish haggis, and to make a spiced wine drink.

complementary flavors

- HARD FRUITS (ESPECIALLY PEARS, APPLES, AND ORANGES)
- DAIRY PRODUCTS (CHEESE SAUCE, CUSTARD, EGGS, RICOTTA CHEESE)
- MEAT (ESPECIALLY LAMB AND CHICKEN)
- ROOT VEGETABLES (ESPECIALLY POTATOES AND PARSNIPS)
- PASTA
- SPINACH
- DRIED FRUIT
- SHELLFISH (POTTED)
- FISH
- HONEY

In the rest of Europe, nutmeg is most usually found in sweet dishes such as rice puddings, honey cakes, fruit cakes, pastries, and occasionally mulled wine. Nutmeg is also used, along with cloves, to spice up eggnog, a popular wintertime drink, commonly served on holidays such as Christmas and New Year.

Note! Never be tempted to add too much, as excessive nutmeg can be poisonous. A couple of pinches should suffice and is perfectly safe.

OTHER USES

Nutmeg has been used as a component in certain medicines and drinks for convalescents for years. Both nutmeg and mace have been used for treating flatulence and to allay nausea. Grated nutmeg mixed with lard is apparently an excellent treatment for piles. It is also thought to aid digestion and improve appetite.

turbot with fried nutmeg brioche crumbs

Butter for greasing
4 x 6 oz. turbot fillets
1/4 cup dry vermouth
1 cup dry white wine
2/3 cup well-flavored fish broth
1/4 cup heavy cream
1/4 cup (1/2 stick) chilled unsalted butter, cut into small pieces
3 oz. sorrel, finely chopped
2 eggs, hard-boiled, shelled, and diced
Salt and freshly ground black pepper

FOR THE NUTMEG BRIOCHE CRUMBS:
1/4 cup (1/2 stick) unsalted butter
2 oz. (1 1/4 cups) fresh brioche crumbs
1/4 teaspoon freshly grated nutmeg

Lightly butter a large shallow pan, big enough to hold the turbot fillets in a single layer. Season the fish with salt and pepper and place it in the pan. Pour the vermouth, white wine, and fish broth over them, cover with buttered foil, then place over medium heat and bring to a boil. Reduce the heat to just below simmering point and poach for 5–6 minutes.

Meanwhile, make the nutmeg brioche crumbs. Heat the butter in a frying pan until foaming, add the crumbs, and cook until golden and crisp. Stir in the nutmeg, remove from the heat, and set aside.

When the fish is done, remove from the pan using a slotted spoon and keep warm. Return the pan to the heat, add the cream, and bring to a boil. Remove from the heat and whisk in the butter, a little at a time, until the sauce thickens. Add the sorrel and let cook for 1 minute. Add the hard-boiled eggs and adjust the seasoning.

To serve, arrange the fish on serving plates, pour the sauce over them, and sprinkle the nutmeg brioche crumbs on top. I like to serve the fish on a bed of buttered asparagus tips.

potted shrimp

This basic recipe can be used for lobster or crab as well. It is very simple, and 100 percent better than the commercial variety, which tends to use frozen shrimp and cheap butter.

7 oz. (1 3/4 cups) good-quality unsalted butter
1 small bay leaf
1/2 teaspoon freshly grated nutmeg
A good pinch of sea salt (kosher salt)
A pinch of cayenne pepper
1 teaspoon brandy (optional)
11 oz. peeled fresh shrimp
Juice of 1/2 lemon
1 tablespoon chopped flat-leaf parsley
Freshly ground black pepper

FOR SERVING:
Fingers of toast or Melba toast
Lemon wedges

Place the butter in a small saucepan, heat slowly to boiling point, and boil for 2 minutes. Strain through a small strainer lined with cheesecloth and return to the pan. Add the bay leaf, nutmeg, salt, cayenne, black pepper to taste, and brandy, if using. Leave on a low heat for 5 minutes to infuse, then remove the bay leaf. Add the shrimp and lemon juice and leave for 4–5 minutes longer, then stir in the parsley.

Fill 4 individual ramekins with the shrimp and top with the butter, which should just cover the shrimp. Let cool and then place in the fridge.

Serve with sticks of toast or Melba toast, and lemon wedges. The shrimp are best served at room temperature in order to appreciate their flavor at its best.

creamy parsnip and nutmeg gratin

$1^3/4$ lbs. baby parsnips
$1^1/4$ cups whole milk
2 cups heavy cream
2 garlic cloves, crushed
1 egg yolk
Freshly grated nutmeg
Butter
Salt and freshly ground black pepper

Preheat the oven to 450°F. Peel the parsnips and cut them into 2-inch lengths. Blanch in a large pot of boiling water for 1 minute, then drain. Return to the dried-out pot, along with the milk, cream, garlic, and some salt and pepper. Bring to a boil, reduce the heat to a simmer, and cook until the parsnips are just tender and the sauce is well reduced. Stir in the egg yolk and season to taste with nutmeg, salt, and pepper.

Butter well a shallow gratin dish and pour in the parsnips and their sauce. Dot with a little more butter and add a sprinkling of nutmeg. Bake for about 15 minutes, until golden and crisp.

nutmeg and cheese custard tart

Soft cheese and nutmeg work extremely well together as long as you don't overdo the spice. Although this is not classically a custard filling, it has all the ingredients and is simply put together in minutes. It's also nice to make small tartlets to serve with tea or coffee.

1 quantity of Sweet Pastry Dough (see page 129)
$^2/3$ cup ricotta cheese
3 eggs
$^1/2$ cup superfine sugar
$^1/3$ cup heavy cream
2 tablespoons honey
Freshly grated nutmeg

Preheat the oven to 375°F. Roll out the dough on a lightly floured surface to $^1/8$-inch thick and use to line an 8-inch tart tin. Prick the base lightly all over with a fork. Line with parchment paper or foil, fill with baking beans, and bake blind for 10 minutes, or until the dough is set but not colored. Remove the paper and beans and return the pie shell to the oven for 5 minutes longer.

Beat all the remaining ingredients except the nutmeg together in a bowl until smooth. Pour into the pie shell, grate enough fresh nutmeg over the surface to cover it lightly, then return to the oven for 40 minutes or until the top is a deep golden brown. Serve warm or at room temperature.

eggnog and orange peel icecream

3/4 cup whole milk
1 3/4 cups heavy cream
1/4–1/2 teaspoon freshly grated nutmeg
6 egg yolks
2/3 cup superfine sugar
Grated zest of 1 orange
1/2 cup dark rum

Put the milk, cream, and grated nutmeg in a pan and bring to a boil. In a bowl, beat the egg yolks, sugar, orange zest, and rum together until light and fluffy. Pour in the cream mixture, beating all the time. Return to the pan and cook gently, stirring constantly, until the mixture thickens enough to coat the back of the spoon; do not let it boil or it will curdle. Let it cool, then pour into an icecream machine and freeze according to the manufacturer's instructions. If you don't have an icecream machine, refer to the tip on page 180.

old-fashioned rice pudding

When I was a child, my favorite dessert was rice pudding, a great British classic, which I loved topped with a dollop of jam. Mum always made plenty; she knew it wouldn't be wasted. Here is the recipe, which must have a nutmeg-crusted skin—what memories!

2 tablespoons unsalted butter
2/3 cup pudding rice (or other short grain rice)
1 vanilla bean
2 1/2 cups whole milk
1/2 cup superfine sugar
1/2 teaspoon grated orange zest
2 1/4 cups heavy cream
2 egg yolks
Freshly grated nutmeg

Preheat the oven to 300°F. Use the butter to grease a 2 1/2-pint baking dish or casserole dish. Scatter the rice into the dish and set aside.

Slit the vanilla bean open lengthwise and scrape out the seeds with the tip of a sharp knife. Put the pod and seeds in a pan along with the milk, sugar, orange zest, and 18 fl oz. of the cream. Bring to a boil, then pour the mixture over the rice and stir well. Cover with a lid or foil and bake for 1 1/2–2 hours, until the rice is just tender. Remove from the oven and cool slightly.

In a bowl, whip the remaining cream with the egg yolks until just beginning to thicken. Stir into the rice pudding and grate fresh nutmeg over the surface (you will need about 1/4–1/2 teaspoonful). Return to the oven and bake, uncovered, for 15 minutes, until a skin has formed and the top is golden and slightly crusty. Serve plain, or with milk, fresh fruit, or a dollop of jam.

apple and nutmeg croustillant

Apples and nutmeg have a great affinity, which is highlighted in this easily prepared dessert.

4 Granny Smith apples
1/3 cup demerara (or light brown) sugar
2 tablespoons unsalted butter
1/2 teaspoon freshly grated nutmeg
1/3 cup Calvados (or other apple brandy)
1 1/2 tablespoons cornstarch
2/3 cup whole milk
1/2 cup good-quality apple juice (not from concentrate)
2 egg yolks
1/4 cup sugar
2/3 cup heavy cream, semi-whipped

Peel the apples, cut them in half, and remove the core, then cut each half into 5 sections. Heat a frying pan over a medium heat, add 1 tablespoon of the sugar and heat until lightly caramelized. Add the butter and apples and toss together for 3–4 minutes, until the apples are just cooked and lightly golden. Season with the nutmeg, then pour half the Calvados over them and toss with the apples. Turn the apples onto a plate and let cool.

Mix the cornstarch with 2 tablespoons of the milk and set aside. Put the apple juice in a pan along with the remaining milk and bring to a boil. Whisk in the cornstarch mixture and cook for 30 seconds, then remove from the heat. In a bowl, beat together the egg yolks and white sugar. Gradually mix in the hot milk and then return to the pan. Bring to a boil quickly, then pour into a bowl and let cool. When cold, fold in the whipped cream and add the remaining Calvados.

Divide the caramelized apples between 4 individual glass dishes, then cover with the cream mixture, spreading it out neatly to cover the apples completely. Sprinkle with the remaining raw (or brown) sugar and glaze under a hot broiler or with a blowtorch until caramelized and crunchy.

date and nutmeg cake

6 oz. (1 cup) dried dates, pitted, and chopped
3/4 oz. (1 1/2 tablespoons) preserved ginger, chopped
1/2 teaspoon baking soda
1 teaspoon baking powder
1/2 teaspoon vanilla extract
5 tablespoons softened unsalted butter
1/4 cup sugar
2 eggs, lightly beaten
1 1/2 cups all-purpose flour, sifted
1/2 teaspoon freshly grated nutmeg

Preheat the oven to 375°F. Mix together the dates and ginger in a bowl, then stir in 1 cup of boiling water. Add the baking soda, baking powder, and vanilla extract, and let stand.

Meanwhile, beat the butter and sugar together until pale, then beat in the eggs, one at a time. Fold in the flour and nutmeg. Stir in the date mixture and its liquid and mix well.

Pour into a well-greased 8-inch round cake pan and bake for 45–50 minutes, until risen and firm to the touch. When it is done, a toothpick inserted in the center of the cake should come out clean. Cool slightly, then turn out onto a wire rack to cool completely.

pepper *Piper nigrum*

The king of spices, pepper is the oldest known spice. Originally from the Malabar coast of India, it appeared in Sanskrit literature over 3,000 years ago. Although common today, it was so highly valued in ancient times that it served as an offering to the gods, a trading medium, and a tax; in fact, Attila the Hun and Alaric I the Visigoth demanded pepper as a major part of Rome's ransom.

Today pepper is grown widely, the most important areas of cultivation being India, Malaysia, Brazil, Sri Lanka, China, Vietnam, Thailand, and Madagascar.

recipes

CRUSHED GOAT CHEESE WITH PEPPER AND BLACK CHERRY JAM (PAGE 93)

AROMATIC THAI QUAILS (PAGE 93)

RASAM (PAGE 94)

BLACK PEPPER-CURED LAMB WITH EGGPLANTS, PEPPERS, AND FETA (PAGE 94)

ANTON'S STEAK AUX QUATRE POIVRES (PAGE 95)

PEPPER-WHITE CHOCOLATE FUDGE (PAGE 95)

BLACK PEPPER YOGURT SEMI-FREDDO (PAGE 96)

TWO-PEPPER RED WINE STRAWBERRIES (PAGE 96)

SEE ALSO:

TWICE-COOKED DUCK WITH LAVENDER HONEY (PAGE 23)

GLAZED BARBECUE MUSTARD SQUABS WITH SWEET POTATOES AND FENNEL (PAGE 54)

DESCRIPTION

Peppercorns are the fruit of the evergreen vine, *Piper nigrum*. Green, black, and white pepper all grow on the same plant but are harvested at different stages of development. The familiar black peppercorn is picked while green and left to dry, which is when it wrinkles and blackens. Green peppercorns are unripe fresh corns which are preserved by bottling in brine or vinegar, or, more recently, by freeze-drying. White peppercorns are mature berries which have been soaked in water and had their outer shells removed.

The peppery flavor and odor come from the essential oils and peperin (which also gives the heat). Black pepper is the most fiery and pungent, followed by white and then green pepper, which is mild with a clean, fresh taste. Pink peppercorns are not peppercorns at all but aromatic berries from the plant *Schinus terebinthfolius*. This species is native to Brazil, where the locals know it as *aroreira*. Pink peppercorns have a pungent sweetish flavor, followed by a peppery aftertaste, and a brittle, slightly bitter skin.

BUYING, STORING, AND PREPARATION

The best black peppercorns are said to be Tellicherry, Lampong, and Malabar. White pepper varieties include Munkok and Siam. Pink peppercorns, or berries, are available dried or bottled in vinegar. I find the bottled variety has a better flavor. Green and pink peppercorns are most likely to be found in speciality food shops.

Peppercorns can be stored for up to a year in airtight containers away from sunlight. Since pepper quickly loses its freshness, flavor, aroma, and heat after it has been ground, it is best to buy whole peppercorns and to grind them yourself when needed. **Cracked pepper** is simply partially broken up peppercorns, crushed using a mortar and pestle or a rolling pin.

CULINARY USES

Pepper has for centuries been used as a standard spice to flavor sauces, pickles, and marinades throughout the world.

In Europe, most dishes are seasoned with salt and pepper—a tradition that dates back to medieval times. In addition to being used as a condiment, however, it is also used as a major ingredient, in dishes like the French Steak au Poivre where the steak is coated in freshly ground black pepper before cooking. A pepper crust on tuna also works very well. While peppercorns (ground, crushed, or whole) have traditionally been used in savoury dishes, they are now also increasingly being added to desserts, cakes, and cookies. They marry particularly well with strawberries (drawing out the sweetness of the fruit) and chocolate. White rather than black pepper is used in light-colored dishes (such as white sauces and icecream) to avoid a speckled appearance.

In India, pepper is used extensively. In the north, it is added particularly to meat and in the

complementary flavors

SALT

HERBS (DILL, THYME AND ROSEMARY)

LEMON AND LIME

SOFT CHEESES

STRAWBERRIES

south, to lentil and legume recipes; and to fish in the east. Pepper is often fried or roasted to extract the aroma and flavor, and added to pastes and spice mixes like garam masala. Black pepper-corns are an optional ingredient in Masala tea (a spicy hot beverage that includes cardamon, cloves, and cinnamon) and is a key player in the soup Rasam (which literally translates "pepper water").

Green peppercorns are an important addition to the culinary palette. Less biting than black pepper, their piquancy and strikingly fresh aroma go wonderfully well with seafood and grilled meats. They can also simply be added to a cream sauce to accompany fish, or used whole in patés and terrines, and curries. In India, green peppercorns are pickled alone in brine or in a wonderful blend of oil, green mango, chile, and ginger. Green pepper-corns can also be mashed with garlic or cinnamon to make a spiced butter. Pink pepper-corns are used in the same way as green.

Pepper is best ground directly onto food or added towards the end of cooking, to preserve its heat and aroma.

MEDICINAL USES

Pepper stimulates the appetite and salivation, improving digestion and blood circulation. It also calms nausea and has an anti-inflammatory and fever-reducing effect. Warm milk with pepper and honey is an ancient home remedy for treating colds, and white pepper mixed with butter is said to cure sore throats.

crushed goat cheese with pepper and black cherry jam

This is a great summer treat. It can be served on its own but is also very good with charbroiled vegetables, hot from the grill. The black cherry jam is an idea I saw in the south of France, and it works really well.

12 oz. (3 cups) soft goat cheese
1 teaspoon cracked black pepper (see page 90)
Juice and grated zest of 1 lemon
1 teaspoon thyme leaves
2 tablespoons virgin olive oil
1 baguette, cut into slices and toasted
1/2 cup good-quality black cherry jam
Coarse salt

Place the cheese in a bowl, add the pepper, lemon juice and zest, and crush together with a fork. Add the thyme and season with a little salt to taste. Let stand for up to 1 hour for the flavors to meld.

Spoon the cheese into a serving dish, drizzle the olive oil, over it, then serve with the toasted baguette and the black cherry jam.

aromatic thai quails

Ideally these should be charbroiled on hot coals, but a grill pan does a good job too. This dish is a common Thai street food, and each region has a different version. Coconut gives a succulent flavor.

8 quails
2 garlic cloves, chopped
2 teaspoons black peppercorns, freshly ground
2 tablespoons cilantro root (from about 2 bunches of cilantro)
1 teaspoon ground coriander
1/2 teaspoon ground turmeric
1 1/4 cups unsweetened coconut milk
1/4 cup *nam pla* (Thai fish sauce)
Olive oil for brushing
Salt

Cut the quails in half by cutting along the breastbone and then along the backbone. Meanwhile, soak 4 bamboo skewers in warm water. With a mortar and pestle, pound the garlic with the peppercorns, cilantro root, and a pinch of salt. Add the ground cilantro and turmeric and pound for another minute. Transfer to a dish, add the coconut milk and fish sauce, and mix together well. Add the quail halves and let marinate at room temperature for 1 hour.

Thread the quail halves onto the soaked skewers. Prepare a barbecue, or heat a ridged grill pan and brush it with olive oil. Grill the quails, skin-side down, for about 8–10 minutes, until cooked through and lightly charred, brushing occasionally with the marinade. Serve with steamed rice.

rasam

A hot and colorful soup from India, whose name translates as "black pepper water." It is highly peppery, with a base of lentils and tamarind.

1 onion, finely chopped
2 garlic cloves, chopped
1-inch piece of fresh galangal or ginger, finely chopped
1 heaped teaspoon black peppercorns
1/4 teaspoon cumin seeds
1/4 teaspoon cilantro seeds
4 cups well-flavored chicken broth
3/4 cup yellow lentils
2 plum tomatoes, peeled, seeded, and chopped
2 oz. sweetcorn kernels
4 scallions, shredded
1 red chile, seeded and thinly sliced
1 teaspoon tamarind paste
1 teaspoon brown sugar
2 tablespoons chopped cilantro
Salt

Crush the onion, garlic, galangal or ginger, black peppercorns, cumin and cilantro seeds with a mortar and pestle. Place in a saucepan, pour in the broth, and bring to a boil. Reduce the heat, add the lentils, and simmer gently for 40–45 minutes, until the lentils are tender. Add the vegetables, red chile, tamarind paste, and sugar, and cook for another 5 minutes. Season with a little salt, add the chopped cilantro, and serve.

black pepper-cured lamb with eggplants, peppers, and feta

4 lamb leg steaks
2 tablespoons black peppercorns, cracked (see page 90)
1/4 cup olive oil
1 onion, finely chopped
2 garlic cloves, crushed
1 1/2 teaspoons tomato paste
1/4 cup tomato puree
1 teaspoon sugar
3–4 tablespoons vegetable oil
1 eggplant, cut in half lengthwise and cut into 1-inch thick slices
2 red peppers, roughly chopped
2 tablespoons balsamic vinegar
1 teaspoon oregano leaves
Salt

FOR GARNISHING

3 oz. (3/4 cup) feta cheese, chopped
Fresh basil leaves

Season the lamb with salt, then sprinkle with the cracked peppercorns. Using the flat of your hand, push the peppercorns into the meat. Leave at room temperature for up to 2 hours.

Heat half the olive oil in a pan, add the onion and half the garlic, and cook gently for 5 minutes. Stir in the tomato paste, puree, and sugar, and cook for 10 minutes longer.

Meanwhile, heat 2–3 tablespoons of the vegetable oil in a large frying pan, add the eggplant, and fry for 3–4 minutes. Add the red peppers and cook for 5 minutes. Add the eggplant and peppers to the tomato sauce, reduce the heat, then cover and cook for 5 minutes or until the vegetables are just tender. Stir in the balsamic vinegar.

Broil or fry the lamb in 1 tablespoon of the vegetable oil until done to your liking. Heat any remaining olive oil and add the rest of the garlic and the oregano. Stir into the vegetables. Slice the lamb thickly and serve it on top of the vegetables, garnished with basil leaves and the feta.

anton's steak aux quatre poivres

I have many great memories of my time at The Dorchester, and working with Anton Mosimann was one of the highlights of my career. Here is a dish Anton created, blending four varieties of pepper harmoniously with brandy and cream. A take on the classic pepper steak.

1/2 teaspoon white peppercorns, coarsely ground
1/2 teaspoon black peppercorns, coarsely ground
4 x 6 oz. sirloin steaks or fillet steaks
2 tablespoons groundnut or vegetable oil
2 tablespoons cognac
7 fl oz. veal broth (or beef broth)
3 1/2 fl oz. heavy cream
1/2 oz. chilled unsalted butter, chopped
1 teaspoon green peppercorns
1 teaspoon pink peppercorns
Salt

Mix together the white and black peppercorns. Season the steaks with salt, then roll them liberally in the peppercorns.

Heat the oil in a large frying pan, add the steaks and cook them to your preferred degree. Remove from the pan and keep warm. Remove any excess fat from the pan and pour in the cognac. Set it alight with a match, standing well back, then when the flames have died down pour in the broth. Simmer until reduced by half. Add the cream and simmer again until the sauce is thick enough to coat the back of a spoon. Whisk in the chilled butter and season with salt to taste. Add the green and pink peppercorns to the sauce, pour it over the steaks and serve.

pepper-white chocolate fudge

Ever since I was a child, I've loved fudge—it's soft, sugary, and totally irresistible. The inclusion of a little black pepper cuts the sweetness without harming the flavor.

2 3/4 cups sugar
2 1/2 cups heavy cream
1/4 cup liquid glucose or corn syrup
1 x 3 1/2 oz. bar good-quality white chocolate, cut into small pieces
1/3 cup (3/4 stick) chilled unsalted butter, cut into small pieces
1 teaspoon black peppercorns, cracked (see page 90)
1/2 teaspoon vanilla extract
A pinch of salt

Mix the sugar, cream, and glucose together in a heavy pan, place on the heat, and stir constantly until it comes to a boil. Continue to cook, without stirring, for about 10–15 minutes, until the mixture reaches the "soft-ball stage" (239°F on a sugar thermometer). If the mixture does not reach this stage, the fudge will not set properly.

Remove the pan from the heat, stir in the chocolate and butter pieces, then set aside until the temperature drops to around 150°F. Finally add the cracked pepper, vanilla extract, and salt, and beat for 1 minute. Line a 10-inch square shallow dish or baking pan with waxed paper and pour in the fudge. Level the surface.

Let cool in the pan, then cut into small squares. The fudge will keep for up to a week in an airtight container. Great served with coffee after dinner.

black pepper yogurt semifreddo

This black pepper parfait topped with a warm tomato, vodka, and pineapple sauce is simple and inspiring. It makes a real dinner-party conversation piece.

SERVES 8

3 organic or cage-free eggs, separated
2 tablespoons sugar
1/2 teaspoon vanilla extract
Grated zest of 1 orange
2/3 cup heavy cream
2/3 cup thick, whole-milk yogurt
3 oz. meringues, broken into pieces
1 teaspoon black peppercorns, lightly cracked (see page 90)

FOR THE SAUCE:

3 tablespoons unsalted butter
1 tablespoon sugar
3 oz. fresh pineapple, cut into 1/4-inch pieces
2 firm, ripe tomatoes, peeled, seeded, and cut into 1/4-inch pieces
1 tablespoon vodka
Juice of 1 orange

Put the egg yolks, sugar, vanilla, and orange zest in the top of a double boiler. Whisk with an electric beater until the mixture doubles in volume and becomes pale and thick. Remove the top pan of water and let it cool, whisking frequently to prevent a skin forming.

In one bowl, whip the cream, and in another, whip the egg whites until stiff. Add the yogurt to the egg yolk mixture and then fold in the whipped cream, followed by the egg whites. Finally add the meringue pieces and the black pepper. Pour into 8 small ramekins and place in the freezer overnight.

To serve, dip the ramekins briefly in hot water and run a knife around the edge to loosen the semifreddo. Turn them out onto serving plates and defrost for 10 minutes while you prepare the sauce.

For the sauce, heat the butter in a frying pan, add the sugar, and cook until lightly caramelized. Add the pineapple and tomatoes, cook for 1 minute, then pour in the vodka and orange juice and boil for another minute. Pour the warm sauce over the semifreddo and serve immediately.

two-pepper red wine strawberries

Black pepper and strawberries are made for each other. Here they are served chilled, with vanilla icecream, which makes a refreshing combination.

2/3 cup good-quality red wine, preferably Cabernet Sauvignon
4 tablespoons sugar
1/2 teaspoon black peppercorns, coarsely cracked (see page 90)
2-inch piece of vanilla bean, slit open lengthwise
1 teaspoon cornstarch
2 tablespoons unsalted butter
1 lb. strawberries
1/2 teaspoon green peppercorns, drained
Vanilla icecream, for serving
Mint leaves, for decorating

Put all but 2 tablespoons of the wine in a saucepan, and add the sugar and half the black pepper. Scrape in the seeds from the vanilla bean, and add the bean too, and stir over medium heat to dissolve the sugar. Bring to boil. Mix the 2 tablespoons of wine with the cornstarch and add to the pan. Cook gently for 1–2 minutes, until the mixture has thickened slightly. Remove the sauce from the heat and take out the vanilla bean.

Melt the butter in a frying pan over a high heat, add the strawberries and the remaining black pepper, and cook for 1 minute, just to warm the strawberries through. Pour the wine sauce over the strawberries and return to boil. Add the green peppercorns, then pour into a bowl and let it cool. Refrigerate overnight to allow the flavors to develop.

To serve, put the strawberry mixture in cocktail glasses, top with vanilla icecream and decorate with mint leaves.

ginger *Zingiber officinale*

It is important not to confuse fresh ginger with the powdered form that is widely used throughout the world. While the powder is a ground version of the same plant, the drying significantly reduces the intensity of the flavor.

recipes

DESCRIPTION

An aromatic rhizome that is rather ugly in appearance, ginger is thought to have originated in southern Asia. Today most of the world's ginger is cultivated in India and China, although it is also grown in the West Indies, Hawaii, parts of Africa (the best quality coming from Kenya), and northern Australia. Jamaican ginger is regarded as the best.

The ginger plant (*Zingiber officinale*), with its bright green leaves, pretty yellow and purple flowers, and creeping rhizome, is a perennial that grows to around 3 feet tall. The roots are tan or pale beige in color, bulbous, and firm. Plants shoot after a couple of weeks and the rhizomes are harvested at 6 months when they are still tender, to be used fresh. Ginger that is left for another 3 months becomes very fibrous and needs to be dried or made into ground ginger.

Fresh ginger, when fully mature, can be fibrous with a warm, fresh aroma and a pungent, biting flavor—with a hint of turmeric. The flesh is yellow. Young ginger is milder, less fibrous, has a thinner skin, and more delicate flavors. It has a light brown toughish skin with a pale yellow flesh.

BUYING, STORING, AND PREPARATION

When buying ginger, look for plump, firm, fresh-looking roots with no sign of wrinkles, which are a sign of age. I find it best to store ginger in a dark cupboard or pantry area where it will stay fresh for up to one month. Discard when it begins to wrinkle and soften.

When using fresh ginger, peel it well. Despite its knobbly crevices, I find a potato peeler is ideal for this job as the best flavor lies just below the skin so you want to remove as little flesh as possible. Once peeled and chopped, it will keep well in the fridge, covered with a little lemon juice and topped with plastic wrap. For natural ginger juice, I grate it and squeeze through cheesecloth. When grating you will find that the tougher fibers get caught in the grater; these should be discarded.

CULINARY USES

Ginger is a versatile ingredient, and is as happy to act as perfect partner (to chile and garlic, for example), as it is to dominate.

It is an essential ingredient in the cooking of most Asian countries, and, combined with garlic and chile (sizzled in hot sesame oil), is used in most Chinese dishes, such as stir-fries, noodles, and soups (hot and sour). So diverse are its properties that ginger can be briefly cooked in stir-fries or, in contrast, slow cooked as a base ingredient in many Indian curries and masalas. Ginger is also added to Indian pastes, chutneys, and marinades. In Japan, raw, grated ginger is often served as a side dish. It is also added to fish dishes, sauces, and marinades. Galangal (see below) is a particularly popular ingredient in Japan.

One of my favorite combinations is ginger added to carrots cooked in butter with lemon.

Although ginger is more generally associated with savory dishes, it has properties that are shown to best advantage in sweet dishes and cakes; in fact a lot of great cakes from the past

include ginger—gingerbread and parkin (see page 105) to name but two. In medieval times, ginger was as common and as expensive as pepper, but was always only used in a sweet form.

Beverages include ginger beer, ginger ale, and ginger wine—in fact ginger used to be an essential ingredient in all early wine-making.

OTHER FORMS

Preserved/Stem ginger: Chunks of peeled ginger, cooked in a heavy syrup, known also as glacé ginger, preserved ginger, or stem ginger. It is exported from China and is traditionally sold in elegant pottery jars around Christmas time. Preserved ginger is a very useful ingredient to keep on hand as it can be added to sweet recipes such as icecream, steamed pudding, cakes, and cookies. It is also wonderful in orange or apricot marmalade.

Crystallized ginger: Pieces of candied ginger, rolled in a crunchy sugar coating—and sometimes dipped in chocolate. Again, a great ingredient to have on hand that is used extensively in baking.

Galangal and pickled pink ginger: These are used extensively in Asian cooking and are now becoming more readily available. Galangal, known as Laos or Thai ginger, is a camphorized member of the ginger family, sometimes also known as Lesser ginger. It has a pink, knobbly fleshed appearance, a more lemony flavor and a peppery taste. Only use fresh young galangal as it gets tougher as it gets older and more difficult to peel. Otherwise, use and prepare as for ginger root.

Pink ginger is a specialty of the Japanese. It is very thinly sliced ginger that is pickled with vinegar, resulting in a pinkish color that not only looks magnificent but tastes fantastic. Generally, it is served with raw shashimi and sushi. I like to use it in dressings and in marinades.

OTHER USES

Ginger didn't get the name "the great medicine", for nothing. Long before it was used in cooking, it was prized for its medicinal properties. The famous Greek physician, Pedanius Dioscorides (around A.D. 70), recommended ginger for the stomach and as an antidote to poison. An ancient headache remedy was to roast ginger root over an open fire and then to apply slices of it to the temples and forehead. Ginger was also widely prescribed by Indian and Chinese herbalists for a number of ailments from gout to paralysis. Because ginger is a diaphoretic, it was used during the Great Plague in London (1665-6). Fresh and crystallized ginger is said to ease travel sickness.

For a delicious ginger tea that will relieve sore throats and head colds, simply add chunks of peeled ginger to a mug of boiling water, sweeten with a little honey (if desired), and drink. Ginger tea granules are also available from health food stores.

complementary flavors

- VEGETABLES (ESPECIALLY GARLIC, ONIONS, AND CELERY)
- FRUIT (RHUBARB, MELON, PINEAPPLE, LIMES, PLUMS, AND APPLES)
- SPICES (ESPECIALLY CHILE AND CUMIN)
- HERBS (ESPECIALLY CILANTRO AND LEMONGRASS)
- DAIRY PRODUCTS (CREAM AND YOGURT)
- HONEY AND MOLASSES
- SHELLFISH (SCALLOPS, LOBSTER, CRAB, AND MUSSELS)
- MEAT (CHICKEN, PORK, AND BEEF)

chilled avocado and ginger soup

2 large, ripe avocados, pitted and peeled
1 garlic clove, chopped
1 onion, chopped
1 green chile, finely chopped
Juice of 2 lemons
3 cups well-flavored vegetable broth (or chicken broth), chilled
1/2 teaspoon coriander seeds
Juice from a 2-inch piece of fresh ginger root (see page 98)
2 tablespoons sour cream
1/4 cup olive oil
Salt and freshly ground black pepper

Place the avocado flesh in a blender along with the garlic, onion, chile, lemon juice, and broth, and blitz to a smooth purée.

In a small hot frying pan, dry toast the cilantro seeds for 20 seconds. Add them to the blender with half the ginger juice and blitz again to give a smooth, silky consistency. Transfer the soup to a bowl and whisk in the sour cream. Season with salt and pepper to taste and chill well.

To serve, pour into chilled soup bowls, mix the remaining ginger juice with the olive oil, and drizzle it over the soup.

sashimi salmon with teriyaki ginger dressing

What I love about this dish, apart from its wonderful flavor, is that no cooking is needed. However, that does mean it is vitally important to use the freshest possible salmon.

1 lb. very fresh skinless, boneless salmon fillet, well chilled
1 fennel bulb, thinly sliced
1/4 English cucumber, cut in half lengthwise, seeded and thinly shaved into ribbons
A handful of cilantro leaves
1 bunch of watercress, trimmed
2 oranges, segmented
1 teaspoon black sesame seeds
Salt and freshly ground black pepper

FOR THE DRESSING;

1 garlic clove, crushed
Grated zest of 1 orange
3 tablespoons rice wine vinegar
1 teaspoon cumin seeds, toasted in a dry frying pan
1 tablespoon pickled pink ginger, finely chopped
2 tablespoons teriyaki sauce
1 small red chile, finely chopped
1 teaspoon sugar
1/4 cup olive oil
1 tablespoon sesame oil

Using a very thin, sharp knife, cut the salmon into slices 1/4-inch thick and set aside.

For the dressing, place the garlic, orange zest, rice wine vinegar, and cumin seeds in a bowl and whisk well. Mix in the pink ginger, teriyaki sauce, chile, and sugar and then gradually whisk in both oils to form a light emulsion.

In a large bowl, toss the fennel, cucumber, cilantro leaves, watercress, and orange segments with a little of the dressing and season to taste. Add the salmon and gently toss again, being careful not to break the salmon slices.

Arrange on individual plates, pour the remaining dressing over it, sprinkle the sesame seeds on top, and serve.

steamed mussels with spicy gremolata

The Italian gremolata is traditionally a mixture of finely chopped parsley, garlic, lemon zest, and bread crumbs, sprinkled generously over fish, meat, or vegetables to add extra texture and flavor. Here, with a little poetic license, I include fresh ginger, which makes a perfect topping for the mussels.

2¼ lbs. fresh mussels
1 tablespoon olive oil
1 onion, finely chopped
2 garlic cloves, crushed
1 teaspoon ground cumin
4 plum tomatoes, skinned, seeded, and chopped
1¼ cups dry white wine
¼ cup ginger wine

FOR THE GREMOLATA:

1-inch piece of fresh ginger root, finely chopped
2 tablespoons finely chopped parsley
1 teaspoon finely grated lemon zest
1 garlic clove, crushed

Combine all the ingredients for the gremolata in a bowl and set aside.

Clean the mussels under cold running water and pull out the beards. Discard any open mussels that don't close when tapped hard on the counter.

Heat the olive oil in a large, heavy pan, add the onion, and cook over a medium heat until translucent. Add the garlic, cumin, and tomatoes, reduce the heat, and cook until fragrant. Add the mussels to the pan, then pour in the white wine and ginger wine. Add a ½ cup of water and bring to a boil. Cover the pan and cook over a high heat for 4–5 minutes, until the mussels open. Discard any that remain closed.

Serve the mussels and their cooking liquor in warmed deep bowls, sprinkled with the gremolata.

scallops with ginger, scallions, and sugar snap peas

1 tablespoon light soy sauce
2 teaspoons arrowroot
2 tablespoons vegetable oil
1 tablespoon light sesame oil
10 scallions, cut into 2-inch lengths
1 teaspoon finely grated fresh ginger root
½ garlic clove, crushed
12 large scallops (ideally diver-caught)
5 oz. baby sugar snap peas, trimmed
⅔ cup well-flavored chicken broth
1 teaspoon *nam pla* (Thai fish sauce)
Salt and freshly ground black pepper

Mix together in a small bowl the soy sauce, arrowroot, and 4 tablespoons of water to form a paste. Set aside.

In a wok or large, shallow frying pan, heat both the oils until fairly hot. Add the scallions, ginger, and garlic, and cook for 1 minute. Add the scallops and fry over high heat for about 1 minute per side. Add the sugar snap peas and toss for a minute longer, then remove the scallops from the pan and keep warm.

Pour the broth into the pan and bring to a boil. Stir in the arrowroot mixture and cook for about 1 minute, until slightly thickened. Return the scallops to the pan, add the fish sauce, and adjust the seasoning.

Put the scallops on serving plates, top with the vegetables, then pour the sauce over them, and serve immediately.

Paul's Tip Frozen scallops can be used as a substitute for fresh but they tend to contain loads of water and certainly don't have the same flavor.

pork chops with sage and caramelized ginger apples

4 pork loin chops
2 tablespoons vegetable oil
2 tablespoons unsalted butter
8 sage leaves, shredded, plus a few leaves for garnishing
2 tablespoons cider vinegar (or white wine vinegar)
1/2 cup dry cider
2/3 cup heavy cream
1/2 cup well-flavored chicken broth
1 teaspoon Dijon mustard
Salt and freshly ground black pepper

FOR THE CARAMELIZED GINGER APPLES:

2 Granny Smith apples
2 tablespoons unsalted butter
1-inch piece of fresh ginger root, finely chopped
1 tablespoon demerara (or light brown) sugar

Season the pork chops on both sides with salt and pepper. Heat the oil in a large frying pan, add the chops, and fry for about 3–4 minutes on each side, until golden and cooked through. Remove from the pan and keep warm. Add the butter to the pan, then add the sage and cook for 30 seconds. Stir in the vinegar and cider and boil rapidly, until reduced by about half. Pour in the cream and chicken broth, and stir well to scrape up any residue on the bottom of the pan. Whisk in the mustard, then reduce the heat and simmer until the sauce is thick enough to coat the back of a spoon.

Meanwhile, peel the apples, remove the cores with a corer, and slice each apple into 4 rings, about 3/4-inch thick. Heat the butter and ginger in a large frying pan until foaming, add the apple slices and sprinkle over the sugar. Let them caramelize before turning them over to caramelize the other side. When beautifully golden and tender, remove from the pan and drain on paper towels.

To serve, place the pork chops on 4 serving plates and pour the sage cream sauce over them. Top each chop with 2 caramelized ginger apples and garnish with sage leaves.

roasted pears in ginger butter

Serve these wonderful roasted pears with a little mint-flavored ricotta cheese, or with a scoop of good lemon sorbet or sherbet.

2 tablespoons sugar
2 tablespoons honey
1-inch piece of fresh ginger root, finely grated
1/4 cup white wine
1-inch piece of cinnamon stick
4 ripe but firm pears, preferably Bartlett
1/4 cup (1/2 stick) unsalted butter
2 tablespoons rum
1 teaspoon finely chopped preserved ginger

Put the sugar, honey, grated ginger, wine, cinnamon, and 2/3 cup of water in a pan and bring to a boil, stirring. Simmer until the syrup has reduced by half, then strain and set aside.

Peel and core the pears and cut them in half vertically, but leave the stalks on. Heat a large frying pan (big enough to take the 8 pear halves lying flat), add the butter, and heat until it begins to foam. Add the pears, laying them flat around the pan, core-side down. Cook for 2–3 minutes, until golden underneath, then turn and cook the other side. Add the strained syrup and the rum to the pan and cover with a lid. Reduce the heat and let the pears caramelize in the buttery syrup, turning occasionally—this will take 4–5 minutes.

Arrange the pears on serving plates, add the preserved ginger to the syrup, and pour it over the pears.

parkin

This recipe originates from Yorkshire and is similar to Welsh gingerbread, except it contains oatmeal. It is sometimes served with cheese, particularly Wensleydale, which may sound strange but is surprisingly good. Originally it was made with black treacle but the lighter flavor of golden syrup is more popular now. You could use half treacle and half syrup. Store parkin in an airtight container; the longer you keep it, the stickier it will become.

3/4 cup all-purpose flour
2 cups medium oatmeal
2 tablespoons brown sugar
1-inch piece of fresh ginger root, finely grated
A pinch of ground ginger
A pinch of salt
2/3 cup golden syrup
1/3 cup (3/4 stick) unsalted butter
1 teaspoon baking soda
1/4 cup whole milk, warmed

Preheat the oven to 325°F. Mix all the dry ingredients together in a large bowl. Place the syrup and butter in a saucepan and heat gently until the butter has melted. Dissolve the baking soda in the warm milk, then pour both liquids into the flour mixture and stir well.

Pour into a greased and lined 8-inch square cake pan and bake for 45–50 minutes; when it is done, a toothpick inserted in the center should come out clean. Let cool in the pan, then turn out and cut into squares.

plum, ginger, and yogurt puddings

1/2 cup (1/2 stick) unsalted butter
1/2 cup plain yogurt
1/4 cup sugar
1/4 cup vanilla sugar (see page 143)
2-inch piece of fresh ginger root, finely grated
2 eggs
1/3 cup cornstarch
1/2 cup all-purpose flour
1 teaspoon baking powder
2/3 cup maple syrup
8 ripe but firm plums, pitted, and cut into 1/2-inch pieces

In a bowl, beat together the butter, yogurt, both sugars, and ginger until light and fluffy. Beat in the eggs, one by one. Sift together the flours and baking powder and fold into the mixture.

Take 4 large soufflé or custard cups, about 1 cup in capacity, and divide the maple syrup between them. Top with the plums. Spoon the ginger mixture over the plums, then cover the dishes with plastic wrap and place in a wide pan. Pour enough boiling water into the pan to come half way up the sides of the dishes, then cover the pan and simmer gently for 25–30 minutes, until a knife inserted in the center of a pudding comes out clean. Remove the puddings carefully and let cool slightly before turning them out onto serving plates. Serve with vanilla icecream or crème fraîche.

garlic *Allium sativum*

Originating in central Asia, garlic has been cultivated for over 6,000 years. Garlic was, and still is, prized for its aphrodisiacal and therapeutic properties, in addition to its culinary uses; the ancient Egyptians took it to increase their strength and endurance.

recipes

GARLIC AND THYME BISQUE (PAGE 108)

GARLIC TARTINES WITH GRILLED SCALLOPS AND CRISPY BACON (PAGE 108)

GARLIC, SHALLOT, AND PORTABELLO CURRY (PAGE 110)

CHICKEN WITH 40 CLOVES OF GARLIC (PAGE 110)

CAESAR STEAK SANDWICH (PAGE 111)

SCAMPI PROVENÇALE (PAGE 111)

SPICY GARLIC AND TOMATO PICKLE (PAGE 112)

POTATOES WITH GARLIC, LEMON, AND WALNUTS (PAGE 112)

SEE ALSO:

SOUPE AU PISTOU (PAGE 36)

GOATS CHEESE AND BASIL MOUSSE (PAGE 38)

PORK ADOBO (PAGE 75)

LINGUINE WITH PUMPKIN SEED-MINT SAUCE (PAGE 31)

SLOW-ROAST LAMB WITH ROSEMARY AND ANCHOIADE (PAGE 46)

ANDALUSIAN FISH SOUP WITH SAFFRON AÏOLI (PAGE 67)

SALT-GRILLED SHRIMP WITH LIME AND GARLIC (PAGE 168)

SALT COD PÂTÉ WITH BALSAMIC PEPPERS AND OLIVES (PAGE 170)

DESCRIPTION

Garlic (*Allium sativum*) is a member of the lily family. It grows underground in bulbs or heads, each composed of some eight to twenty smaller inner units called cloves. These are covered in a thin papery skin. Garlic contains a liquid called allecin, which is the compound that gives garlic its aroma, and is also the culprit of smelly garlic breath.

All garlic is harvested and stored for up to one month prior to use, to undergo a drying or curing process in which its natural inner moisture evaporates to prevent it from rotting. It is during this time that the flavor of the garlic develops and strengthens. There are over 300 different garlic varieties. All are white inside, but the outer skin can be white, purple, pink, and sometimes red. White is the most common and has the strongest flavor. Purple and red varieties are milder and have a shorter shelf life. Elephant garlic is the name given to a very large variety of garlic with an intense flavor. The bulbs of elephant garlic can grow to the size of a small apple and are ideal when you want a lot of garlic in a dish. Use as you would normal garlic. I've tried some amazing pickLed garlic from Spain. Smoked garlic is also available but I am not a great lover of it.

BUYING AND STORING

Choose garlic that feels firm and heavy for its size and there should be no sign of mold, shriveling, or sprouting. Available all year round, garlic has a long shelf life if stored correctly. It is best kept in a cool, dark, well-ventilated, dry place. Do not refrigerate as this promotes rot as well as a smelly fridge. Occasionally garlic will germinate producing green sprouts that will taste bitter. If the cloves are still firm, however, the garlic will be fine, so simply cut away the sprouts.

PREPARATION

Garlic has long had a reputation for being difficult to handle, which is simply not the case if you follow simple guidelines. First you need to break up the bulbs. Simply set the garlic head upside down on a flat surface and use the palm of your hand to press down hard on the root end. All the cloves will break loose, ready to be peeled.

Lots of recipes call for crushed or chopped garlic. To my mind, crushing is a finer, more refined way to use it. I personally always crush it as I find it unpleasant to bite into chunks of chopped garlic. Chunky pieces don't cook well, tend to burn, and can entirely ruin a dish with bitterness. Although there are numerous garlic gadgets on the market, all you will need to crush garlic is a large cook's knife—nothing beats the result.

First, chop the garlic as fine as you can on a board, sprinkle a little salt overt it to aid chopping, and to form a paste. Pull your knife back over the garlic and salt at a 20° angle, crushing and rubbing the garlic into a smooth paste with the inside of your blade. Store it in a little oil if not using immediately. For occasions when you need to peel a large amount of garlic, as for my Garlic and Thyme Bisque (page 108), microwave the cloves or blanch in boiling water for 30–40 seconds to loosen the skins. This makes them easier to peel once they have cooled.

CULINARY USES

For me, the scent of fresh garlic, whether raw or cooked, is the aroma and promise of great food to come. It has been used for centuries to invigorate dishes (such as Chicken with 40 Cloves of Garlic, page 110), soups (like Tourin Blanchi), and sauces, and is even surprisingly delicious in desserts and icecream. Where would the French be without aïoli, North Africans without harissa, or the Americans without their famous Caesar salad dressing? Also take a moment to think of pesto and garlic bread, and the many recipes, too numerous to contemplate, that begin with sautéing a little garlic in oil or butter.... We are talking about a major player on the culinary scene.

The flavor of garlic depends on how you use it, whether raw, smoked, sautéed, roasted, or infused into oils or vinegars. Each provides a distinctive taste and range of flavor. Add raw garlic when you want the most bite from the smallest amount, or cook it in fat to sweeten the flavor and make it milder (don't burn it, though: it becomes bitter). As a rule, the smaller you chop it, the more potent the taste and aroma. I love to roast whole cloves in the oven, the roasting caramelizes the natural sugars, giving a wonderful almost nutty flavor. In fact, when roasting garlic cloves, I suggest you roast extra. They are delicious used in all sorts of things—salads, dressings, marinades, or with roasted vegetables.

OTHER PRODUCTS AND THEIR USES

Garlic vinegar: for dressings.
Garlic salt: a blend of dried garlic and salt used as a seasoning.
Garlic powder: dried garlic, crushed into a powder and used as a flavoring.
Garlic flakes: dried garlic, cut into flakes, great with roasted meats.
Garlic oil: for dressings and for dressing.
Garlic purée: manufactured purée. Fine as a substitute when time is short but not as flavorful as fresh crushed garlic.
Garlic leaves: wonderful and fragrant in salads and soups.

OTHER USES

Apart from its culinary versatility, garlic has long been regarded as one of the best all-round healing plants. It is credited with diuretic, antiseptic, and cleansing properties, and it is an excellent antibiotic, antihistamine and expectorant. Reputed to give strength and courage in ancient days, it is nowadays widely available as an over-the-counter treatment for high cholesterol.

complementary flavors

TOMATO
MUSTARD
PARMESAN CHEESE
BALSAMIC VINEGAR
BASIL
ONIONS AND SHALLOTS
MUSHROOMS
OLIVE OIL
LEMON

garlic and thyme bisque

A wonderful soup for all garlic lovers who have no qualms about the effect on others!

2 tablespoons unsalted butter
1 onion, chopped
1 small leek, chopped
1 head of garlic, cloves separated and peeled
14 fl oz. whole milk
2 teaspoons thyme leaves
3/4 pint chicken broth (or vegetable broth)
5 slices of baguette, cut 3/4-inch thick
2 tablespoons olive oil
3 1/2 fl oz. heavy cream
Freshly grated nutmeg
Salt and freshly ground black pepper

Heat the butter in a heavy pan, add the onion and leek and cook gently until soft and tender. Add the garlic cloves and cook for 10 minutes, until the vegetables and garlic have become slightly caramelized and very tender. Add the milk, half the thyme, and the broth, and bring to a boil.

Lightly toast the bread and rub it with the olive oil. Cut into smallish pieces, add to the boiling soup, and reduce the heat to a simmer. Cook for about 30 minutes, for the flavors to meld. Pour into a blender and blitz to a creamy purée, then strain through a strainer as well, to give an even smoother finish. Return to the pan, add the cream, and reheat gently. Season with nutmeg, salt, and pepper, and sprinkle the remaining thyme leaves over it, for garnishing.

Paul's Tip Garlic is great but, jokes aside, the after-effects can be harsh on others. After eating garlic, chew some parsley, which helps sweeten the breath.

garlic tartines with grilled scallops and crispy bacon

2 large garlic cloves, peeled
1/2 cup whole milk
1/4 cup heavy cream
Olive oil
8 large, fresh scallops
4 strips of bacon
4 slices of baguette, cut 3/4-inch thick
2 oz. (1 1/2 cups) arugula
2 oz. Parmesan cheese, thinly shaved
Salt and freshly ground black pepper

FOR THE DRESSING:

1 tablespoon sherry vinegar (or red wine vinegar)
2 tablespoons walnut oil
2 tablespoons olive oil

Put the garlic cloves in a small pan of boiling water, blanch for 1 minute, then drain and repeat. Return to the dry pan, cover with the milk, and cook for 12–15 minutes, until tender. Drain off excess milk, add the cream, and return to a boil for 2 minutes. Blitz in a blender to obtain a thick garlic purée.

Make the dressing by whisking all the ingredients together and seasoning with salt and pepper.

Heat a ridged grill pan, brush it with a little olive oil, then season the scallops and cook them for 1–2 minutes on each side, until just done. Set aside and keep warm. Grill the bacon on the grill pan until crisp.

Toast the baguette slices on the grill pan. Spoon the garlic purée liberally over each piece, top with the scallops, and then with the bacon. Toss the arugula with most of the dressing and serve alongside or on the tartines, drizzling the remaining dressing over the tartines and scattering the Parmesan shavings over them.

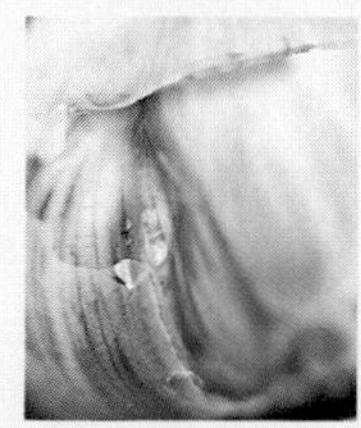

garlic, shallot, and portobello mushroom curry

1-inch piece of fresh ginger root, chopped
2 onions, chopped
6 garlic cloves, thinly sliced
3 tablespoons thick, whole-milk yogurt
1/2 cup vegetable oil
1 lb. large portobello mushrooms, thinly sliced
2 teaspoons ground cilantro
1/2 teaspoon chili powder
A pinch of turmeric
1 teaspoon tomato paste
2 tablespoons chopped cilantro
Salt and freshly ground black pepper

In a blender or food processor, blitz together the ginger, onions, garlic, yogurt and a 1/2 cup of water until smooth.

Heat half the oil in a large frying pan, add the mushrooms, and stir-fry until cooked. Remove from the pan and set aside. Heat the remaining oil in the pan, add the spices, and cook for 2–3 minutes, until they start to brown. Stir in the yogurt mixture and tomato paste, and cook for another minute. Then add 1 1/4 cups of water, return the mushrooms to the pan, and simmer for 8–10 minutes. Sprinkle the cilantro on top and serve.

chicken with 40 cloves of garlic

A traditional French dish, perfect for vampires! You may be put off by the thought of so much garlic but in fact, the flavor mellows as it cooks.

1 x 3 1/2–4 lb. organic or cage-free chicken
2 sprigs each of rosemary, thyme, and sage
1 small bay leaf
40 garlic cloves, unpeeled
2/3 cup olive oil
Salt and freshly ground black pepper

FOR SEALING THE CASSEROLE DISH:

1/4 cup all-purpose flour
1/4 cup water mixed with 1 tablespoon oil

Preheat the oven to 350°F. Season the chicken liberally with salt and pepper and place it in a large casserole dish. Tuck the herbs and the garlic cloves in around the bird, then pour the oil over them and toss all the ingredients, ensuring the chicken is on top.

Mix together the 2 ingredients for sealing the casserole dish until you have a smooth paste. Place the lid on the casserole dish and seal with the paste, pressing it around the join (this ensures that all the flavor and juices are kept in the casserole dish). Place in the oven and cook for 1 3/4 hours.

To serve, transfer the casserole dish to the table and remove the lid to release the wonderful garlicky fragrance inside.

caesar steak sandwich

Olive oil
4 x 5 oz. beef minute steaks
2 Bibb lettuces
1 oz. Parmesan cheese, freshly grated
1 focaccia bread, about 10 inches in diameter, cut into quarters
4 plum tomatoes, thinly sliced
Salt and freshly ground black pepper

FOR THE DRESSING:

2 yolks from organic or cage-free eggs
1 teaspoon Dijon mustard
1/4 teaspoon sugar
1 tablespoon red wine vinegar
3 garlic cloves, crushed
1/4 cup extra virgin olive oil
2 tablespoons vegetable oil
A drop of Tabasco sauce
Juice of 1/2 lemon

First make the dressing. Put the egg yolks, mustard, sugar, and vinegar in a bowl and mix well. Add the garlic, then slowly beat in the oils to form a thick sauce. Mix in the Tabasco and lemon juice, and season to taste.

Heat a little olive oil in a ridged grill pan or large frying pan. Season the steaks, cook until done to your liking, then remove from the heat and keep warm.

Break up the lettuce leaves, put them in a bowl, and toss with a little of the dressing to bind them. Add the grated Parmesan and season to taste.

Cut the focaccia quarters horizontally in half and grill on the ridged grill pan or warm them through briefly in the oven. Place a little lettuce in each quarter of focaccia, top with sliced tomato, and then with the steak. Drizzle the remaining dressing over them. Finish with lettuce, replace the top half of the bread, and serve immediately.

scampi provençale

32 scampi (fresh or frozen), shelled and de-veined (see page 119)
Juice of 1/2 lemon
2 tablespoons olive oil
1/4 cup (1/2 stick) unsalted butter
4 garlic cloves, crushed
7 oz. sunblush tomatoes
3 tablespoons chopped flat-leaf parsley
Salt and freshly ground black pepper

Defrost the scampi, if frozen, and dry thoroughly. Season the scampi with salt and pepper and squeeze the lemon juice over it. Heat the olive oil in a large frying pan, add the scampi, and fry for 1 minute. Add the butter and garlic and cook for another minute. Remove the scampi from the pan and keep warm. Add the sunblush tomatoes and parsley, cook for a few minutes, then return the scampi to the pan and toss gently together so that all the ingredients are spread evenly. Serve immediately.

spicy garlic and tomato relish

This makes a delicious summer relish, especially when served with cheese, cold meat, or fish.

2 1/4 lbs. tomatoes, skinned and quartered
2/3 cup white wine vinegar
1/2 teaspoon ground cloves
1 teaspoon ground cumin
1-inch piece of fresh ginger root, chopped
20 plump garlic cloves, peeled but left whole
2 red chiles, finely chopped
2/3 cup brown sugar
1 teaspoon ground cardamom
2 tablespoons *nam pla* (Thai fish sauce)

Put all the ingredients in a large pot and bring slowly to a boil, stirring occasionally. Reduce the heat and simmer for up to 1 hour or until the mixture is very thick. Let cool to room temperature before serving. Leave in the fridge for up to 2 days before using, for best results. Or you can put it in sterilized jars (see page 23) and seal if you want to store it for longer.

potatoes with garlic, lemon, and walnuts

1 1/2 lbs. medium-sized waxy new potatoes
2 tablespoons vegetable oil
2 tablespoons walnut oil
2 tablespoons unsalted butter
A pinch of freshly grated nutmeg
4 garlic cloves, crushed
2 tablespoons chopped parsley
Grated zest of 1/2 lemon
2 tablespoons chopped walnuts
Salt and freshly ground black pepper

Cook the whole, unpeeled potatoes in boiling salted water until almost tender. Drain in a colander and leave until cool enough to handle, then carefully peel off the skins and slice the potatoes 1/2-inch thick.

Heat the oils together in a large frying pan, add the potatoes, and fry quickly to develop the color. Add the butter and, when it is foaming, gently toss the potatoes in it until beautifully golden in color. Season with nutmeg, salt, and pepper. Add the garlic, parsley, lemon zest, and walnuts, toss with the potatoes, and serve.

chiles

Capsicum annuum, C. frutescens

Following my book, *Raising the Heat*, which expounds the virtues of chiles and other "hot" ingredients, I still relish the opportunity to cook with chiles at any time, so you will see them regularly throughout these pages.

recipes

NUOC CHAM MACKEREL SALAD (PAGE 116)

SPICE-GRILLED PUMPKIN SALAD (PAGE 1116)

CRISP CHILE-COCONUT SEA BREAM (PAGE 118)

ASIAN-STYLE DIRTY RICE (PAGE 119)

CHILE-CRAB NOODLE OMELETTE (PAGE 119)

SEE ALSO:

MONKFISH CURRY WITH GREEN MANGO AND THAI BASIL (PAGE 40)

MOLE POBLANO (TURKEY IN CHOCOLATE SAUCE) (PAGE 175)

AZTEC EGGS (PAGE 11)

SPICY GARLIC AND TOMATO RELISH (PAGE 112)

TIRITAS (PAGE 123)

MINTED CHICKEN AND EGGPLANT SALAD (PAGE 28)

STIR-FRIED NOODLES THAI STYLE (PAGE 139)

WOK-FRIED MONKFISH IN SOUR SAUCE (PAGE 140)

CILANTRO-MARINATED SARDINES WITH COCONUT MILK (PAGE 12)

DESCRIPTION

All chiles and peppers belong to the Capsicum family. While most sweet peppers (along with a few of the hot varieties, like the Carliston pepper) come from *Capsicum annum*, most of the small, pungent chile varieties fall under the category *Capsicum frutescens.* There are hundreds of varieties of chile grown widely throughout the world (in Mexico, China, Japan, and Indonesia), of all different shapes, sizes, and colors—not to mention pungencies. To the average cook, chiles are merely hot, very hot, or mind-blowing, but to the true chile lover each has a particular aroma and flavor. Unfortunately, however, relatively few varieties of chile have yet beaten a path to the average Western supermarket or grocery store.

The most common chiles are listed below, but, as a general rule, the smaller the chile, the hotter the beast! For example, the small red Thai chile (also known as Birds Eye chile), is hot and mind-blowing. Scotch Bonnet or Habanero have extremely hot qualities that will probably only really be appreciated by chile aficionados. Do not to be fooled by the color: some small green chiles can also be extremely hot. And long chiles are generally hotter than round ones. When recipes in this book simply call for red chiles, use larger red or green chiles unless otherwise stated.

Small red chiles (or Birds Eye chiles): These are tiny, blisteringly hot, pointed chiles, usually not more than 1 inch long. Traditionally used in Thai and Chinese cooking. Use with care.

Large red chiles (Lombok): These long, red chiles originate from Indonesia and are now commonly found in food stores simply labelled mild chiles. They provide a good starting-out variety for those taking the plunge with chiles for the first time.

Small green chiles (Jalepeños): A torpedo-shaped, bright green chile from Mexico. It was originally a very hot chile, although it now seems to vary and can be mild. The Jalepeño can also be sold ripe and red, when it is slightly sweeter and less hot. These chiles should be used with care as they vary from batch to batch. Cutting one open and running your fingers over the seeds will generally give an indication of the intensity of that particular lot: this test should merely cause a slight tingle.

Large green chiles: Again, the larger variety is less hot than the smaller green variety; use for general recipes throughout the book.

Dried chiles: Buying dried chiles can be as confusing as buying fresh ones, and specialty food stores stock numerous varieties. They are generally used in Mexican cooking and vary tremendously in heat. In some of the recipes I have used dried chili flakes, which are a safe bet for most dishes because the vein and seeds have been removed.

Chili powder is also available, and although it takes a lot of the hard work out of preparation, I do not recommend it except as a last resort.

BUYING AND STORING

When buying fresh chiles, select only those that are plump, firm, shiny and, unwrinkled, especially close to the stem. Stored in the fridge, they will last for several weeks. Remove any that seem to be getting soft as they will quickly rot and spoil the rest. Buy dried chiles in small quantities and store in a cool dark place.

PREPARATION

Chiles have little aroma, but vary enormously in taste. Capsaicin, the pungent irritant constituent that gives chiles their ultimate kick, is present in the vein and seeds of the chile (more so than the skin), depending on the species and the state of ripeness. To reduce the heat in a dish, I suggest removing both the vein and seeds before using.

One word of caution: when handling chiles, wash your hands well and avoid touching your eyes, or any sensitive areas or cuts.

CULINARY USES

Fresh chiles are generally associated with Asian and Mexican cooking, but they are also widely used across South America, the Caribbean, and West Africa, where many regional recipes call for the more dramatic chiles (such as the Habanero and Scotch Bonnet). Mexican Tex Mex, chili con carne, and chili rellenos (deep-fried, whole, stuffed chiles cooked in batter) have become firm favorites in the West, too. Chiles are also, of course, used extensively in Chinese (particularly Szechuan), Thai, and other Southeast Asian cooking—from salads (like the particularly fiery *Som Tam*) to traditional sambals. The seeds are also often left in, for extra heat!

Many curry pastes (such as red, green, and yellow Thai pastes) and sauces have a chile base. In Morocco, couscous is traditionally served with a fiendishly hot chile sauce called harissa. Chiles also form the base of many commercial products such as chile sauce and Tabasco, and seasonings such as paprika and cayenne pepper.

HOW TO SOFTEN THE BLOW

Beware of over indulgence—chiles can burn and cause considerable discomfort. Another word of warning: never drink water to dull the pain after eating very hot chili—it only heightens the heat. Instead, eat some bread or yogurt, or drink some milk, to neutralize the effect.

OTHER USES

Chiles have antiseptic properties and are apparently a constituent of bandaids. They are said to stimulate digestion and awaken appetite. They also have a very high vitamin C content. Chiles are used in meat preservation and, in some cultures, were used as a means of torture!

complementary flavors

GARLIC

NAM PLA (THAI FISH SAUCE)

SHALLOTS

LIMES

BLACK BEANS

COCONUT MILK

LEMONGRASS

YOGURT

GINGER

nuoc cham mackerel salad

Nuoc cham (or sometimes *nuoc mam*) is a condiment based on the fish sauce of the same name. Used as freely as salt and pepper, it is popular all over Vietnam, although it does vary slightly in character from place to place.

In Asia, fresh mackerel is a popular fish because it is cheap and widely available. Here I have substituted smoked mackerel, which gives the dish an unusual smoky flavor that permeates the dressing.

1/2 English cucumber
1/2-inch piece of fresh ginger root, peeled and finely chopped
14 oz. smoked mackerel fillet, skinned and flaked
4 scallions, shredded
7 oz. (3–3 1/2 cups) bean sprouts
1 teaspoon black sesame seeds

FOR THE NUOC CHAM:
3 tablespoons palm sugar (or light brown) sugar)
4 garlic cloves, crushed
2 red chiles (or 1 Thai chile), finely sliced
Juice of 2 limes
2 tablespoons *nuoc mam* (Vietnamese fish sauce) or *nam pla* (Thai fish sauce)
3 shallots, thinly sliced

Put all the ingredients for the *nuoc cham* in a bowl and mix until the sugar has dissolved. Leave for 2 hours for the flavors to meld.

Cut the cucumber in half lengthwise and scrape out the seeds with a teaspoon. Thinly slice the cucumber into long strips lengthwise, using a vegetable peeler. Place in a bowl, add the ginger, flaked mackerel, scallions, and bean sprouts, and pour the *nuoc cham* dressing over them. Toss lightly together. Place on a serving plate, sprinkle the sesame seeds on top, and serve.

spice-grilled pumpkin salad

1 garlic clove, crushed
1 teaspoon ground cumin
2 red chiles, finely chopped
1/4 cup rice wine vinegar
1 tablespoon soft brown sugar
2 tablespoons *ketjap manis* (Indonesian soy sauce)
3 tablespoons olive oil
1 tablespoon dark sesame oil
1 small pumpkin (or butternut squash), seeded and cut into wedges
2 tablespoons chopped cilantro (optional)

To make the marinade, place the garlic, cumin, chiles, vinegar, and sugar in a saucepan, bring to a boil, then reduce the heat and simmer until the mixture has reduced to a light syrup. Transfer to a large bowl and add the *ketjap manis*, olive oil, and sesame oil.

Cook the pumpkin wedges in boiling salted water for 10 minutes, then drain well and place in the marinade. Let marinate for 1 hour.

Heat a ridged grill pan, place the pumpkin pieces on it, and cook for 10–12 minutes, until caramelized, turning regularly. Serve warm, sprinkled with the cilantro, if you like.

crisp chile-coconut sea bream

1 lb 10 oz. sea bream (porgy) fillets, skinned
2 red chiles, seeded and finely chopped
1/4 cup light soy sauce
1 tablespoon finely chopped cilantro
Juice of 2 limes
1/2 cup *nam pla* (Thai fish sauce)
1/4 cup beer
1 tablespoon olive oil
1/3 cup all-purpose flour
1/2 cup cornstarch
Vegetable oil for deep-frying
3 tablespoons unsweetened dried coconut

FOR SERVING:

Steamed jasmine rice (or basmati rice)
2/3 cup *nam jim* (see page 124)
Cilantro leaves
2 limes or lemons, cut into wedges

Cut the bream fillets into thumb-sized strips. Place in a bowl, add half the chile, plus the soy sauce, cilantro, lime juice, and half the fish sauce. Cover and let marinate at room temperature for 30 minutes.

In a blender, blitz the remaining chile with the remaining fish sauce, plus the beer, olive oil, flour, and cornstarch. Add enough water to form a light batter and then let stand for 10 minutes.

Heat the vegetable oil in a deep-fat fryer or large, deep pot to 350°F (or until a cube of day-old bread browns in 30 seconds). Remove the pieces of fish from the marinade and dip them into the batter so they are lightly coated, then into the coconut. Fry in the hot oil for 2–3 minutes, until golden and crisp (do this in batches, if necessary). Serve with rice and lots of *nam jim* dressing, garnished with cilantro leaves and lime or lemon wedges.

asian-style dirty rice

Dirty rice is a Cajun dish, usually made with chicken livers and lots of pepper, and served with chicken. This is my own, Asian-inspired, style of dirty rice, using the cooking liquid from fermented black beans to give the rice a dark gray color.

Fermented black beans, available in cans from Chinese grocery stores, are small soybeans that have been preserved with salt and spices and cooked. I cook them for another 30 minutes to create a wonderful, fragrant broth in which to cook the rice.

14 oz. fermented black beans, roughly chopped
1/4 cup (1/2 stick) unsalted butter
1 2/3 cups long grain rice
1 green chile, seeded and sliced
1 red chile, seeded and sliced
18 oz. raw tiger shrimp, shelled, de-veined (see Tip below), and finely chopped
1 teaspoon ground cumin
2 tablespoons chopped cilantro
6 scallions, chopped
2 tablespoons *nam pla* (Thai fish sauce)
2 tablespoons light soy sauce

Put the fermented black beans in a saucepan, cover with 3 cups of water, then bring to a boil and simmer for 30 minutes. Drain well, reserving the cooking liquid.

Gently heat the butter in a large, wide pan, add the rice, and cook for 1 minute. Add the chiles, shrimp, and cumin and cook for a minute longer. Add the cooking liquid from the beans and bring to a boil. Reduce the heat, cover, and cook for 20 minutes, until the rice is tender. Add the cooked black beans, cilantro, and scallions. Mix well, season with the fish sauce and light soy sauce, and serve.

Paul's Tip To de-vein shrimp, remove the shells, then run the tip of a sharp knife down the back of the shrimp and lift out the thin black thread (intestinal vein).

chile-crab noodle omelette

5 oz. (2-2 1/2 cups) fresh rice noodles
8 organic or cage-free eggs
2 teaspoons *nam pla* (Thai fish sauce)
1 red chile, seeded and finely chopped
1 tablespoon chopped cilantro
Oil for frying
4 scallions, shredded on the diagonal
5 oz. (3/4 cup) fresh crabmeat
Salt and freshly ground black pepper

Cook the rice noodles in a large pot of boiling water for about 5 minutes, until tender, then drain well and dry. Set aside.

Beat the eggs in a bowl along with the fish sauce, chile, half the cilantro, and some salt and pepper.

Heat 2 tablespoons of oil in a frying pan, add the scallions, and cook for 1 minute. Add the crab and warm through, then season to taste. Keep warm.

Heat a little oil in an omelette pan, add a quarter of the noodles, and toss for 30 seconds to reheat them. Pour in a quarter of the beaten egg mixture and cook, drawing in the egg mixture from the sides of the pan, until set underneath. Spoon a quarter of the crab mixture down the center of the omelette, fold in half, and turn out onto a warm plate and keep warm while you cook the remaining 3 omelettes in the same way. Serve immediately, sprinkled with a little of the remaining cilantro.

lemons and limes

Citrus aurantifolia or *C. limon*

I have always tended to think of lemons as being truly Mediterranean, but they were, in fact, discovered in Southeast Asia. Both China and India claim to be their birthplace, although according to history India seems the more logical choice.

The Romans used lemons as an antidote to poison as well as a moth repellent, rather than as a food during the first century A.D. From Rome, lemons found their way to Persia, from where they spread to Spain and North Africa.

recipes

DESCRIPTION

Lemon trees (*Citrus limon*) are fairly small with glossy, dark, evergreen leaves and fragrant blossom. The fruit ripens in winter and lemons taste best when left to ripen on the tree, then picked and used quickly as their fragrance tends to disappear after a day or two. Limes, fruit of the *Citrus aurantifolia*, are always picked unripe and green; if left on the tree longer, they would turn yellow. While both Lemons and limes are rich in vitamin C, lemons contain almost twice as much as limes.

LEMONS

Lemons must surely be the most versatile and indispensable food item for any cook. They provide a range of effects: sharp juice for a clean, fresh flavor; zest for scented sharpness to a mousse or sauce; they are wonderful in tarts, puddings, refreshing sorbets, and long summer drinks. They also add a piquant sour tang to salad dressings, give a lift when squeezed over grilled meat, while fish and seafood could not live without an accompanying wedge of lemon.

As well as adding flavor to a range of foods, lemon juice is also used as a tenderizer for fish and meat. It can be used as a bleach, too, and when rubbed on cut surfaces of fruits and vegetables, such as apples, pears, artichokes, and salsify, stops them turning brown before cooking. Also adding a few drops to the water during cooking keeps them beautifully white.

There are numerous varieties of lemons grown and used throughout the world. In Spain, the Verna lemon is held in great affection, while in Italy chefs have particular regard for the Ferminetto, brought over by the Arabs in the ninth century. Invernali has a soft skin and is a very juicy variety, and the prized Verdelli is much sought after. The Meyer lemon is adored by Americans who love its tart yet sweet flavor in creamy desserts.

LIMES

Limes prefer a hotter, wetter climate than lemons and flourish in the tropics, where they replace lemons. They originated in Malaysia but are also now grown in Mexico, the Caribbean, Florida, and tropical Africa.

British sailors consumed copious amounts of lime on long sea voyages during the late nineteenth century to ward off scurvy, a deadly maritime disease. This practice actually became law with the Merchant Shipping Act of 1894 which required each crew member, after ten days at sea, to consume 2 tablespoons of lime juice daily. Thankfully for the sailors, a little rum was added to it, by way of preservation, and coaxing! Sailors thus acquired the nickname "Limeys." Fortunately scurvy is unheard of these days as our vitamin C intake is more readily under control.

There are a number of varieties of lime, most notably the American Key Lime, a West Indian variety which grows in the Florida Keys, and is

adored by Americans in their Key Lime Pie. Another one is the Tahitian (sometimes also called the Persian lime).

The dark green, knobbly skinned kaffir or wild lime (*Citrus hystrix*) is an essential ingredient in many Thai dishes. These limes do not have much juice, but both the skin and the distinctive, "winged" leaves are frequently used. The leaves are added whole to curries and soups (like Tom Yam) to infuse flavor and should be removed before serving. They are also shredded very finely and added to salads. The leaves are best used fresh. The zest of kaffir tends to be even more intense than that of limes.

BUYING AND STORING LEMONS AND LIMES

Always try to buy organic lemons and limes where possible, as they are the two fruit that I think are all the better for it. When buying lemons from supermarkets, do bear in mind that most (commercially grown) lemons are unfortunately picked unripe as their high acid content helps them last longer in storage. They are therefore treated with ethylene oxide, which turns their chlorophyll green into an enticing lemon yellow.

So remember, the juciest lemons and limes will never look good but will undoubtably have the best flavor. When buying lemons and limes, thin-skinned varieties tend to be juicier whereas thicker-skinned varieties are better for zesting. When purchasing, they should feel weighty—an indication of their juiciness. Keep them in a bowl in the kitchen: they will not only stay at their best, but will brighten up the room no end.

A common practice is to wax lemons to give a wonderful shiny gloss, so if you plan to zest them, first wash them well in boiling water and dry thoroughly before using.

USING LEMONS AND LIMES

Lemon skins contain an oil which is used in confectionery and in perfumery. Twenty drops of lemon oil is equivalent to the juice of an average lemon, so you can see why the finely grated zest is such an effective flavoring.

To extract the most juice from lemons and limes, here's a tip. Simply roll them under the palm of your hand for a while to help release the inner juices. Another trade secret in these modern days is to place the fruit in the microwave for 30 seconds, or some chefs suggest immersing them in warm water for 20 seconds will give a better yield.

As a guide, one medium lemon equals 2–3 tablespoons of juice and approximately 1 tablespoon of freshly grated zest or rind.

complementary flavors

FOR LEMON:

VANILLA

SEAFOOD

MEAT (ESPECIALLY LAMB, CHICKEN, VEAL, AND DUCK)

HONEY

NUTS

HERBS (ESPECIALLY THYME AND ROSEMARY)

FRUIT (ESPECIALLY RASPBERRIES, STRAWBERRIES, AND BLACK CURRANTS)

FOR LIME:

COCONUT MILK

CHILES

LEMONGRASS

CILANTRO

AVOCADO

TOMATO

HONEY

SHELLFISH

The acid in lemons and limes has a pickling effect on fish and seafood, such as my Tiritas (page 123), where the acid cooks the fish during the marinating process. Keep in mind that limes are more acidic than lemons.

Use lemon juice for a sharper flavor or to counteract oiliness or greasiness. It is more aromatic than vinegar, and is an essential ingredient in mayonnaise, hollandaise, and béarnaise sauces.

Lime juice can be used for almost all the same purposes as lemon, although it has a rather sweeter flavor.

CULINARY USES

Lemons and limes are used throughout the world. In the Middle East, cooks use lemon as a souring agent. They love to make fresh lemonade using the rind and pulp of freshly picked lemons, with added water and sugar. They add lemon to their dips such as Baba Ghanoush, Moutabel, and Hummus. The Greeks add lemon to Skordalia, a highly aromatic garlic sauce that accompanies vegetables.

Limes add a wonderful sweet sharp flavor to Asian dressings such as my Nam Jim (page 124). In India, limes are salted like lemons or preserved as a relish, highly seasoned with chiles.

In Morocco, lemons are preserved in salt (page 128), before being added to their tagines and rice dishes. The juice is added to tea to make a refreshing drink in the hot climate.

The Italians have a great affection for lemons, too, which they add to pasta sauces and dips, and make their wonderful lemoncello drink from zest and pulp of lemon mixed with sugar, water, and 30 percent natural alcohol. (I first experienced this when it was added to an icecream by the chef of the Hassler Hotel in Rome during one of our many guest chef promotions. I use it to this day.) Lemons are also a major ingredient in Italian cakes, cocktails, and desserts.

In Mexico, limes are the god of fruits, added to *mojos* (pronounced *mohos,*) a sauce similar to a salsa for grilled meats and fish; they are also squeezed over fruits such as strawberries with a dash of tequila, used in marinades, soups, and, well, just about anything.

As a chef, I use lemons daily in one form or another: I add them to sauces to give a discerning sharp flavor, to help balance the concentrated flavors of a reduced sauce, to give a lift to desserts, to soups, to dressings, etc. All in all, citrus fruits hold unlimited use in cooking.

LEMON AND LIME TIPS

• When grating lemons and limes, place a sheet of waxed paper between the fruit and the grater before grating normally. The zest will stick to the paper and not the grater, and can be just scooped up with a knife.
• Wrap lemon and lime halves in cheesecloth. The cheesecloth stops the seeds falling out and prevents the juice from spurting everywhere. Your guests will be impressed when served with fish dishes.
• Excess lime and lemon juice freezes well, so keep in plastic ice cube trays and store in the freezer for use at any time.
• Use lemon and lime leaves to wrap fish and meat prior to grilling.
• 3 tablespoons of lemon or lime juice equals 1 average lemon or lime.

OTHER USES

Lemons and limes have a very high vitamin C content, which explains why they have been used to treat everything from scurvy to the common cold. Aside from medicinal applications, lemons can also be used as a bleaching and cleaning agent. Adding a few slices of lemon to boiling water when cooking eggs, prevents a ring forming in the pan. Rubbing cut lemon over your cutting board after chopping onions, crushing garlic, etc., will remove the smell. Lemons are also said to be great for cleaning copper, bleaching blond hair, and balancing greasy skin!

tiritas

Tiritas is the first cousin of the Mexican dish, ceviche — white fish "cooked" in a lime juice marinade. This recipe is from the Yucatán. Tuna, with its vibrant color, makes a pleasant change from white fish.

14 oz. sushi-quality (i.e., extremely fresh) blue fin tuna, cut into 1/2-inch cubes
Juice of 3 limes
2 tablespoons olive oil
2 tablespoons tomato ketchup
A few drops of Tabasco
1/2 ripe mango, peeled and cut into 1/4-inch pieces
1/4 red pepper, cut into 1/4-inch pieces
1/2 avocado, peeled and cut into 1/4-inch pieces
1 red chile, seeded and finely chopped
2 scallions, roughly chopped
2 tablespoons roughly chopped cilantro
Salt and freshly ground black pepper

FOR SERVING:

Corn tortillas, cut into quarters and fried until crisp
Lime wedges (optional)
Cilantro leaves

Place the tuna in a bowl, pour the lime juice over it, then add a little salt and leave for 30 minutes, until the tuna becomes opaque. Drain off the juice and combine some of it, according to taste, with the olive oil, tomato ketchup, and Tabasco to form a dressing. Add the mango, red pepper, avocado, red chile, scallions, cilantro, and some salt and pepper. Pour this dressing over the tuna, mix well, and chill for 1 hour.

Serve in cocktail-style glasses, garnished with the fried corn tortillas, lime wedges, and cilantro leaves.

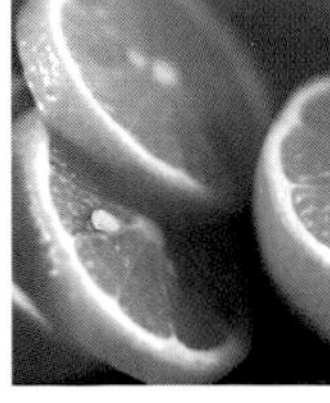

roasted skate with lemon and caper sauce

4 x 10–12 oz. skate wings
1/4 cup olive oil
2 tablespoons unsalted butter
Salt and freshly ground black pepper

FOR THE SAUCE:
1/4 cup olive oil
2 shallots, chopped
1 garlic clove, crushed
1 tablespoon chopped preserved lemons (see page 128)
2 tablespoons superfine capers, drained and rinsed
A pinch of ground cumin
1 tablespoon chopped cilantro
1/2 tablespoon chopped mint
1/2 cup hot fish broth (or water)
2 tablespoons chilled unsalted butter, chopped

Preheat the oven to 400°F. Season the skate wings with salt and pepper. Heat the oil in a large ovenproof frying pan, add the butter and, when it begins to foam, add the skate wings. Cook for 2 minutes on each side, until golden, then place in the oven for 5–6 minutes, until cooked through.

Meanwhile, for the sauce, heat the oil in a pan, add the shallots, garlic, preserved lemon, capers, and cumin, and cook over a gentle heat for 2 minutes. Add the herbs and hot broth, then whisk in the chopped butter over low heat to form a light sauce. Adjust the seasoning and keep warm.

Put the skate on serving plates and spoon the sauce over it. Serve with plain potatoes and buttered spinach.

nam jim (lime and green chile dressing)

This power-packed dressing from Southeast Asia combines sour, sweet, hot, and salty flavors to great effect. I love it with crab, shrimp, chicken, and vegetables. For a spicier dressing still, leave the chile seeds in.

2 tablespoons palm (or light brown) sugar)
2 tablespoons sea salt or kosher salt
3 garlic cloves, chopped
A good handful of cilantro leaves
5 hot green chiles, seeded and finely chopped
1/2-inch piece of fresh ginger root, finely grated (optional)
4 large shallots, chopped
3 tablespoons *nam pla* (Thai fish sauce)
Juice of 8 limes

Put the palm sugar into a small pan and melt over low heat, then set aside.

With a mortar and pestle, crush the sea salt, garlic, and cilantro leaves to a pulp. Add the chopped chiles, sugar, and ginger, if using, and pound again. Mix in the shallots, fish sauce, and lime juice. Leave for up to 1 hour before using to let the flavors develop. It will keep in the fridge for about a week.

sea bream with anchovy, mozzarella, and roasted lemons

4 x 6 oz. sea bream (porgy) fillets
2 tablespoons olive oil
2 small lemons, cut into 3/4-inch-thick slices
2 plum tomatoes, peeled and sliced
1 buffalo mozzarella, cut into 4 slices
1/2 teaspoon lemon thyme leaves
Salt and freshly ground black pepper

FOR THE ANCHOVY SAUCE:

1/4 cup extra virgin olive oil
1 shallot, finely chopped
2 anchovy fillets, finely chopped
1 garlic clove, crushed
1 tablespoon lemon juice
1 tablespoon sherry vinegar
8 basil leaves

Preheat the oven to 400°F. Season the fish liberally with salt and pepper. Heat the oil in a large ovenproof frying pan, place the fish in it skin-side down and cook for 2 minutes, without turning. Remove from the pan and set aside, skin-side up. Add the lemon slices to the oil and cook for 3–4 minutes on each side, until colored. Remove from the pan and set aside.

Return the fish to the pan and add the lemon slices. Place 2 slices of tomato on each fish fillet, top with a slice of mozzarella, then season with salt and pepper and sprinkle with the lemon thyme leaves. Place in the oven for 5–6 minutes, until the fish is cooked and the cheese is melting.

Meanwhile, make the sauce. Heat the oil in a small pan over low heat, add the shallot, anchovies, and garlic, and cook gently for 2–3 minutes. Stir in the lemon juice, sherry vinegar, and basil, and season to taste.

To serve, place the fish on serving plates, pour the anchovy sauce around and top with the roasted lemons. Great served with wilted spinach.

veal chops with lemon sauce and swiss chard

4 x 7-inch thick veal cutlets
2 tablespoons olive oil
1/4 cup (1/2 stick) chilled unsalted butter, chopped
Juice and grated zest of 1 lemon
1 tablespoon brown sugar
1/2 cup dry white wine
1 1/4 cups brown veal broth (or other meat broth)
1 lemon, peel and pith removed, cut into slices
Salt and freshly ground black pepper

FOR THE SWISS CHARD:

1 tablespoon olive oil
1 large head of Swiss chard, leaves only, coarsely chopped
1 garlic clove, crushed
2 tablespoons raisins, soaked in warm water until swollen, then drained
2 tablespoons pine nuts, toasted

Season the veal with salt and pepper. Heat the oil in a frying pan, add half the butter and, when it foams, add the veal chops. Cook over medium heat for about 4–5 minutes on each side, until just tender. Remove from the pan and keep warm.

Remove any excess fat from the pan, add the lemon juice and sugar, and cook until lightly caramelized. Pour in the white wine, raise the heat and boil for 2 minutes. Add the broth, return to a boil and stir in the lemon zest. Reduce the heat and simmer until the sauce is reduced by half.

Meanwhile, for the Swiss chard, heat the olive oil in a pan, add the chard, garlic, and raisins, and cook for 1 minute. Stir in a 1/2 cup of water, cover and cook for 4–5 minutes, until the chard is tender and all the liquid has evaporated. Add the pine nuts and season with salt and pepper.

Finish the lemon sauce by whisking in the remaining butter, a little at a time. Taste, and adjust the seasoning.

Put the Swiss chard on 4 serving plates and top with the veal. Put a lemon slice on each veal chop, pour the lemon sauce over them, and serve.

poached asparagus with avgolemono

Avgolemono, meaning egg and lemon, is a staple of Greek cooking. The name often refers to a soup made from chicken broth and rice, and finished with egg and lemon but it can also be a sauce, served with fish and vegetables.

32 asparagus spears

FOR THE AVGOLEMONO:

2 egg yolks
Juice of 2 lemons
2 teaspoons cornstarch
2 tablespoons heavy cream
Salt and freshly ground black pepper

Peel the asparagus spears, reserving the peelings, and snap off the bottom of each spear at its natural breaking point (about 1 inch from the end). Tie the asparagus into 4 bundles with string and set aside. Bring 4 cups of water to a boil in a large saucepan, add the asparagus peelings and simmer for 20 minutes to form a light asparagus broth. Strain into a clean pan and return to a boil. Poach the asparagus spears in the broth for 4–5 minutes, until just tender. Remove from the pan with a slotted spoon and keep warm. Boil the broth until it has reduced to about 1 cup and a bit.

To make the sauce, whisk the egg yolks and lemon juice together in a heavy pan, off the heat. Mix the cornstarch to a paste with 1 tablespoon of water and add to the egg yolks. Gradually add the hot asparagus broth, whisking constantly. Place over a low heat and cook, stirring, until the mixture has thickened just enough to coat the back of a spoon. It should not boil.

Remove from the heat, add the cream, and season to taste. Pour the sauce over the asparagus and serve immediately.

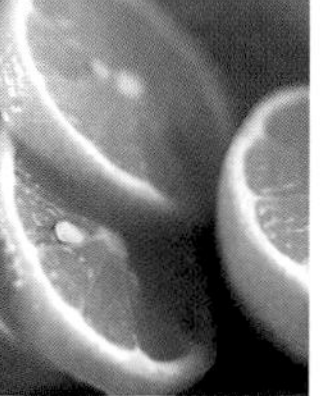

preserved lemons

Some recipes for preserved lemons are too salty for my taste. Here's a milder version that can be used in all sorts of dishes. They will keep, unopened, for up to 1 year, and for up to a month once opened. Try preserving limes in the same way.

12 medium lemons
12 oz. coarse sea salt of kosher salt
3 bay leaves
2 tablespoons sugar
15 allspice berries
15 cilantro seeds
5 star anise

Slit 6 of the lemons into quarters vertically, taking the cuts to within a 1/2 inch of their base. Open them out carefully with your hands. Pack some of the salt into the center of each lemon and press together to re-form its shape.

Sterilize a 1 quart-canning jar (see page 23) and fill with half the remaining salt. Pack the lemons in tightly, pushing them down well to release their juices. Push the bay leaves in between the lemons. Mix the remaining salt with the sugar, allspice berries, cilantro seeds, and star anise, and sprinkle it over the lemons. Squeeze the juice from the remaining 6 lemons and strain into the jar. Seal and leave in a cool place for at least 1 month, turning the jar on end each day. When using the preserved lemons, cut off the flesh and use only the peel.

lemon chiffon cream

If you are searching for a very light and refreshing dessert, look no further. This is so airy and delicate that it might just float away if left unattended—beware! It's a delicious summer dish served with fresh berries. You could make it with limes instead of lemons.

2 gelatin leaves
Juice and grated zest of 2 lemons
3/4 cup superfine sugar
3 large eggs, separated
1 1/4 cups heavy cream, semi-whipped

Cover the gelatine leaves with cold water for 5 minutes, then squeeze out excess water with your hands. Place the gelatin in a small pan with half the lemon juice and warm very gently, stirring until dissolved. Remove from the heat and set aside.

In a bowl, beat the sugar and egg yolks together until thick and creamy. Add the lemon zest and the remaining juice, then stir in the dissolved gelatin.

In a separate bowl and using clean beaters, beat the egg whites until stiff. Fold the semi-whipped cream into the lemon mixture and then, with a metal spoon, carefully fold in the egg whites. Pour into a bowl, cover with plastic wrap, and chill until set.

lemon and almond butter tart

SERVES 6

2 large eggs
1/2 cup sugar
Juice and grated zest of 2 lemons
4 1/2 oz. unsalted butter, melted
1 cup ground almonds
Confectioners' sugar for dusting

FOR THE SWEET PASTRY DOUGH:
2 1/2 cups all-purpose flour, sifted
1 cup (2 sticks) unsalted butter (at room temperature), cut into small pieces
A pinch of salt
3/4 cup confectioners' sugar, sifted
Finely grated zest of 1/2 lemon
1 egg

First make the dough. Put the sifted flour on a work surface and make a well in the center. Put the chopped butter, salt, sugar, and lemon zest in the well, and then add the egg. With your fingertips, gradually bring the flour into the center until all the ingredients come together to form a soft dough. Knead lightly for 1 minute, until completely smooth, then shape the dough into a ball, place in a bowl, and cover with plastic wrap. Let rest in the fridge for 2 hours.

Preheat the oven to 375°F. Roll out the sweet pastry dough to 1/8 inch thick and use to line a 10-inch tart pan. Prick the bottom lightly all over with a fork. Line with parchment paper, fill with baking beans, and bake blind for 10 minutes or until the crust is set but not colored. Remove the beans and paper and return the pie shell to the oven for 5 minutes, then let cool. Reduce the oven temperature to 350°F.

For the filling, beat the eggs and sugar with an electric, or hand-held beater until light and creamy and thick enough to leave a trail when the beater is lifted. Fold in the lemon juice and zest and the melted butter, then finally add the ground almonds. Pour the mixture into the pie shell, return to the oven, and bake for 25–30 minutes, until golden and set. Let cool and then dust with confectioners' sugar before serving.

lime posset with champagne red berry jello

1 tablespoon sugar
1 1/4 cups heavy cream
Juice and grated zest of 2 juicy limes, plus a little extra grated zest for decorating
2 small egg whites
1 1/2 teaspoons confectioners' sugar

FOR THE JELLO:
2 gelatin leaves
1/3 cup sugar
1 cup champagne (or sparkling wine)
11 oz. mixed red berries (such as raspberries, strawberries and blackberries), plus a few extra for decorating

First make the jello. Cover the gelatin leaves with cold water for 5 minutes to soften them. Meanwhile, put the sugar and champagne in a saucepan and bring to a boil, stirring occasionally to dissolve the sugar. Remove from the heat, add the berries, and stir well. Squeeze out excess water from the gelatin. Add the gelatin to the hot fruit syrup and stir until dissolved. Let cool, then divide the fruit jello between 4 tall sundae glasses; it should come almost halfway up them. Place in the fridge to set.

For the posset, bring the sugar and cream to a boil in a pan and cook over high heat for 3–4 minutes. Remove from the heat, add the lime juice and zest, then pour into a large bowl and let cool. Beat the egg whites with the confectioners' sugar until stiff, then fold into the chilled cream. To finish, top each jello-filled glass with the lime posset and decorate with lime zest and a few red berries. Serve chilled.

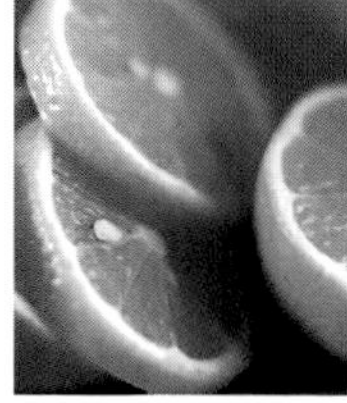

olives *Olea europaea*

Olives are one of the oldest cultivated fruits known to man. They have been grown and used around the Mediterranean for over 2,500 years, whether picked for eating or as a source of oil for cooking.

recipes

DESCRIPTION

The olive tree (*Olea europaea*) is an evergreen, usually around 15 feet in height. The bark is gray and the trunks tend to be gnarled and twisted. The leaves are long and narrow, gray-green on top and white underneath. The olive fruit do not all ripen at the same time and will ripen earlier or later according to the tree's position, the soil, and, of course, the weather.

Olives come in numerous varieties. Their textures vary from firm to fleshy and their shape and size from tiny ovals and half moons to the large, fat, round varieties. Their color is always a measure of ripeness; green olives being picked younger than black. During the ripening process, as the olives become oilier, they pass through a spectrum of shades from pale green to tan, to violet, and finally to reddish brown or black before they start to wrinkle under the rays of the hot sun.

Black olives are picked when they are fully formed and ripe. At this point, they are harvested and then treated. They are either picked by hand (the best method, as it minimizes bruising and damage, but very labor intensive) or shaken from the tree and caught in a large net that is placed underneath. Freshly picked olives are bitter and virtually inedible. They are cracked and immersed in cold water for up to 15 days, with the water changed daily. During this procedure they lose their bitterness, and are then salted and flavored with, for example, aromatics or spices.

A NOTE ON OLIVE OILS

Of equal importance, if not more so, in cooking is the use of olive oil. I have had the pleasure of seeing French olive oil produced. Once the olives are picked, they are transported to the olive mill with all haste before they start to ferment and their acidity increases, thereby affecting the quality of the oil.

They are then crushed once between huge millstones (without breaking their pits), and pressed with a mat which releases their natural oils. The resulting pulp produces the finest flavored virgin olive oil. To be labeled "extra virgin," the oil needs to have an acidity level of less than 1 percent. A second pressing produces a liquid, usually cleaner in color, simply called "olive oil." A third pressing, with water added, and additional pressings only produce oil suitable for soaps and cosmetics.

The current interest in quality olive oils for health reasons means that they have become an expensive commodity. Connoisseurs are at pains to argue over the best available, and olive oil tastings have become nearly as popular as wine tastings. Greece and Spain are believed to be the world's leading olive oil producers.

BUYING

The practice of tasting before we buy is nowadays much more common, and none too soon, I may add! There is such a variety of olives available that I firmly believe in tasting them first. I tend to buy my olives loose rather than bottled, as they are fresher, unadulterated, and free from additives. I also find the best are those packed in olive oil and not in brine solution, which does nothing for the flavor.

Generally, green olives tend to be lighter and more delicate in flavor and the flesh clings more to the pits. Black olives are stronger and more complex in flavor, and softer in texture.

Choosing a good olive oil depends, again, on

individual taste—you might prefer a spicy Tuscan oil, a sweet Spanish one with fruity overtones, or a pungent power-packed Greek one. Your choice should also be guided by what you intend using it for. For general cooking, an inexpensive, mild-flavored oil is fine but try to use a quality, extra-virgin oil where it will benefit—in sauces, drizzled over a tomato and basil salad, or on meat that is to be grilled...

STORING AND PREPARATION

Contrary to popular opinion, olives do not have to be refrigerated; just store in an airtight container in a dark place. Olive oil should be kept in a dark, cool place as it can quickly go rancid.

If you are going to use olives in cooking, I'm afraid there is no way of avoiding the chore of pitting them. Ready-pitted ones are available, but they tend to be rejects from the curing process. To pit olives, I find the best way is simply to cut a slit lengthwise along the olive using a sharp knife and pry out the pit within.

CULINARY USES

Olives are wonderful not only as a nibble before a meal (often stuffed with red pepper or anchovy or, in Spain, almonds) but also as an ingredient in sauces, soups, and salad dressings. The Italians have long partnered olives with pasta and used them to adorn their pizzas. In France, especially in the south, they are used in all sorts of dishes and tasty dips like tapenade (black olives, capers, anchovies, and garlic blended with olive oil) which is spread on crusty bread. In the Middle East and other parts of the Mediterranean, they are an indispensable part of the cuisine. In Morocco, olives are added to tagines and salads, and mixed with various spices (such as cumin) for slow-cook chicken. I find it best to add olives at the end of the cooking, to ensure the retention of their shape and texture but, more importantly, so that their salty flavor does not overpower the dish.

You may be surprised to see olives used in a sweet form (try my Calves' Liver with Candied Olives and Grapefruit, see page 134), but they can even be added to icecream, sweet sauces, and desserts—with a little imagination!

Olive oil has an underlying flavor which it imparts to a dish. In France, it is used as a condiment, as the base of vinaigrette, in sauces such as anchoïade (a piquant dressing with crushed anchovies, garlic, and herbs), and drizzled over steamed vegetables or grilled meats and fish. In Italy it is drizzled over all sorts of rustic soups and pasta. In the Middle East and eastern Mediterranean, olive oil is used to make pastries, cookies, cakes, and dips such as hummus (with chickpeas and garlic).

Using olive oil in your day-to-day diet, rather than animal fat, is believed to significantly reduce cholesterol levels (thereby lowering the risk of heart disease), and to slow down the signs of aging. Having said this, over-consumption of oils and fats is not good for you so, as in all things, moderation is the key.

complementary flavors

- ANCHOVIES
- GARLIC AND ONIONS
- LEMON
- CAPERS
- TOMATOES
- PEPPERS
- MEAT (ESPECIALLY VEAL)
- FISH (ESPECIALLY TUNA)
- GOAT CHEESE AND FETA CHEESE

cauliflower and olive soup

1 medium cauliflower, cut into florets
3 tablespoons virgin olive oil
2 teaspoons unsalted butter
1 onion, chopped
1 small leek, white part only, chopped
3 cups well-flavored chicken broth (or vegetable broth)
2/3 cup whole milk
1/3 cup heavy cream
6 black olives, pitted, rinsed, dried, and very finely chopped
1 tablespoon chopped chives
Salt and freshly ground black pepper

Blanch the cauliflower florets in a pan of boiling salted water for 2 minutes, then drain well.

In a large pan, heat 1 tablespoon of the oil along with the butter, add the onion and leek, and sweat until tender. Pour in the broth and milk and bring to a boil. Add the cauliflower, then reduce the heat and simmer for 15–20 minutes, until the cauliflower is almost puréed. Place in a blender or food processor and blitz until smooth. Return to the pan, add the heavy cream and olives, and lightly season to taste—remember the olives are already salty.

To serve, pour into soup bowls, drizzle the remaining olive oil over it, and sprinkle the chives on top.

chicken with green olives and saffron

3 garlic cloves, chopped
1 teaspoon cumin seeds
1/2-inch piece of fresh ginger root, grated
1 teaspoon smoked paprika
1 x 4 lb. organic or cage-free chicken, cut into 8 portions
3 tablespoons olive oil
2/3 cup white wine
1 lemon
A good pinch of saffron strands
5 oz. (about 20) green olives, pitted
2 tablespoons chopped cilantro
Salt and freshly ground black pepper

Crush the garlic, cumin seeds, and ginger to a paste in a mortar. Add the paprika and some salt and then rub the chicken pieces with this mixture. Heat the olive oil in a large, heavy pan, add the seasoned chicken pieces, and cook until golden brown all over. Pour in the wine and bring to a boil, then squeeze the juice of the lemon over it. Add the saffron, olives, and cilantro, and mix in with the chicken.

Pour in 2 1/2 cups of water, then cover and simmer for 30–40 minutes, until the chicken is cooked and tender and the pieces are coated in the sauce. If the sauce is not at a coating consistency, remove the chicken pieces and boil the sauce until it thickens. Adjust the seasoning if necessary, and serve.

calf's liver with candied olives and grapefruit

Candied olives might not appeal to everyone initially but once you taste them you'll be converted. The idea comes from the famous French chef, Jacques Chibois, who serves them at his eponymous restaurant near Nice. I now experiment with them regularly in all sorts of dishes. In this one, their sweetness is balanced with sharp-tasting grapefruit. Between them, they act as a foil for the rich calf's liver.

1 pink grapefruit
3 tablespoons sugar
1/3 cup (3/4 stick) unsalted butter
1 tablespoon olive oil
8 x 4 oz. slices of calf's liver
1 tablespoon white wine vinegar
1/4 cup dry white wine
1/2 cup veal broth (or beef broth)
Salt and freshly ground black pepper

FOR THE CANDIED OLIVES:
3/4 cup black olives
1/4 cup clear honey
1 sprig of rosemary

First prepare the candied olives, which have to be done 2 days in advance. Cut the olives in half and pit them, then place them in a pan of boiling water and cook for 2 minutes. Drain well and repeat the process 3 times to de-salt them fully.

Put the honey, rosemary sprig and a 1/2 cup of water in a pan and bring to a boil. Add the olives and simmer for 10 minutes. Remove from the heat and let soak for 48 hours in the syrup, ready for use.

Using a zester, pare the zest off the grapefruit, place it in a small pan and cover with water. Bring to a boil, then drain the zest and return it to the pan. Add 4 tablespoons of water and 1 tablespoon of the sugar and cook for 2 minutes to glaze the zest in the syrup. Remove from the heat and set aside.

Cut off all the peel and pith from the grapefruit, then cut out the segments from between the membranes—do this over a bowl to catch the juice, squeezing out the membrane after you have taken out all the segments. Set aside the juice and the segments.

Heat 2 tablespoons of the butter in a large frying pan along with the olive oil. When it begins to sizzle, season the calf's liver and add it to the pan. Cook over a high heat for 2 minutes on each side, keeping it rosy pink in the center. Remove the meat from the pan and keep warm. Pour away the fat but do not wash the pan. Add the white wine vinegar and remaining sugar and cook until caramelized. Then add the wine and boil for 2–3 minutes, until reduced. Add the grapefruit juice and broth, bring to a boil, and simmer until thick enough to coat the back of a spoon. Dice the remaining butter and beat it into the sauce, then adjust the seasoning.

Arrange the calf's liver on 4 serving plates, garnish with the grapefruit segments and zest, and top with a teaspoon of the candied olives. Pour the sauce over them and serve. I like to serve this with Risotto or a selection of baby vegetables.

roasted lamb rib eye with red wine and olive caviar

1/4 cup olive oil
2 x 6-bone racks of lamb, bones removed (you can ask your butcher to do this)
1/2 cup red wine
1 1/4 cups lamb broth (or other meat broth)
2 tablespoons chilled unsalted butter, chopped
Salt and freshly ground black pepper

FOR THE OLIVE CAVIAR:
2 tablespoons olive oil
1 onion, finely chopped
2 garlic cloves, crushed
1 small red pepper, finely chopped
5 oz. black olives, pitted and finely chopped
2 anchovy fillets, finely chopped
2 tablespoons chopped basil
2 tablespoons chopped flat-leaf parsley
1 tablespoon honey

FOR SERVING:
Mashed potatoes
A bunch of watercress

Preheat the oven to 400°F. To make the olive caviar, heat the oil in a frying pan, add the onion and garlic, and cook until soft but not colored. Add the red pepper and cook for 2–3 minutes, then add the olives and anchovies and cook for 2 minutes more. Stir in the basil, parsley, and honey. Adjust the seasoning and keep warm.

Heat the olive oil in a flameproof roasting pan until smoking. Season the lamb, add to the pan, and seal on both sides, until golden. Transfer to the oven and roast for 10–12 minutes, until pink. Remove from the roasting pan and keep warm.

Wipe out any excess oil from the roasting pan, pour in the red wine and boil on the stove for 2 minutes. Add the broth and boil rapidly until reduced by half. Remove from the heat, beat in the butter a little at a time, and then season to taste.

Slice each rib eye into 4 pieces and arrange on a bed of mashed potatoes. Pour a little sauce around them, garnish with the olive caviar on the lamb and a little watercress alongside.

fig tapenade

I use this classic variation on tapenade in all sorts of ways. Try it with fish or chicken, tossed with pasta, or simply on toasted baguette slices as a canapé.

5 oz. (about 14) dried figs
14 black olives, pitted
4 anchovy fillets, drained and rinsed
3 tablespoons superfine capers, drained and rinsed
3 garlic cloves, crushed
Juice of 1/2 lemon
1/2 cup virgin olive oil
2 tablespoons chopped parsley
Freshly ground black pepper

Soak the figs in warm water for 1 hour until swollen, then drain them and dry well. Chop finely.

Blitz together the olives, anchovies, capers, garlic, lemon juice, and a little black pepper in a blender or food processor. Gradually add the olive oil to form a paste, then add the parsley and chopped figs.

Paul's Tip You can vary the tapenade by adding chopped sun-dried tomatoes and basil.

tamarind *Tamarindus indica*

Up to five years ago, you would probably only have heard of tamarind as an ingredient found or used in Indian restaurants. Nowadays, with the growing interest in multicultural food, tamarind is becoming an ingredient chefs and food lovers alike are savoring. It has an endearing quality that cooks are discovering with delight, a subtle sweet and sour pulp that works deliciously well in savory and sweet dishes.

recipes

DESCRIPTION

Tamarind trees (*Tamarindus indica*) are native to East Africa and are now grown throughout India, across Southeast Asia, and in the tropics. The pods, which grow on the large, evergreen, tropical trees are about 2–6 inches long. They are green when young and dark brown when fully ripe, which is when they are harvested. Within the bean-shaped pods are shiny seeds surrounded by a reddish-brown, sticky, intensely sour pulp, somewhat similar in looks to dates.

BUYING AND PREPARING

Tamarind can occasionally be bought fresh in the pod from Indian and Oriental stores but is more readily available as a pulp in pre-packed, compressed 1 lb. blocks and as a smooth purée in jars.

To make a purée from the fresh pods, break them open, remove the inner flesh and place everything in a pan. Add an amount of cold water, equal to half the amount of the pods and flesh. Simmer 5 minutes or longer, depending on the age and hardness of your pods. Strain through a strainer to remove the seeds and tough fibers. If using tamarind blocks, cut it up in pieces and proceed as for fresh.

Fresh tamarind pods and tamarind water can be kept in the fridge for up to 5 days. Tamarind blocks and paste last indefinitely if stored in a cool dark place. The paste is my preferred version for its ease of use.

CULINARY USES

Tamarind is traditionally found in Indian, East Indian, and Asian cooking where it contributes a gentle sour flavor with undercurrents of tropical fruits. It is used in Indian lentil dishes, curries, and rasans (spicy Indian soup, highly flavored with black pepper, see page 94). It is also added to sweet chutneys, and tamarind water is used to flavor rice. In Thailand, tamarind water is more frequently used than the paste, and is added to hot and sour soups and curries. In Jamaica, tamarind is added to rice dishes, stews, and desserts. The natural pectin extracted from the tamarind fruit is also used in jams and jello preparations.

In Britain, where it is still a largely unfamiliar ingredient, it has, ironically, long been used as a main ingredient of Worcestershire sauce, one of Britain's favorite condiments.

Today, with the ever-increasing availability of new ingredients, tamarind is used with more creativity. I have successfully made a wonderful tamarind water icecream (served with mango tart), and fruit syrups. I also like to add it to dressings with Asian flavors, such as ginger and lime.

If tamarind is not readily available, as a last resort lime or lemon may be substituted, but the taste is really not similar, and will consequently not have the same effect.

OTHER USES

Tamarind is a mild laxative and is used in ayurvedic medicine to treat bowel and bronchial disorders. It is rich in vitamins and is reputed to be good for the liver and kidneys. Tamarind is also said to be an outstanding polish for brass and copper.

complementary flavors

- CHILES
- COCONUT MILK
- *NAM PLA* (THAI FISH SAUCE)
- HERBS (THAI BASIL AND MINT)
- CHICKEN
- FISH (FIRM VARIETIES)
- SPICES (GINGER AND STAR ANISE)

tamarind and date chutney

This versatile chutney makes a great accompaniment to all sorts of dishes, especially grilled salmon and chicken, or can be served as a dip for spicy poppadoms.

2 tablespoons palm (or light brown) sugar)
1 teaspoon cumin seeds
3 tablespoons tamarind paste
1/2 cup dates, chopped
1/2 teaspoon *nam pla* (Thai fish sauce)
1-inch piece of fresh ginger root, finely grated
A pinch of cayenne pepper
Salt

Put the sugar in a small pan and place over low heat until melted. Heat a small frying pan over medium heat, add the cumin seeds, and toast for 10 seconds to release their fragrance. Grind the seeds in a spice grinder or with a mortar and pestle. Place the ground seeds in a blender or food processor along with the tamarind, dates, sugar, fish sauce, and ginger, and blitz until smooth. If using as a dip, add enough boiling water to give a spreadable consistency. Season with the cayenne pepper and some salt and use as needed. The chutney will keep for up to 1 month in a sealed sterilized jar (see page 23), or for 3–4 days in the fridge.

grilled tuna with green papaya salad

A healthy and beautifully flavored dish. Green papaya salad (*som tam*) is a staple dish from northeast Thailand, prepared daily by roadside traders.

$1^1/_2$ lbs. small tuna fillet, trimmed
2 tablespoons tamarind paste
2 tablespoons brown sugar
2 red chiles, seeded and finely chopped
1 tablespoon *nam pla* (Thai fish sauce)
A little oil for grilling
Salt and freshly ground black pepper
1 lime, cut into wedges, for garnishing

FOR THE GREEN PAPAYA SALAD:

1 garlic clove, chopped
2 red chiles, seeded and chopped
1 teaspoon brown sugar
2 green papayas, peeled, seeded, and shredded
Juice of 2 limes
2 tablespoons *nam pla* (Thai fish sauce)
4 oz. (about 10–12) green beans, cooked
2 tablespoons roasted peanuts
10 red cherry tomatoes, cut in half
10 yellow cherry tomatoes, cut in half

Cut the tuna into 4 steaks across the fillet. In a bowl, combine the tamarind with the sugar, chiles, fish sauce, and some salt and pepper. Pour this mixture over the tuna and set aside for 1 hour for the flavors to meld.

For the salad, roughly crush the garlic, chiles, sugar, and a quarter of the shredded papaya in a mortar. Transfer to a bowl, add the lime juice and fish sauce, and stir well. Add all the remaining ingredients, including the rest of the papaya, toss well, and season to taste.

Heat a ridged grill pan until very hot and brush with a little oil. Season the tuna steaks again with salt and pepper and grill for 2 minutes on each side, keeping them rare. Remove from the pan and cut each steak into 4 slices.

Arrange a pile of salad on each serving plate, top with the seared tuna, then garnish with the lime wedges and serve.

stir-fried noodles, thai style

8 oz. dried rice noodles
2 red chiles, seeded and finely chopped
2 shallots, sliced
3 tablespoons *nam pla* (Thai fish sauce)
2 tablespoons brown sugar
2 tablespoons tamarind paste
1 teaspoon lime juice
$^1/_4$ cup vegetable oil
$4^1/_2$ oz. pork tenderloin, cut into small, thin strips
5 oz. fresh shrimp, peeled
2 oz. ($^1/_2$ cup) shiitake mushrooms, sliced
3 oz. ($1^1/_2$ cups) beans prouts
2 tablespoons *ketjap manis* (Indonesian soy sauce)
Salt and freshly ground black pepper

Soak the noodles in a bowl of warm water for about 10 minutes, until softened, then drain in a colander.

Place the chiles, shallots, fish sauce, and sugar in a mortar and crush to a paste. Add the tamarind and lime juice and pound until smooth. Mix in 2 tablespoons of water and set aside.

Heat the oil in a wok until very hot, add the spice paste, and stir-fry for 1 minute. Add the pork and shrimp, mix well with the paste, and cook for 2–3 minutes. Add the noodles, mushrooms, bean sprouts, and *ketjap manis,* and season with salt and pepper. Stir-fry for 2 minutes and then serve immediately.

wok-fried monkfish in sour sauce

$1^1/_2$ lbs. monkfish (angler fish) fillet
$^1/_4$ cup vegetable oil
2 shallots, thinly sliced
3 garlic cloves, crushed
$^2/_3$ cup cooked, salted, fermented black beans (see page 119), washed and drained
1-inch piece of fresh ginger root, finely chopped
2 tablespoons soy sauce
2 teaspoons *nam pla* (Thai fish sauce)
$^1/_4$ cup tamarind paste
2 red chiles, seeded and thinly sliced
2 tablespoons brown sugar
Salt and freshly ground black pepper

FOR GARNISHING:
2 tablespoons coarsely chopped cilantro
3 scallions, shredded

Cut the monkfish into $^1/_2$-inch slices along the fillet, season with salt and pepper, and set aside.

Heat a wok until almost smoking, add the oil, then add the shallots, garlic, fermented black beans, and ginger. Cook for 1 minute, until lightly golden. Add the monkfish pieces and cook over medium heat for 5 minutes. Remove the fish from the wok and keep warm. Add the soy sauce, fish sauce, tamarind paste, chiles, and sugar to the wok, and mix well. Add $^1/_2$ cup of water and boil for 2 minutes, then return the monkfish to the wok and toss well with the sauce.

Serve in bowls with white rice, garnished with the cilantro and scallions.

tamarind-baked winter fruits with star anise

1 vanilla bean, split open lengthwise
$^2/_3$ cup palm (or light brown) sugar
2 lemongrass stalks, outer layers removed, tender inner core finely shredded
$1^1/_2$ teaspoons finely grated fresh ginger root
4 star anise
2 tablespoons tamarind paste
$^1/_4$ cup ($^1/_2$ stick) unsalted butter
2 ripe pears, peeled, cored, and quartered
6 ripe plums, cut in half and pitted
8 prunes, pitted
8 dried figs
12 dried apricots
$3^1/_2$ fl oz. sweet white wine
Juice of 1 lime

Preheat the oven to 375°F. Combine the vanilla bean, sugar, lemongrass, ginger, star anise, and tamarind in a pan with $^2/_3$ cup of water, bring to a boil, and simmer for 10 minutes. Remove from the heat and set aside.

Heat a deep, heavy, flameproof and ovenproof pan on the stove, add the butter, then add all the fruit and fry for 1–2 minutes, until lightly caramelized. Pour the wine, lime juice, and tamarind mixture over them, and stir to coat the fruit. Place in the oven for 10–12 minutes, until the fruit is tender and lightly glazed. Serve warm.

vanilla *Vanilla planifolia*

Fresh natural vanilla, despite its reputation as one of the world's most expensive ingredients, is one that is certainly well worth buying. Since it is always used in small amounts, it is really not too pricey to pay for top quality.

Europeans first tasted vanilla in the sixteenth century when Mexico was invaded by the Spanish, where the Aztec Indians had used it as a flavoring for centuries.

recipes

PORK LOIN COOKED IN VANILLA MILK (PAGE 145)

CURRIED TURBOT WITH VANILLA AND GINGER (PAGE 145)

STRAWBERRY AND VANILLA CUSTARD TART (PAGE 146)

REAL VANILLA ICECREAM (PAGE 146)

VANILLA AND ORANGE MARMALADE PUDDING (PAGE 147)

SEE ALSO:

SLOW-BAKED TAMARILLOS IN CINNAMON-WINE SAUCE (PAGE 61)

COFFEE AND FENNEL SEED BISCOTTI (PAGE 158)

LEMONGRASS, COCONUT, AND VANILLA PANNA COTTA (PAGE 19)

FRUIT TABBOULEH (PAGE 32)

OLD-FASHIONED RICE PUDDING (PAGE 88)

TAMARIND-BAKED WINTER FRUITS WITH STAR ANISE (PAGE 140)

The Spanish explorers of the New World returned home with the fruit and gave it its name. They loved its aroma and flavor and soon it was being consumed in vast quantities. Today it is perhaps the most popular flavoring, the world over, with the French and Germans the biggest importers. Many countries, including Mexico, Puerto Rico, and Tahiti, now produce vanilla, and the island of Madagascar, off Africa's east coast, is the world's largest commercial exporter.

DESCRIPTION

The vanilla plant (*Vanilla planifolia*) is a type of orchid (and the only edible one) that must be pollinated and harvested. The orchids are only pollinated unaided in Mexico—on the one day in the year when the flowers bloom. Elsewhere, they have to be pollinated by hand, which highlights why real vanilla is such an expensive commodity. The pods are picked unripe when green, and there follows a lengthy and complicated curing process to extract the vanillin, the primary flavor of vanilla. The oxidization of the pods causes browning which helps to develop their tobacco-like flavor.

Vanilla has a fabulous tropical scent and a wonderful aroma, sweet smelling and utterly alluring. I once visited the market at Marigot on the island of St. Martin in the Caribbean to look at the local produce. The sight, scent, and aroma of the vanilla, sold in bunches by market traders that day, will stay with me for the rest of my life.

BUYING, STORING, AND PREPARATION

When buying fresh vanilla, look for beans that are dark in color, plump, and pliable. Store them away from heat and light. I suggest also wrapping them in plastic wrap, and placing in an airtight container, which will ensure they keep their flavor indefinitely.

Vanilla can be best utilized in two ways; whole, to flavor creamy puddings, custards, crème brûlée, etc.; or by extracting the seeds. The latter is the best way to extract the vanilla's intense flavor: split the pods lengthwise with a small knife and scrape out the thick paste-like inner seeds that hold the vanilla's intense flavor, then use the seeds as directed in the recipe.

OTHER PRODUCTS

As real vanilla is so expensive, cheap imitations such as vanilla flavoring are commonplace, as are the not-cheap extracts and pure essences, but they have limited use in real cooking, to my mind. However, such commercial products now satisfy 78 percent of the word's demand for a real vanilla flavor. I recommend you use fresh vanilla (there are some pleasures you just can't put a price on!) or, if this is not possible, the next best thing is vanilla extract.

VANILLA EXTRACT AND PURE VANILLA ESSENCE This is the extracted flavor and aroma of the vanilla bean. Pure vanilla extract and essence have a rich perfume and a deep amber

color, and contains at least 35 percent alcohol. Mexican vanilla extract is the best. As a guide, I suggest 1 teaspoon of extract could replace one vanilla bean in a recipe. For a wonderful, rich, home-made extract, simply place 6 split vanilla beans in a jar (with a lid). Top with a solution of 2 tablespoons sugar, dissolved in 2 1/2 cups warmed, dark rum. Cover and store in a cool dark place. Leave for up to one month before using.

VANILLA FLAVORING A much inferior product, chemically produced, which has no relevance to the real thing; use only in desperate circumstances.

CULINARY USES

This sweet, perfumed spice with its tobacco-like aroma and its wonderfully mellow fragrance, is ideally suited to enhance sweet flavors. For this reason, it is added to all sorts of desserts, confectionery, syrups, and jams. Vanilla is also an essential ingredient in much baking.

Although vanilla's primary use is in sweet recipes, it can also successfully become an unusual flavoring in savory dishes—particularly in conjunction with fish, chicken, and pork.

Only a few drops of vanilla extract are needed to transform a recipe. Try a little in crêpe batters, fruit salads, mayonnaise, béarnaise sauce and meat glazes. The beans can be used to flavor jars of sugar (see below) and coffee.

Vanilla is an ingredient in many beverages from the intoxicant (vanilla schnapps, Mexican vanilla liqueur, Galliano, sangria...) to the non-alcoholic (coca cola, for example, is packed with vanilla). One of the earliest beverages to use vanilla was the Aztec cocoa drink, *xocolat*.

Vanilla sugar

Throughout this book you will see recipes that include vanilla sugar, which is simply sugar perfumed with vanilla beans. This has two advantages; first, the sugar helps keep the vanilla at its best, dry and in good condition. Second, the resulting perfume of the sugar is indispensable in baking or as a mild flavoring. Leave the beans in the sugar for 1 week before using on breakfast cereals, in coffee, and to flavor desserts and soufflés. One bean can scent a jar of sugar for year.

Vanilla yogurt

Blend 2/3 cup thick, whole-milk yogurt with the seeds of one fresh vanilla bean, and 1 tablespoon of honey. Great for pies, tarts, and fruit.

OTHER USES

Vanilla has long been regarded an aphrodisiac. It is also an effective calmative and for this reason, it has (and still is) used for treating nervous disorders and to settle stomachs.

complementary flavors

- DAIRY PRODUCTS (ESPECIALLY CUSTARD AND ICECREAMS)
- SOFT CHEESES (RICOTTA AND MASCARPONE)
- FRUIT (LEMON, APRICOTS, STRAWBERRIES, PEACHES AND NECTARINES)
- TEA AND COFFEE
- CHOCOLATE
- CARDAMOM
- MEAT (PORK, CHICKEN)

pork loin cooked in vanilla milk

2 plump, soft vanilla beans
3¼ lbs. boneless loin of pork, skin and most of the fat removed
A pinch of ground cinnamon
A pinch of freshly grated nutmeg
2 tablespoons olive oil
3 garlic cloves, unpeeled
1 quart whole milk
½ cup heavy cream
1 bay leaf
3 sprigs of thyme
2 large carrots, peeled and cut into segments
1 teaspoon Dijon mustard
Salt and freshly ground black pepper

Cut the vanilla beans in half lengthwise. Season the pork loin with the cinnamon and nutmeg and some salt and pepper. Place the vanilla on the pork and tie it down with string, around the pork.

Heat the olive oil in a large, heavy, ovenproof pan that has a lid, add the pork, and cook until sealed and golden all over. Add the garlic cloves and cook for 2 minutes, until colored. Bring the milk and cream to a boil in a pan, pour them over the pork, then tuck in the bay leaf and thyme and cover with a lid. Cook for 30 minutes, either in an oven preheated to 350°F or on top of the stove over a low heat.

Add the carrots to the pan and cook for 1 hour, until the pork and carrots are very tender. Remove the pork and carrots from the pan and keep warm.

Press the garlic cloves free from their skin and add to the cooking liquid along with the mustard. Pour into a saucepan and simmer for 2 minutes. Strain the sauce through a strainer and adjust the seasoning.

Carve the pork into thin slices, garnish with the carrots, pour the vanilla sauce over it, and serve.

curried turbot with vanilla and ginger

4 x 6 oz. turbot fillets, skinned
1 teaspoon mild curry powder
½ cup heavy cream
1 cup fish broth
¼ cup dry white wine
2-inch piece of fresh ginger root, finely chopped
1 vanilla bean, chopped
4 tablespoons (½ stick) unsalted butter
4 tablespoons vegetable oil
7 oz. (1½ cups) baby zucchini, sliced
7 oz. (5 cups) spinach, well washed and dried
12 cherry tomatoes, cut in half
Salt and freshly ground black pepper

Season the turbot fillets, rub the curry powder over both sides, then set aside.

Put the cream, fish broth, wine, and ginger in a pan, bring to a boil and simmer until reduced by half. Pour into a blender or food processor, add the vanilla bean and blitz to a smooth purée. Strain through a fine strainer into a clean pan, whisk in 2 tablespoons of the butter, then season to taste and keep warm.

Heat 2 tablespoons of the oil in a frying pan and add another tablespoon of the butter. When it starts to foam, add the turbot fillets, curried-side down, and cook for 2–3 minutes. Turn the fillets over and cook for another 2–3 minutes, then remove from the pan and keep warm.

Heat the remaining oil and butter in a separate pan, add the zucchini, and fry until golden. Add the spinach and cook together for 2–3 minutes. Finally add the cherry tomato halves and season to taste.

Place a pile of the spinach, zucchini, and tomato mixture in the center of 4 plates, top with the turbot fillets, and pour the sauce around it.

strawberry and vanilla custard tart

SERVES 6-8

1 quantity of Sweet Pastry Dough (page 129)
1 lb. strawberries, hulled and cut in half
1/4 cup strawberry jam

FOR THE VANILLA CUSTARD:
2 vanilla beans
2/3 cup whole milk
2/3 cup light cream
1 egg
2 egg yolks
1/2 cup vanilla sugar (see page 143)
3 tablespoons all-purpose flour, sifted

Preheat the oven to 375°F. Roll out the pastry on a lightly floured surface to 1/8-inch thick and use to line a 9-inch tart pan with it. Prick the bottom lightly all over with a fork. Line with parchment paper, fill with baking beans, and bake blind for 10–15 minutes, until the crust is set but not colored. Remove the paper and beans, reduce the oven temperature to 300°F, and return the pie shell to the oven for 10 minutes. Remove from the oven and let cool.

For the vanilla custard, split the vanilla beans open lengthwise and scrape out the seeds with a small teaspoon or the point of a sharp knife. Put the beans and seeds in a pan, add the milk and cream, and bring to a boil. Remove from the heat and let infuse for 15 minutes.

In a bowl, beat the egg and egg yolks with all but 1 tablespoon of the vanilla sugar until pale and fluffy. Add the flour and mix well. Strain the vanilla cream onto the egg mixture, stirring constantly. Return to the pan and bring back to a boil, stirring all the time. Simmer for 1–2 minutes, until thickened, then pour into a bowl and let cool.

Fill the pie shell with the vanilla custard and arrange the strawberry halves on top, cut-side down. Put the strawberry jam in a pan along with 4 tablespoons of water, bring to a boil, and strain through a fine mesh strainer. Brush the jam over the strawberries and let cool. Sprinkle the remaining vanilla sugar over it before serving.

real vanilla icecream

There is only one icecream I would die for and this is it. Fragrant, rich, and creamy. Always use good, plump vanilla beans; it really does make such a difference.

1 cup whole milk
1 1/2 cups heavy cream
2 plump, soft vanilla beans
6 egg yolks
1/2 cup sugar
A pinch of salt

Heat the milk and cream in a pan until almost at boiling point, then remove from the heat. Split the vanilla beans open lengthwise and scrape out the seeds with a small teaspoon or the point of a sharp knife. Add the seeds and pods to the milk and let infuse for 20 minutes on the lowest possible heat.

Beat the egg yolks and sugar together in a bowl until light and fluffy. Remove the vanilla beans from the milk and gradually beat the milk into the egg yolk mixture. Return to the pan, add the salt, and cook, stirring constantly, over a low heat until the mixture has thickened enough to coat the back of the spoon (do not let it boil or it will curdle).

Remove the mixture from the heat immediately and strain through a strainer into a bowl. When cool, chill in the fridge, then freeze in an icecream machine according to the manufacturer's instructions. (If you don't have a machine, refer to the Paul's Tip on page 180.)

vanilla and orange marmalade pudding

SERVES 8

2/3 cup sugar
2/3 cup (1 1/4 sticks) unsalted butter
1 teaspoon vanilla extract
3 eggs, separated
3/4 cup self-raising flour, sifted
1/4 cup golden syrup
1/4 cup good-quality orange marmalade
2 vanilla beans

Preheat the oven to 375°F. In a bowl, beat 1/3 cup of the sugar with the butter until pale and creamy. Add the vanilla extract, then beat in the egg yolks one at a time. Fold in the flour. In a separate bowl, beat the egg whites with the remaining sugar until they form stiff peaks. Stir a quarter of the whites into the egg yolk mixture to loosen it, then carefully fold in the rest.

Gently heat the golden syrup and marmalade together in a pan. Slit the vanilla beans open lengthwise and scrape out the seeds with a small teaspoon or the point of a sharp knife. Add to the marmalade and syrup and mix well.

Grease 8 ramekins and place 2 tablespoons of the vanilla marmalade in the bottom of each one. Top with the pudding mixture, filling them three-quarters full, and tap the ramekins to release any air pockets. Cover with foil and place in a roasting pan of hot water (the water should come halfway up the side of the remekins). Place in the oven and bake for 40–45 minutes.

Run a knife around the edge of each pudding and turn out onto a serving plate. Serve with copious amounts of clotted cream or other cream.

balsamic vinegar *aceto balsamico*

Food is like fashion: styles come and go from month to month, year to year. Every so often a new ingredient hits the stores and takes off. Balsamic vinegar, or *aceto balsamico*, is one such ingredient, finding instant appeal with chefs, cooks, and food lovers alike. Its presence can now be seen on menus from London to New York to Sydney. However, this vinegar is not new to the world: it has been a staple in Italy for many centuries.

recipes

DUCK WITH BALSAMIC CHERRIES AND SHIITAKE MUSHROOMS (PAGE 150)

BALSAMIC BRAISED RED CABBAGE WITH CRANBERRIES (PAGE 151)

GRILLED PORK WITH BALSAMIC ONIONS AND BEETS (PAGE 151)

BUTTERNUT SQUASH AND PORCINI RISOTTO WITH BALSAMIC CARAMEL (PAGE 152)

BALSAMIC BUTTER ICECREAM WITH CITRUS SALAD AND PASSIONFRUIT JELLO (PAGE 153)

SEE ALSO:

SUMMER VEGETABLE SALAD (PAGE 36)

ROSEMARY-SKEWERED SCALLOPS WITH FENNEL AND ORANGE SALSA (PAGE 44)

ROSEMARY-GRILLED VEGETABLES WITH FETA (PAGE 47)

LOBSTER, SAFFRON, AND MANGO SALAD (SEE PAGE 68)

SALT COD PÂTÉ WITH BALSAMIC PEPPERS AND OLIVES (SEE PAGE 170)

This thick, radiant, dark brown essence with its extraordinarily complex fragrance has nothing in common with other vinegars we know. It has a unique character, with sweet and sour overtones, and an almost velvet-like consistency.

At this point I should explain that I am talking about the authentic and fabulously expensive balsamic vinegar, which bears the words *tradizionale* or *naturelle*, and not the cheap imitations available in some supermarkets.

DESCRIPTION

Balsamic vinegar is made in the area around Modena and Reggio nell' Emilia in Italy. Unlike other vinegars, it is made from wine marc (a liquid produced from the grape skins, seeds, and stalks that remain after pressing) and not wine itself. This marc comes from the Trebbiano grape, an Italian variety, which ripens on the slopes nearby.

Its manufacture is a lengthy process, which begins with crushing the must (freshly harvested grape berries and juice). This produces 8½ gallons) of marc per 220 lbs. of fruit, which is first heated to 180°F and then simmered until almost 50 percent has evaporated to concentrate the natural sugars.

Once cooled, it is poured into casks called *demijohns* (generally made of ash, cherry, or chestnut), and blended with some balsamic vinegar from an earlier vintage. It is then aged in rows in airy attics called *acetaia*. Here, over a period of years—even decades—it is exposed to changes in the weather and seasons: warmth and cold, dryness and dampness, all of which enhance and develop the vinegar, according to connoisseurs.

Through gradual fermentation, the liquid is transformed into a deep, rich, brown, syrupy vinegar to which no flavorants or additives are added. About 10 percent of the liquid evaporates each year. Generally the older the vinegar, the better the flavor, the thicker the intensity, and, of course, the more expensive it is to buy.

The name Aceto Balsamico Tradizionale has been legally protected since 1983 for vinegar from Modena, and since 1987 for that from Reggio nell' Emilia, both of which have a minimum age of 12 years.

BUYING

The quality of industrially-produced balsamic vinegar varies greatly. I generally use a moderately priced eight-year-old, which generally has all the qualities I need, but as a rule always buy the best you can afford.

CULINARY USES

Although Italian chefs have long admired the qualities of this wonderful vinegar and used it for flavoring many traditional dishes (such as Coniglio con Aceto Balsamico), today chefs are using it to create exciting new tastes. Balsamic vinegar's distinctive flavor goes well with fish, meat, and vegetables, in salad dressings, and on

complementary flavors

MUSTARD

VEGETABLES (ESPECIALLY RED CABBAGE, RED ONIONS, AND TOMATOES)

FRUIT (ESPECIALLY STRAWBERRIES, RASPBERRIES, AND APRICOTS)

OYSTERS

carpaccio. It can even be used in icecream (try my Balsamic Butter Icecream on page 153—you won't be disappointed!) and marries particularly well with strawberries and apricots.

If you get your hands on a bottle of balsamic vinegar that has been aged for more than 25 years (these are prized in Italy and treated with the respect of old wine vintages), be aware that you should use it sparingly as it will have a complex and very intense taste.

A recent introduction to the market is white balsamic vinegar. Although not technically an actual vinegar, it is a clear liquid with a sweet, delicate flavor, similar to cider vinegar. The only advantage I can see with it is that its clear color mixes well with other ingredients as, for example, in salad dressings. Watch out for its progress in the near future.

A few sips of balsamic vinegar were traditionally taken to improve digestion.

duck with balsamic cherries and shiitake mushrooms

Duck served with sweet cherries has long been a classic of French cuisine, the sauce made from a sugar and vinegar base. Here, balsamic vinegar and dried sour cherries do a wonderful job. The shiitake mushrooms give an interesting twist and, more importantly, a good, meaty-flavored sauce. Serve on a bed of Swiss chard, bok choy, or spinach.

2 tablespoons demerara (or light brown) sugar
1/4 cup balsamic vinegar (preferably aged)
3 oz. (1/2 cup) dried sour cherries
2/3 cup red wine
1 tablespoon five-spice powder
3 tablespoons honey
4 x 6 oz. duck breasts, skin on
3 tablespoons olive oil
12 shiitake mushrooms, thickly sliced
1/2 cup well-flavored duck broth (or chicken broth)
2 tablespoons unsalted butter, chopped
Salt and freshly ground black pepper

Preheat the oven to 400°F. Put the sugar in a heavy saucepan and melt over low heat. Raise the heat and cook, stirring frequently, until the sugar becomes a light amber color. Add the balsamic vinegar, dried cherries, and red wine, and simmer over low heat for 6–8 minutes, until reduced and syrupy. Set aside.

Mix together the five-spice powder, honey, and a little cracked black pepper (see page 90), and spread this mixture liberally over the skin side of the duck breasts. Heat the olive oil in a large ovenproof frying pan until very hot. Add the duck breasts, skin side down, and cook over medium heat for 2–3 minutes, until golden; take care or the honey will caramelize too quickly and burn. Turn the duck breasts over, then transfer to the oven and cook to your liking—about 4–5 minutes for rare, longer if you prefer them more cooked. Remove from the pan and keep warm.

Drain off most of the fat from the pan, leaving about 2 tablespoons. Add the shiitake mushrooms and place in the oven for about 5 minutes to brown. Remove the pan from the oven, place on the stove, and add the duck or chicken broth. Bring to a boil and simmer for 4–5 minutes. Add the balsamic cherries, mix well, and cook for 5 minutes longer, stirring to scrape up the caramelized residue from the bottom of the pan. Swirl in the butter to enrich the sauce, then adjust the seasoning.

Carve the duck breasts and arrange on serving plates. Pour the cherry and shiitake sauce over them, and serve.

balsamic braised red cabbage with cranberries

1½ lbs. red cabbage, cored and finely shredded
1¾ cups red wine
5 tablespoons balsamic vinegar
1 tablespoon brown sugar
1⅓ cups fresh or frozen cranberries
2 tablespoons cranberry jello (or red currant jello)
Salt and freshly ground black pepper

Preheat the oven to 400°F. Place the shredded cabbage in a large, heavy flameproof and ovenproof pan, pour in the red wine and balsamic vinegar, and place over a medium heat for 5 minutes. Sprinkle over the sugar and season lightly. Pour in 2½ cups of water and bring to a boil, then add the cranberries. Cover with a tight-fitting lid and transfer to the oven. Braise for 1 hour or until the cabbage is very tender. If any liquid remains, place the pan on the stove and cook, uncovered, until it evaporates. Stir in the cranberry jello, adjust the seasoning, and serve immediately.

grilled pork with balsamic onions and beets

A light dish with sweet and sour flavors, simple to prepare.

12 baby beets
2 tablespoons unsalted butter
¼ cup virgin olive oil
4 pieces of pork tenderloin, about 6–7 oz. each
1 teaspoon ground cilantro
1 tablespoon chopped fresh cilantro
Salt and freshly ground black pepper

FOR THE BALSAMIC ONIONS:

¼ cup (½ stick) unsalted butter
3 red onions, thinly sliced
3 tablespoons demerara (or light brown) sugar
½ cup balsamic vinegar
¼ cup red wine

For the balsamic onions, heat the butter in a saucepan, add the onions, and cook gently until soft but not colored. Add the sugar, vinegar, and red wine, raise the heat, and cook for 25–30 minutes, until the mixture is thick and syrupy. Season to taste and keep warm.

Cook the baby beets in boiling salted water until tender, then drain well and peel. Heat the butter in a pan, add the beets and toss to glaze with the butter. Season to taste and keep warm.

Heat a ridged grill pan or heavy frying pan until very hot, and brush with half the olive oil. Season the pork with the ground cilantro and some salt and pepper, and cook for 7–8 minutes, turning regularly until golden, cooked through, and slightly charred. Remove from the heat and keep warm.

Mix the remaining olive oil with the chopped cilantro and some seasoning. Quickly reheat the beets if necessary. Arrange a bed of balsamic onions on each serving plate, slice each pork tenderloin into 5, and place on top. Arrange the glazed beets on the pork, pour a little of the cilantro oil over them, and serve.

butternut squash and porcini risotto with balsamic caramel

1 oz. dried porcini mushrooms
1/4 cup olive oil
1 small butternut squash, peeled, seeded, and cut into 3/4-inch cubes
1/3 cup (3/4 stick) unsalted butter
3 garlic cloves, cut into 1/8-inch thick slices
1 sprig of thyme
2 1/4 cups well-flavored vegetable broth (or chicken broth)
2 shallots, finely chopped
1 1/4 cups *vialone nano* risotto rice
1/3 cup dry white wine
Salt and freshly ground black pepper

FOR THE BALSAMIC CARAMEL:
1/4 cup sugar
1/4 cup balsamic vinegar

Soak the dried porcini in a 1/2-cup of hot water for 30 minutes. Meanwhile, heat half of the oil in a large sauté or frying pan, add the butternut squash, and fry until golden all over. Add 2 tablespoons of the butter, then the garlic and thyme, and fry over medium heat for 5 minutes. Season with salt and pepper, then remove from the pan and set aside.

Drain the mushrooms, reserving the soaking water, and chop them coarsely. Put the soaking water and broth in a saucepan and bring to a boil. Keep at simmering point while you make the risotto.

Wipe out the sauté pan, add the remaining oil and 2 tablespoons of the remaining butter, then add the shallots and chopped porcini, and cook for 2 minutes. Add the rice and stir well to coat the grains with the butter. Increase the heat, then stir in the wine and boil for 1 minute. Then start adding the hot broth, a ladleful at a time, waiting until it has been absorbed before adding more. Keep the risotto simmering as you add the broth and stir constantly until the rice is tender but still retains bite; this will take 20–25 minutes. Add the cooked butternut squash, season to taste, and stir in the remaining butter.

For the balsamic caramel, put the sugar in a small, heavy pan and heat gently until melted. Raise the heat and cook, without stirring, until it becomes a golden amber color. Add the balsamic vinegar (stand well back, as it will splutter) and boil for 3 minutes. Divide the risotto between 4 plates, drizzle the balsamic caramel over it, and serve.

balsamic butter icecream with citrus salad and passionfruit jello

SERVES 8

3/4 cup sugar
2 1/4 cups whole milk, hot
1/3 cup (3/4 stick) unsalted butter
6 egg yolks
1 teaspoon cornstarch
1/4 cup balsamic vinegar
12 tiny mint leaves

FOR THE CITRUS SALAD AND PASSIONFRUIT JELLO:
2 blood oranges
2 pink grapefruit
2 oranges
1 cup passionfruit pulp (you will need about 10 fruits)
2 tablespoons sugar
3 gelatin leaves
1/3 cup sugar syrup (see Tip below)
2 tablespoons Cointreau

Put all but 1 tablespoon of the sugar in a small, heavy pan and heat gently until melted. Raise the heat and cook, without stirring, until it becomes a golden amber color. Pour in the hot milk (stand well back, as it will splutter), stir well, and boil for 1 minute, then remove from the heat and set aside. In a separate pan, heat the butter until it foams up and gives off a nutty fragrance. Quickly strain it through a fine mesh strainer or cheesecloth into a bowl, then cover and set aside.

In a separate bowl, beat together the egg yolks and remaining sugar until pale and creamy. Beat in the cornstarch. Gradually pour in the caramelized milk and beat until smooth. Finally, beat in the melted butter and balsamic vinegar and let cool. Place in an icecream machine and freeze according to the manufacturer's instructions. Transfer to a container and freeze overnight to let the flavors to strengthen.

For the citrus salad and jello, cut off all the peel and pith from the citrus fruits, then cut out the segments from between the membranes—do this over a bowl to catch the juice, squeezing out the membrane from each fruit after you have taken out all the segments. Set aside the juice and the membrane-free segments.

Place the passionfruit pulp in a saucepan along with the sugar and a 1/4-cup of water. Crush the passionfruit skins with your hands and add them, too (they give a wonderful pink color). Bring to a boil and simmer for 3–4 minutes. Meanwhile, cover the gelatin leaves with cold water for 5 minutes Strain the passionfruit mixture into a bowl and stir in a 1/2-cup of the reserved citrus juice, the sugar syrup, and Cointreau. Squeeze out excess water from the gelatin and add to the passionfruit mixture, stirring until dissolved. Strain into 8 shallow bowls and leave in the fridge overnight.

To serve, top the jello with the citrus fruit segments, place a scoop of balsamic icecream on top, then decorate with the mint leaves.

Paul's Tip To make sugar syrup, put 1 cup superfine sugar in a saucepan with 1 1/4 cups of water and bring slowly to a boil, stirring until the sugar has dissolved. Boil rapidly for 2 minutes to form a light syrup. Let cool, then store in a cool place. Use for sweet sauces, icecreams, sorbets, etc.

coffee

Coffea arabica

Over the last five years, coffee has undergone something of revival. Speciality coffee shops and delicatessens are popping up in cities worldwide, and coffee is very much in vogue today.

This was not, however, always the case. Both in America and Britain, coffee consumption dropped rapidly and steadily in the 1970s and 80s by 30–40 percent, mainly because of growing health concerns. Evidence had begun to surface that linked high coffee consumption with cancer and a number of other serious medical conditions.

recipes

COFFEE RISOTTO (PAGE 156)

COFFEE-ROASTED SPARE RIBS (PAGE 156)

VEAL FILLET WITH MOCHA PORCINI SAUCE (PAGE 157)

PEAR GALETTES WITH COFFEE AND HAZELNUT MERINGUE (PAGE 158)

COFFEE AND FENNEL SEED BISCOTTI (PAGE 158)

CAFFE LATTE WITH ESPRESSO GRANITA (PAGE 159)

Now coffee bars are offering better quality and a greater variety of blends than ever before, so those like me, who could not live without it (especially to wake up morning spirits!), are now drinking a better tasting brew and becoming more sophisticated in our tastes. Familiarity with cappuccinos, espressos, caffe lattes, mochacinos, and other specialty coffees is increasing.

Coffee originated over 1,000 years ago in North Africa and the wild coffee arabica bush is believed to have been cultivated by African tribesman from the sixth century A.D. It is likely that the first berries were chewed, and only later crushed to a wet paste and infused with water. Later still, a more sophisticated coffee was made by fermenting the juice from the ripe berries. Following its inception in Africa, coffee-drinking soon spread quickly to the Middle East (even though the practice was prohibited in Iran in the 1920s as, among other things, coffee was thought to loosen men's tongues), then to central Europe, and eventually to Martinique in the West Indies. However, the modern drink, as we now know it, was not invented until the thirteenth century, when the beans were cleaned and roasted before infusing.

DESCRIPTION

Coffee grows in the tropics on small, evergreen trees (genus *Coffea*) which bear a fruit that looks like a wild cherry. Each berry contains two small green pods or beans that are released from the fruit by being steeped in water or dried in the sun (wet or dry processing). The manufacturing, wet or dry, affects the final flavor. Wet processing is common in Latin America and parts of Africa where there is plenty of water. The flavor tends to be slightly acidic with citrussy overtones. Countries such as Sumatra and Ethiopia employ the dry method which results in beans with a more earthy, spicy flavor. One tree produces enough beans in one year to yield 1 lb. of finished product.

All the world's coffee is grown in a wide band between the Tropics of Cancer and Capricorn. As well as liking warmth, coffee needs moderate rainfall, some shade, and good drainage, therefore hillsides are considered the best plantation sites. A coffee tree takes five years to crop. Each tree produces 2¼ lbs. beans per annum.

QUALITIES OF COFFEE

Some of the world's best coffee comes from South America, where Brazil and Columbia are the first and second largest producers in the world. Yet there are more than 100 kinds of coffee from 40 different countries. Quality coffee comes from the coffee arabica plant which is grown at high altitude. The beans from the hardy robusta variety are generally higher in caffeine, inferior in taste and flavor, and used for making instant coffees.

Pure arabica coffees have distinctive flavors. Brazilian coffee, for example, is noted for its smooth richness and somewhat chocolatey taste. Costa Rica produces a mild, popular breakfast

coffee. Jamaican coffee is recognized for its quality and flavor, with famous names such as Blue Mountain. African varieties include Ethiopian (long considered among the best in the world) and an especially popular Kenyan (noted for its richness and full, fresh flavor). Heavier coffees from Java (smoky and rich with spicy overtones) and Sumatra are particularly favored in France.

ROASTING COFFEE

Roasting coffee beans develops the flavor and body of the coffee, and brings out the aroma. The beans are only roasted for ten minutes, as any longer would make the coffee bitter.

- Light or pale roasted coffee is good with milk.
- Medium roasted produces a stronger, richer coffee.
- Full roasted is often drunk black.
- High roasted is also called Continental coffee.

BUYING AND STORING

Ideally I find it is best to buy coffee from specialty stores that roast their own beans, thus ensuring freshness. Once roasted, coffee beans lose their aroma after 3–4 days. It is undoubtedly best to grind your own coffee just prior to brewing it since the aroma is lost even faster once the beans are ground.

Alternatively, I suggest that you purchase vacuum-packed coffee from supermarkets, which has a decent flavor and aroma. Taste by trial and error, since some smell wonderful but can be disappointing in taste. Store the beans and ground coffee in airtight jars. You can also freeze roasted beans for up to a month in plastic bags, and grind them while still frozen for immediate use.

CULINARY USES

As a beverage, coffee can be blended with cocoa powder as mocha, which is valued as an after-dinner drink; with mysore (from southern India); or served as café brulot (a spicy, citrussy blend); calypso coffee (with rum); and Irish coffee (with whiskey), both topped with cream. It is flavored with spices like cardamom in the Middle East, and with cinnamon, cloves, and orange in Mexico. Iced coffee is particularly delicious in hot weather.

Apart from coffee's obvious appeal as a drink, it also plays an important role in desserts and confectionery, cookies, and biscuits. I confess to being a bit of a coffee lover and, as a flavoring, I think coffee blends beautifully with many ingredients such as chocolate, berries, nuts, and with alcohol such as rum and Tia Maria. The Italians and French are especially fond of coffee in desserts such as mousses and icecream (mousse aux café and gelatti) and all sorts of wonderful preparations. The hugely popular Italian dessert, tiramisu, combines coffee and marscapone cheese. The French also use it to flavor custards (petits pots aux café) and parfaits.

Coffee is used less frequently in savory dishes although I personally believe it has a role to play— try my Veal Fillet with Mocha Porcini Sauce (page 157).

Plenty of people still consider, as I do, a cup of coffee a small taste of heaven, but remember it has more possibilities in cooking than you suspect.

complementary flavors

- CHOCOLATE
- NUTS
- DAIRY PRODUCTS
- FENNEL SEEDS
- PRESERVED GINGER
- ALCOHOL (MARSALA, RUM, TIA MARIA, KAHLUA, AND CRÈME DE CACAO)
- FRESH COCONUT
- FRUIT (BANANAS, PEARS, ORANGES, AND RASPBERRIES)

coffee risotto

I featured this unusual sweet risotto in my book, *Great Value Gourmet* (Weidenfeld & Nicolson, 1996). It was a little heretical then but sweet risottos are more common now, and it makes regular appearances on my menu—sometimes on its own, or with poached pears or glazed oranges.

2 tablespoons coffee-flavored syrup, or 1 tablespoon freshly brewed black coffee
Juice and grated zest of 1/2 orange (not combined)
1/2 cup vialone nano risotto rice
2 1/2 cups milk
2 drops of vanilla extract
1/2 cup superfine sugar
2 tablespooons unsalted butter
3/4 cup whipping cream
2 tablespoons rum (optional)

Place the coffee and orange juice in a saucepan with 2/3 cup of water and bring to a boil. Remove from the heat, add the rice, and let soak for 5 minutes.

Return the pan to the heat and add the milk and vanilla extract. Bring to a boil, then reduce the heat and cook gently for 15–18 minutes, until the rice is tender but still slightly firm to the bite. Remove from the heat and add the sugar, orange zest, butter, cream, and rum, if using. Stir through gently and serve immediately.

coffee-roasted spare ribs

Everyone loves a barbecue and most of us have our favorite marinades and bastes for adding flavor to meat and fish. Here is an unusual glaze for pork ribs using coffee. Its slightly bitter edge, blended with tomato and spices, gives a wonderful flavor that will surprise you. Bring on the summer, I say!

2 teaspoons dried chili flakes
2/3 cup strong freshly brewed black filter coffee
1/2 cup tomato ketchup
3 garlic cloves, crushed
1/2 cup wine vinegar
3 tablespoons brown sugar
1/2 cup rum
1/2 cup vegetable oil
1 teaspoon ground cumin
1/2 teaspoon ground cilantro
1/8 teaspoon ground allspice
2 racks of pork spare ribs
Salt

Put everything except the pork and salt in a blender and blend to a paste. Season with salt, to taste. Coat the racks with the paste, ensuring they are well covered all over. Place in a dish, cover, and let marinate in the fridge overnight or for at least 8 hours.

Preheat the oven to 400°F. Let the pork come to room temperature, then place in a roasting pan and cook in the oven for 1–1 1/2 hours, brushing them regularly with the marinade. Let cool slightly before cutting into individual ribs. Take napkin in hand and begin!

Paul's Tip Cook these for 20–25 minutes on a barbeque remembering to turn them regularly, this gives a lovely smokey flavor to the meat.

veal fillet with mocha porcini sauce

Here, coffee forms the base of a wonderful wild mushroom sauce, enhanced with red wine and sweet marsala. A creamy celeriac or parsnip purée goes particularly well with this dish.

3/4 oz. dried porcini mushrooms
1/3 cup freshly brewed black filter coffee (not espresso)
3 tablespoons vegetable oil
4 x 6 oz. veal fillet steaks or veal cutlets
1 oz. unsalted butter, chilled and cut into small pieces
2 shallots, chopped
1 garlic clove, crushed
1 sprig of thyme
9 oz. fresh porcini mushrooms (or chestnut mushrooms), thickly sliced
1/4 cup good-quality red wine
1/2 cup veal broth (or chicken broth)
1/3 cup sweet marsala wine
Salt and freshly ground black pepper

Put the dried porcini in a bowl, pour the coffee over them, and let soak for 30 minutes, until softened. Strain off the liquid and reserve. Chop the mushrooms finely and set aside.

Heat the oil in a large frying pan until very hot, season the veal steaks and fry for 2–3 minutes on each side. Remove from the pan and keep warm, draining off any excess oil left in the pan. Melt 2 teaspoons of the butter in the pan, then add the shallots, garlic, thyme, and soaked dried mushrooms and cook over a high heat for 1 minute. Add the fresh mushrooms and cook for 2 minutes longer. Pour in the red wine, the mushroom soaking liquid, and broth, and boil until the sauce has reduced by half its original volume. Stir in the remaining chilled butter and the marsala, and season to taste.

Put the veal steaks on serving plates and coat with the mocha porcini sauce.

pear galettes with coffee and hazelnut meringue

1 quantity of Sweet Pastry Dough (see page 129) or 14 oz. shortcrust pastry
4 ripe but firm pears
1/4 cup (1/2 stick) unsalted butter
2 tablespoons sugar
1/4 cup poire William liqueur (if unavailable, use pear brandy)
1 egg, beaten

FOR THE MERINGUE:

2 egg whites
1/2 cup superfine sugar
1 tablespoon freshly ground coffee beans
4 1/2 oz. (1-1 1/4 cups) hazelnuts, coarsely ground

Roll out the pastry to approximately 1/8-inch thick and cut out four 6-inch circles. Place on a lightly greased baking sheet and chill while you cook the pears.

Preheat the oven to 400°F. Peel and core the pears, cut them in half vertically, then cut each half into 4 vertically-cut wedges. Heat the butter in a large frying pan, add the pears and sugar, and cook for 6–8 minutes, until the pear wedges are beautifully golden and caramelized. Pour the poire William liqueur over them and remove from the pan. Let cool.

Arrange the caramelized pear wedges in the center of each pastry dough circle. Fold over the edge of the dough to form a 1-inch border and brush the dough with the beaten egg. Bake for 15 minutes, then remove from the oven and reduce the oven temperature to 350°F.

To make the meringue, beat the egg whites using an electric beater with half the sugar until they form stiff peaks. Add the remaining sugar and the ground coffee and beat again. Finally, fold in the ground hazelnuts.

Top the pear galettes with the coffee meringue and return to the oven for 8–10 minutes to glaze until golden. Serve warm.

coffee and fennel seed biscotti

These delicious, crisp, fragrant cookies are great served with morning coffee or with dessert. Surprisingly, instant coffee powder gives a better flavor than freshly ground coffee, although both work well.

1/2 cup vanilla sugar (see page 143)
1 egg
2 tablespoons anise liqueur, such as Ricard or Pernod
1 teaspoon vanilla extract
3/4 cup all-purpose flour, sifted
1/2 teaspoon baking powder
A pinch of salt
2 tablespoons instant coffee powder
1/4 cup raisins
1/2 cup almonds, toasted
1 teaspoon fennel seeds, toasted

Preheat the oven to 325°F. In a bowl, beat together the vanilla sugar, egg, liqueur, and vanilla until thick and pale. Mix together the flour, baking powder, salt, and coffee powder and add to the bowl. Stir until well combined, then mix in the raisins, almonds, and fennel seeds. Turn the mixture out onto a counter and shape into a flat log, about 10 inches long, 3 inches wide and 1 inch high. Place on a well-greased baking sheet and bake for 25 minutes, until golden brown. Remove and let cool for about 15 minutes, until firm. Meanwhile, reduce the oven temperature to 300°F.

With a serrated knife, cut the log into slices 1/4-inch thick. Arrange the slices flat on the baking sheet and return to the oven for 10–15 minutes. Let cool completely.

caffe latte with espresso granita

FOR THE GRANITA:

1/3 cup sugar
1 cup espresso coffee
2 tablespoons Tia Maria or other coffee liqueur

FOR THE CAFFE LATTE:

1 cup espresso coffee beans, finely ground
2 gelatin leaves
2 eggs
1 egg yolk
1/4 cup sugar
1 tablespoon Tia Maria or other coffee liqueur
1 cup heavy cream, semi-whipped

FOR SERVING:

1/2 cup sweetened whipped cream
A few coffee beans

First make the granita. Put the sugar in a pan with 1 cup of water and bring slowly to a boil. Simmer for 10 minutes, then add the espresso coffee and let cool. Add the coffee liqueur and pour the mixture into a shallow metal tray. Place in the freezer and, as it begins to freeze and ice crystals form, use a fork to scrape up the mixture from the sides and bottom occasionally, to flake the ice crystals.

For the caffe latte, pour 3/4 cup of boiling water over the coffee and let infuse (ideally do this in a cafetière). Meanwhile, cover the gelatin leaves with cold water and let soak for 5 minutes. Drain well, squeezing out excess water. Strain the coffee, add the soaked gelatin, and stir until dissolved. Let cool.

Put the eggs, egg yolk, and sugar in the top of a double-boiler, set over simmering water. Whisk with a hand-held beater until the mixture is creamy, pale, and thick enough to leave a ribbon on the surface when trailed from the beat. Remove the top pan, add the Tia Maria, and whisk until cool. Whisk in the coffee and gelatin mixture and leave until almost set, stirring occasionally. Finally, fold in the whipped cream and spoon into 4 large coffee cups or glasses. Place in the fridge until set.

To serve, top the caffe latte with a good spoonful of the granita, then with some whipped cream and coffee beans. Coffee and Fennel Seed Biscotti (see page 158) make a good accompaniment.

honey *Mel*

Honey is a very rich and concentrated food (70 calories per tablespoon), a natural sweetener and a great source of energy. Its effect on the body is similar to that of sugar and is, therefore, prohibited in certain medical conditions, such as diabetes. None the less, it is recommended for those who prefer a healthier diet and lifestyle, as it undergoes less processing refinement and contains more complex carbohydrates. Honey was the chief sweet food in medieval times, when cane sugar became too expensive and somewhat of a rarity.

recipes

DESCRIPTION

According to a French chef friend of mine, producing honey is easy: you simply take your hives to where the pollen you prefer is abundant, and let the bees loose. They return to the hive, you return home, and wait for the bees to begin the process. It sounds simple enough, but like all things in life, I'm sure there is a lot more to it than that—or is there?

The quality, consistency, color, aroma, and flavor of honey all vary according to where it has been gathered, that is to say, according to the nectar-source, or feeding ground of the bees. Honey aficionados will understand how different honey can taste. The flavor can alter from season to season (spring honey is always superior to winter honey), from location to location, and from one source of nectar to another. In France, especially in Provence, honey is a serious business, one that means beekeepers must relocate their hives at different times of the year in order to place the bees close to the lavender fields when the plants are in full bloom.

There are many distinct types of honey, some collected from a single source (such as Scotland's heather honey), and others from mixed nectars. For me, the best honeys are those with a distinctive flavor, such as lavender (delicate and aromatic), pine nut or chestnut (nutty and mild), heather (with its unique, jello consistency and distinctive full flavor), elderflower and herbs such as thyme and rosemary. Some other favorites are: acacia (a popular, mild honey, delicious on cereals, in icecream, and yogurt), clover (sweet, mild, and vanilla-flavored, usually set), and Greek (a dark, thick honey with a pungent aroma—one of the strongest tasting varieties and superb poured over Greek yogurt).

Honey can be bought either in the edible wax comb, straight from the hive (honeycomb), or with the comb removed by straining or by centrifugal force, in a machine called a spinner.

Different nectars produce honey that sets (or crystallizes) at different rates. Crops such as oil seed rape produce large quantities of nectar that sets very solidly, whereas garden flowers tend to a give a clear, liquid honey. Honey sold as set, creamed, or whipped is honey in its crystallized form.

BUYING AND STORING

When selecting honey, price is generally a good guide to quality. In flavor, they vary immensely from mild flavored cheaper versions to single-flower honeys of intense, sticky rich qualities. The most reputed honeys are those of Hymettus in Greece and the French varieties from Champagne, Savoy, and southern France.

Ideally, honey should be stored in a pantry away from direct heat and light, where it retains its natural flavor. All honey will eventually crystallize or solidify. If this happens, and a recipe calls for runny honey, simply heat gently over low heat until melted.

complementary flavors

HARD FRUITS (LEMONS, PEARS, AND BANANAS)

SOFT FRUITS (GOOSEBERRIES, RASPBERRIES, AND APRICOTS)

CARROTS AND TURNIPS

DUCK AND CHICKEN (FOR GLAZING)

ROSEWATER AND ORANGE FLOWER WATER

NUTS

CHOCOLATE

SPICES (GINGER, CINNAMON, AND SAFFRON)

MUSTARD

CULINARY USES

For many people, honey is merely a delicious spread enjoyed on hot, thickly sliced toast, or in tarts and cakes. However, in the Middle East and parts of the Mediterranean, honey is an important and much-loved cooking ingredient. It is poured over pastries and made into cookies. In Greece it is drizzled over small savory cheese-filled pastries, and over yogurt and fruits at breakfast time. In Morocco, honey is regularly used in sweet, sticky cakes and pastries, on desserts and added to sweet spicy tagines—a distinctive feature of Moroccan cooking.

The French are fanatical about honey: they use it in many dishes: sweet (like Crème Homère, a crème caramel with honey) and savory (such as Duck with Lavender Honey). They also bake it in tarts, use it to flavor bread, icecream, and desserts, and to make their famous white nougats (touvon).

In certain recipes, it may be substituted for sugar, while in others, such as cakes and pastries, it is not a suitable substitute because of its density. Honey makes a great glaze for meats (particularly lamb) and vegetables to be grilled on the barbecue or under the broiler, and is a flavorsome sweetening agent for sauces.

Mead, a drink made from honey and water, has been drunk across Europe and Russia for centuries, and is still common today. In Russia, fruit such as black cherries, currants, and raspberries are added to the mixture.

OTHER USES

Besides its use in cooking, honey is said to be very good for your health, and in combating ailments. I think we have all in our time had a soothing hot toddy made from honey, brandy, and fresh lemon juice to help relieve cold and flu symptoms. It's also said to combat dry skin and aid a good complexion.

Royal jello, a creamy-white substance that is very rich in protein and fatty acids, is produced by the mouth glands in young bees and fed to the queen bee and larvae. It is very expensive as it is made in such small quantities, and is used in some dietary supplements and cosmetics.

duck steaks with five-spice caramel

1 teaspoon cilantro seeds
1 teaspoon cumin seeds
1/2 teaspoon sesame seeds
1/4 cup honey
1/2 teaspoon five-spice powder
1 tablespoon red wine vinegar
2 tablespoons soy sauce
2 tablespoons vegetable oil
4 x 6 oz. boneless duck breasts, skin on
Salt and freshly ground black pepper

FOR THE ORIENTAL VEGETABLES:
1/4 cup sesame oil
2 bok choy, cut in half
6 radishes, sliced
1 carrot, thinly sliced
7 oz. Chinese broccoli, cut into florets
2 tablespoons soy sauce

Lightly crack the cilantro, cumin, and sesame seeds in a mortar and pestle to break them up. Put them in a pan with the honey, five-spice powder, vinegar, soy sauce, and some salt and pepper, and heat gently until the mixture comes to a boil. Remove from the heat and put to one side. Preheat the broiler to its highest setting.

Heat the vegetable oil in a large frying pan, season the duck breasts, and cook them in the hot oil, skin-side down, until golden underneath. Turn and cook the other side for about 4–5 minutes, depending on how well you like it cooked. Remove the duck breasts from the pan and place under the broiler. Brush them liberally with the honey and spice mixture and place under the hot broiler. Reduce the heat and leave until the honey caramelizes.

Meanwhile, for the Oriental vegetables, heat the sesame oil in a wok or large frying pan, add all the vegetables, and stir-fry until tender but still retaining a little crispness. Season to taste with salt, pepper, and the soy sauce. Place the duck breasts on the vegetables and serve.

lavender honey and sauternes lacquered nectarines

The honey and Sauternes syrup is a gorgeous purplish-pink color, with an intense lavender honey aroma and delicate floral flavor. Melon is another favorite for this perfectly balanced syrup.

1/2 cup superfine sugar
1 tablespoon small mint leaves, stalks removed
4 large nectarines
2 tablespoons unsalted butter
1/4 cup lavender honey
Grated zest of 1/4 lemon
1/2 teaspoon lavender pollen (see page 21)
1/2 cup Sauternes or other sweet dessert wine
1/4 cup sliced almonds, lightly toasted

Combine the sugar with 2 1/2 cups of water in a saucepan and bring slowly to a boil, stirring to dissolve the sugar. Add the stalks from the mint leaves, then the nectarines, and simmer for 5 minutes, turning the nectarines occasionally if the liquid doesn't cover them completely. Remove from the heat and set aside. When the nectarines are cool enough to handle, peel them, cut in half, and remove the pits. Return the nectarine halves to the cooked syrup (this may all be done well in advance).

To serve, melt the butter in a large frying pan and stir in the honey, lemon zest, and lavender pollen. Drain the nectarines, toss them in the honey mixture, and then pour in the Sauternes. Turn the nectarines in the pan until glazed all over. Place the nectarines on serving plates, coat with the lavender honey sauce, scatter the toasted almonds and mint leaves on top, and serve.

halvah

This very sweet confectionery is immensely popular in India and Mediterranean countries. There are many variations on the recipe. My own version is flavored with honey, cinnamon, and saffron. It makes a delicious dessert or petit four and can be eaten warm, although I prefer it at room temperature.

1^3/4 cups sugar
A pinch of saffron strands
2 cinnamon sticks
1 teaspoon ground cardamom
1 cup olive oil
2^1/2 cups semolina
^{3}/4 cup sliced almonds
^{1}/3 cup honey
2 tablespoons whole blanched almonds
1 teaspoon ground cinnamon

Place the sugar and saffron in a pan with 2^1/2 cups of water and bring slowly to a boil, stirring from time to time to dissolve the sugar. Add the cinnamon and cardamom, simmer for 5 minutes, then remove from the heat and let infuse.

Meanwhile, in a separate pan, heat the olive oil until quite hot, stir in the semolina, reduce the heat, and simmer for 20 minutes, until lightly golden. Add the sliced almonds and cook for 2 minutes. Strain in the saffron syrup and boil together for 5 minutes. Add the honey, remove from the heat, and let cool slightly. Pour into a greased and lined shallow pan, about 10 x 8 inches, smooth the top and set aside to cool. Cut into small squares, top each one with a blanched almond, and dust with the ground cinnamon.

gooseberry omelette with elderflower honey

6 tablespoons elderflower honey
1/3 cup elderflower syrup
11 oz. slightly underripe green gooseberries
Grated zest of 1/2 lemon
8 eggs, beaten
1/4 cup sugar
2 tablespoons unsalted butter
Confectioners' sugar for dusting
1/4 cup clotted cream (if unavailable, use slightly-whipped, heavy cream)

Put half the honey in a pan with the elderflower syrup and bring to a boil. Reduce the heat to a low simmer, add the green gooseberries and lemon zest, and cook gently for 8–10 minutes, until the gooseberries are soft and the liquid is syrupy.

Beat the eggs together in a bowl, add the sugar and 1 tablespoon of water, and beat again until light and fluffy.

Heat a 1/2 tablespoon of the butter in an 8-inch omelette pan until foaming. Pour in a quarter of the beaten egg mixture and cook for about 30 seconds, lifting the cooked edges of the omelette to allow the uncooked egg to flow underneath. When half set, spoon a quarter of the gooseberries over the top, then fold the omelette over and transfer to a warm serving plate and keep warm. Make the remaining omelettes in the same way. Dust with confectioners' sugar, place the clotted cream on top, drizzle the remaining honey over them, and serve.

persian-style baked figs

4 oz. mixed dried fruit (such as apricots, prunes, dates, and golden raisins)
8 large, ripe figs
1/4 cup honey
Juice and grated zest of 2 oranges
1/4 teaspoon ground cinnamon
Pinch of fennel seeds
1/3 cup anisette or brandy

FOR SERVING:

2 teaspoons rosewater
1/2 cup crème fraîche
1 tablespoon pine nuts, toasted
A few mint leaves

Soak the dried fruit overnight in water until swollen, then drain and cut into small pieces.

Preheat the oven to 350°F. Cut the figs in half, scoop out the center, and fill each fig half with the dried fruit. Place in a shallow baking dish or gratin dish. Combine the honey, orange juice and zest, cinnamon, fennel seeds, and anisette or brandy, and pour them over the figs. Cover and bake for 20 minutes, basting occasionally. Transfer to a serving dish.

Lightly fold the rosewater into the crème fraîche. Serve the figs warm, decorated with the pine nuts and mint leaves and accompanied by the crème fraîche.

salt *Sel*

"Take it with a pinch of salt," "the salt of the earth," "he"s worth his salt": everyday phrases in these days when salt is commonplace and taken for granted.

But in medieval times, salt was so precious that it occupied pride of place in the center of the table, piled in great silver or gold salt cellars. Commoners sat below the salt, dignitaries above. During Roman times it was as valuable as gold, and Roman soldiers were given a ration to buy salt, a "salarium" from which we derive the word salary. Salt has also long been regarded as a symbol of hospitality, and in many countries is offered with bread to welcome people into homes.

recipes

SALT-CURED SALMON (GRAVAD LAX) (PAGE 168)

SALT-GRILLED SHRIMP WITH LIME AND GARLIC (PAGE 168)

SALT COD PÂTÉ WITH BALSAMIC PEPPERS AND OLIVES (PAGE 170)

BURIED SEA BASS IN LEMON SALT (PAGE 171)

HERB-BAKED CHICKEN IN A SALT CRUST (PAGE 171)

SEE ALSO:

TWICE-COOKED DUCK WITH LAVENDER HONEY (PAGE 23)

One thing is for sure; we all need salt in one form or another in our diet. Salt is in our blood, sweat, and tears, and is essential for our well-being. It helps to maintain the body's fluid balance, regulates blood pressure, sparks nerve communication, and aids muscle contraction. Like most things, however, if taken in excess, it can be harmful. There is evidence that links a high salt intake to high blood pressure and heart disease.

Culinary practices influence the consumption or need for salt. Boiling vegetables in a large pot of water, for example, deprives them of much of their natural mineral salts, which we replace by adding salt to the water or at the table. Vegetables steamed in their own juices need much less salt, as do roasted, rather than boiled, potatoes.

How much salt is a matter of taste; some people like lots, others less, some none at all. But for me, any cook worth his or her salt (excuse the pun!) cannot deny its importance in enhancing the taste of food and drawing out natural flavors. Salt is the only mineral condiment we add to our food, and it should be noted by vegetarians especially, that the higher the vegetable content of the diet, the greater the need for salt.

DESCRIPTION

Salt is a mineral consisting mainly of sodium chloride. There are two main types of salt: sea salt, which is distilled from sea water; and rock salt, found in the earth in a crystallised form. In addition to these, there are numerous specialized varieties.

SEA SALT AND KOSHER SALT Sea salt contains tiny amounts of important minerals, such as calcium and magnesium, which occur naturally in the sea. It is odorless, has a more refined flavor than most, and is the costliest of all salts to produce. Kosher salt has a jagged texture and is pure salt with no additives. Although water is involved in its processing, the salt is from underground deposits—it is not a sea salt. It's less salty-tasting than regular table salt and is preferred by many famous cooks. Gray salt (or *sel gris de guérande*) is an unrefined sea salt produced by natural evaporation.

ROCK SALT Mined from dried-up underground saline lakes and processed to different degrees of fineness. In its crude state, it is used to de-ice roads and in icecream machines. In its refined form, it is used for cooking purposes. The flavor cannot, however, be compared with sea salt.

TABLE SALT Basic all-purpose cooking salt. It is refined, finely ground rock salt, with added soda to prevent caking (to keep the crystals free-flowing in humid conditions, add a few grains of rice to the salt shaker). Iodized salt is simply table salt with potassium iodide (an essential trace element that is sometimes missing in our diets).

CURING SALT (sel rosé) A pink refined salt with added nitrates, used in hams, cured meats, and terrines to enhance the color.

BLACK SALT Unusual pink-tan (not black) grains, used in Indian cooking and prized in ayurvedic medicine. It has a slightly smoky flavor.

SPICE SALT (sel épicé) A flavored salt comprising salt, white pepper, and mixed spices.

CANNING OR PICKLING SALT A coarse-grained salt, free of all additives to prevent discoloring and to ensure the liquid doesn't cloud.

VEGETABLE SALTS Fine salt with added vegetable extract, such as celery or onion. If you use vegetable salt, cut down on the amount of salt called for in recipes.

STORING

Salt, unlike herbs and spices, keeps indefinitely without losing its flavor; it is not true that grinding your salt in a mill gives a fresher flavor.

CULINARY USES

Salt is probably the most popular seasoning, is one of the four major components of taste (along with sweet, sour, and bitter), and is a versatile culinary performer.

It was the Romans who first invented the process of salting to preserve meat, fish, cheese, and fruit such as lemons (see page 128)—a technique we still use today. However, there are many other ways to utilize salt in cooking. For example, it can be used as a casing to enclose meat and fish in order to seal in the flavor and moisture while baking.

In addition to its own "salty" flavor, salt has the ability to bring out the natural flavor of other ingredients and make them more vibrant. It also has the capacity to cut the sweetness of very rich flavors (like chocolate) and can soften the sharpness of acidic ingredients such as citrus fruit, pineapple, and tomatoes. Adding salt to sweet dishes is becoming increasingly popular—although it is best to use mellow salts such as *fleur de sel*. Some cooks use salt crystals for their crunchy texture, as well as the flavor, lightly sprinkled on top of chocolate cakes or fruit such as cantaloupe.

Salt slows down fermentation and is used in bread-making to help develop the flavor of the wheat and enhance the texture of the dough. It is also used for disgorging the bitter juices from vegetables such as cucumbers and eggplants. Adding salt to water raises the temperature at which it boils, thereby reducing cooking time.

OTHER USES

Because salt is an effective antiseptic, salt water is an excellent gargle for sore throats. It is also said to boost the immune system and to ease depression. Salt is added to commercially produced sports drinks and is a key ingredient in processed foods—often in alarming quantities. It has also, for years, been used as a cleaning agent to remove stains (rub plenty of salt into red wine stains while they are still fresh) and break down grease. And, of course, you will have heard of superstitious people throwing a pinch of salt over their shoulders to ward off bad luck!

salt-cured salmon (gravad lax)

I could not leave this Scandinavian specialty out of this book. The name *gravad lax* means "buried salmon," and derives from the original method of salt curing—when the fish was prepared in the same manner but buried in a hole in the ground for several weeks.

SERVES 10-12

1 x 4 1/2 lb. salmon, filleted
2 bunches of dill
1/3 cup coarse salt
1/4 cup sugar
2 teaspoons white peppercorns, crushed

FOR THE DILL MUSTARD SAUCE:
4 egg yolks
1 1/2 teaspoons cider vinegar
1 tablespoon brown sugar
1 tablespoon Dijon mustard
1 cup olive oil
2 tablespoons chopped dill
Salt and freshly ground black pepper

Place one salmon fillet skin-side down in a shallow dish. Spread the dill on top. Mix together the salt, sugar, and peppercorns, and sprinkle liberally over the fish. Put the other fillet on top, skin-side up. Cover with foil and then weight down the fish with a plank of wood (or a plate or board), topped with some weights or heavy cans. The pressure applied should be approximately the same weight as the salmon. Place in the fridge and leave for 3 days, turning the salmon and spooning the juices back over the fish every 8 hours or so.

To make the sauce, beat the egg yolks and vinegar together, then beat in the sugar until dissolved. Add the mustard, then gradually beat in the oil, as for making mayonnaise. Stir in the chopped dill and adjust the seasoning.

Take the salmon out of the marinade, clean off the dill and spices, and pat the fish dry. Cut into thin slices on the diagonal and serve with the dill mustard sauce. In Scandinavia it is usually garnished with a small salad, lemon wedges, and sticks of toast.

salt-grilled shrimp with lime and garlic

20 extra-large uncooked tiger shrimp, shell on
1/4 cup virgin olive oil
Juice of 1/4 lemon
1/2 teaspoon chopped thyme
1/2 teaspoon chopped oregano
2 tablespoons coarse salt
1/4 teaspoon garlic salt
Freshly ground black pepper

FOR THE LIME AND GARLIC SAUCE:
1 cup fish broth
Juice of 3 limes
Grated zest of 1 lime
1 garlic clove, crushed
1 small red onion, finely chopped
2 tablespoons chopped flat-leaf parsley
2 tablespoons chilled unsalted butter, chopped

Cut down the back of each shrimp shell with a sharp knife or kitchen scissors and lift out the black intestinal vein, leaving the shell on. Coat the shrimp in the olive oil and lemon juice and season with black pepper. In a bowl, mix together the herbs and salts. Dredge the shrimp in the mixture, ensuring they are well coated. Grill the salt-crusted shrimp on a hot barbecue or a ridged grill pan for 3–4 minutes on each side.

Meanwhile, make the sauce. Put all the ingredients except the butter in a pan and bring to a boil. Remove from the heat and beat in the butter.

Remove the shrimp from the grill and arrange on a serving dish. Pour the sauce around them and serve.

Paul's Tip (left) Once you have perfected the basic recipe, you can experiment. Try flavoring the salmon with orange or lemon zest, or spices such as cumin or cardamom. In Norway, I encountered it marinated with dill and grated raw beets, which gave the fish a wonderfully sweet flavor and a remarkable ruby-red color when sliced.

salt cod pâté with balsamic peppers and olives

I have never been fond of Mediterranean-style salt cod. I much prefer this lighter version, using fresh cod. It has a mellower taste, which lets the flavor of the fish stand out, and is far less salty on the palate.

7 oz. fresh cod fillet, skinned
1/2 cup coarse sea salt or kosher salt
1 cup whole milk
3 garlic cloves, crushed
11 oz. waxy potatoes, peeled and chopped into 1/4-inch pieces
3 tablespoons olive oil
A pinch of cayenne pepper
Salt and freshly ground black pepper
A little paprika, for dusting

FOR THE BALSAMIC PEPPERS:
2 large red peppers
1 tablespoon olive oil, plus extra for brushing
1 garlic clove, crushed
1 tablespoon sugar
1/4 cup balsamic vinegar
20 small black olives

Place the cod in a dish, cover it liberally with the salt, and leave for 2 hours. Wash the salt from the fish by running it under cold water. Place in a pan along with the milk, garlic, and potatoes, and bring to a gentle simmer. Poach until the cod and potatoes are tender. Remove the fish and potatoes from the poaching liquid with a slotted spoon and let them cool slightly. Mash them together in a bowl, then stir in the olive oil and enough of the poaching liquid to give a firm consistency, like stiff mashed potatoes. Season with salt, pepper, and cayenne. Let cool, and then place in the fridge.

Preheat the oven to 400°F. Brush the red peppers with oil, then place on a baking sheet and roast until blackened and blistered. Leave until cool enough to handle, then peel off the skins, remove the seeds, and cut the peppers into large chunks.

Heat the olive oil and garlic in a pan, add the roasted peppers, and fry for 2 minutes. Sprinkle on the sugar, add the balsamic vinegar, then reduce the heat and cook gently for 2–3 minutes, until the peppers take on a sweet and sour flavor. Stir in the olives, season lightly, and let cool.

To serve, arrange a small mound of peppers and olives on each serving plate. Top with a large quenelle (see Tip below) of the pâté, dust with a little paprika, and spoon some of the balsamic syrup around it. Serve with good crusty bread.

Paul's Tip To shape the pâté into quenelles, you will need 2 wet tablespoons. Scoop up some of the pâté in 1 tablespoon and shape it into an oval by scraping it neatly off 1 spoon on to the other several times.

buried sea bass in lemon salt

You might think that burying such a delicate fish as sea bass in salt would ruin the flavor. Wrong! It actually keeps the fish moist and preserves the delicate texture, without making it taste salty. In France, chicken and other fish, such as turbot and mullet, are prepared in a similar fashion.

This is very good served on a bed of roasted vegetables such as peppers, zucchini, and fennel, cooked in the oven at the same time as the fish.

1 x 4 lb. sea bass, cleaned, scaled, and washed clean of all traces of blood
1 lemon, thickly sliced
1/2 cup olive oil
Leaves from 1 small bunch of thyme
1 small bunch of rosemary, chopped
3 1/4 cups coarse sea salt or kosher salt
Grated zest of 1 lemon
1 egg white, lightly beaten
Freshly ground black pepper
Melted butter or lemon wedges, for serving

Preheat the oven to 425°F. Fill the belly cavity of the fish with the lemon slices and season inside with pepper. Heat the olive oil in a large, flameproof and ovenproof baking dish. Carefully add the sea bass and cook for 2–3 minutes on each side, until the skin colors and begins to crisp. Remove from the heat.

In a bowl, mix the herbs with the salt, lemon zest, and beaten egg white. Mold this mixture all over the fish to cover it. Place in the oven and bake for 20–25 minutes. Remove from the oven and carefully brush away the salt. Serve on a large dish with a little melted butter or simply with lemon wedges.

herb-baked chicken in a salt crust

An impressive way to serve chicken to your guests. Take it to the table, crack the salt crust open in front of everyone, and wait for the waft of steamed herbs and garlic to pervade the room. The chicken can be prepared in advance up to the baking stage. Serve with roasted new potatoes and creamed spinach.

4 x 6 oz. organic or cage-free chicken breasts, on the bone
2 garlic cloves, crushed
2 tablespoons chopped mixed herbs (such as rosemary, thyme, and sage)
Salt and freshly ground black pepper

FOR THE SALT CRUST:

4 cups all-purpose flour
1/2 cup coarse sea salt or kosher salt
1 tablespoon chopped mixed herbs (such as rosemary, thyme, and sage)
1 large egg
3/4 cup iced water
Beaten egg, for glazing

For the crust, mix the flour, salt, and herbs together in a bowl. Make a well in the center, add the egg and water, and bring together to form a dough. Wrap in plastic wrap and let rest in the fridge for 30 minutes.

Preheat the oven to 400°F. Season the chicken breasts with salt and pepper, then roll them in the herbs and garlic, ensuring they are evenly coated. Roll out the dough to about 1/4-inch thick and cut it into quarters. Wrap a chicken breast in each piece, enclosing everything except the wing bone. Brush lightly all over with beaten egg.

Place on a baking sheet and bake for 15–18 minutes, then remove from the oven and let stand for 2–3 minutes before serving.

chocolate *Theobroma cacao*

Understandably, chocolate finds favor almost everywhere and it can be prepared and served in all sorts of ways, from luscious desserts to surprisingly interesting fish, meat, and vegetable dishes.

Some may reject chocolate on health grounds: it has been associated with allergic reactions, depression, migraines, ulcers, and is said to heighten hyper-activity in children. Others believe it has aphrodisiac qualities. However, many of these contra-indications are yet to be proven—which is just as well as, let's face it, chocolate is for many (myself included) simply irresistible.

recipes

Sometimes called "the food of the gods", chocolate has a long history. The Mayans were the first to establish cacao plantations (in Yucatán, in Mexico), around A.D. 600. Around the same time, the Aztecs made a bitter drink called Xocolat from roasted crushed cocoa beans beaten into boiling water and flavored with honey and chile. Cocoa was as precious as gold in Aztec towns, where 100 beans could buy a slave, and ten could buy the favors of a woman—even taxes were paid in cocoa beans.

Europe was first introduced to cacao in 1502 by Columbus who, having encountered it in Nicaragua, presented it to the Spanish court of King Ferdinand and Queen Isabella. A little later, Hernando Cortés, a conquistador, tasted Xocolat at the court of King Montezuma, and on his return it soon became the preferred beverage of the Spanish aristocracy, sweetened with a little sugar. Much later, this became the hot chocolate beverage we all know and serve to this day as a warming, comforting drink.

It was not until late in the eighteenth century, however, that the first eating chocolate was produced, flavored with vanilla to cater for European tastes.

DESCRIPTION

Chocolate is made from the beans of the evergreen cacao tree (*Theobroma cacao*), which is mainly indigenous to the rain forests of South America, all within 20° latitude of the equator.

The oval pods are harvested by hand twice a year, in late spring/early summer, and again in winter. As the pods ripen, they turn from light green to vibrant reds and golden yellow, and are then cut from the trees. The harvested fruit is collected, the pods are hooked open to reveal the beans, and they are assessed for ripeness. The beans themselves are covered in a thick, pulpy, white substance, naturally high in sugar but with a tart taste.

The beans are then dried in the sun, and must be continually shuffled to ensure even drying. Next, they are shelled, to expose the nibs or kernels, then roasted and ground to produce a thick, dark brown, viscous matter known as cocoa mass or liquor. This is then refined, and the fat content or cocoa butter is extracted to leave a solid cake, which is then ground into what we know as cocoa powder.

Chocolate-making begins when sugar and natural vanilla are added to the cocoa liquor, which after various processes is cooled and shaped. It is a highly processed commodity which explains why the better qualities are expensive. The better the chocolate, the higher the price. Chocolate is produced plain (dark), milk, white, or as cocoa powder. Plain (dark) chocolate gives the best flavor, milk is sweeter and softer, and white is mainly all cocoa butter.

Plain (Dark): Also known as bitter or unsweetened chocolate, this variety must contain a minimum of 34 percent cocoa solids (mass or butter). The

higher the percentage of solids, the better the quality; look out for 50–70 percent varieties. Usually the higher the percentage, the darker and less sweet the chocolate will be. There are many excellent concentrated varieties available; for me Valrhona is the best with 72+ percent cocoa solids, although it is difficult to find except through specialist kitchen stores or chocolate stores.

Milk (Semi-sweet): This is made in a similar way, but contains less cocoa mass. In its place, milk powder is added, making it sweeter and milder in flavor. It is generally used as an eating chocolate. I sometimes use it in mousses, when dark is not readily available.

White: This does not contain any cocoa mass, and is, in fact, a mixture of cocoa butter and sugar with flavorings and milk powder added. It has nowhere near the depth of flavor of dark chocolate and is more usually eaten in chocolate bar form. The best varieties are always creamy in color, never really white. The Lindt brand is particularly acceptable, I find.

Cocoa powder: The mass that remains when the extraction of the cocoa butter and liquor is completed is ground to form cocoa powder, which is used in cooking or to make a drink.

CULINARY USES

When using chocolate in cooking, I generally break it into bite-size pieces, which makes it easier to melt. Place the chocolate pieces in the top of a double-boiler over simmering water and let it melt, stirring occasionally. When smooth and silky, remove from the heat. If I'm in a hurry, I sometimes melt chocolate in the microwave on a medium heat. Take care not to overheat as it makes the chocolate grainy. In certain dishes, particularly sauces, I find it best to grate the chocolate before adding.

In Italy, a little chocolate is added to a sweet and sour vegetable dish called Caponata. The Europeans, especially the Germans, have long used it in rich sauces served with venison, hare, and game birds. In Mexico, the birthplace of chocolate, the beans are roasted very dark and are mixed with cinnamon or almonds (not just vanilla) and added to molés or sauces to give them a smooth, interesting flavor.

Chocolate adds a mellow silkiness to savory dishes and rounds out flavor—especially when combined with chiles, as in Mole Poblano (Turkey in Chocolate Sauce—see page 175).

Of course, chocolate is also used to flavor a huge number of desserts, cakes, mousses, cookies, and drinks.

CHOCOLATE TIPS

To prepare a simple decoration for chocolate desserts, pull a potato peeler evenly across the surface of a chocolate bar at room temperature to produce chocolate shavings.

Or, take some fresh dry leaves with raised veins (such as bay leaves or rose leaves) and dip their underside in melted chocolate. Let them set hard, then carefully peel away the leaf to reveal the chocolate replica. Basil leaves can similarly be dipped, for a completely edible decoration.

complementary flavors

- NUTS
- CARAMEL
- COFFEE AND TEA (ESPECIALLY EARL GREY)
- DRIED FRUIT (ESPECIALLY DRIED APRICOTS AND PEARS)
- FRESH FRUIT (ESPECIALLY RASPBERRIES AND PEARS)
- ALCOHOL (ESPECIALLY RUM, CRÈME DE CACAO, COGNAC, AND VODKA)
- HERBS (ROSEMARY, MINT, LAVENDER, AND BASIL)
- SPICES (CINNAMON, GINGER, VANILLA, SAFFRON, AND STAR ANISE)
- CHILES

braised monkfish with chocolate sauce

An interesting dish of braised fish in a smooth red wine and chocolate sauce with a hint of spice. Curiously enough, the chocolate gives the sauce a wonderfully silky texture but does not taste too sweet.

2 1/4 lb. monkfish (angler fish) fillet, cut into 1-inch cubes
1/4 cup olive oil
2/3 cup fish broth
2/3 cup veal broth (or chicken broth)
16 pearl onions, peeled
4 oz. bacon, cut into little strips
12 button mushrooms
1 oz. best-quality dark chocolate (at least 70% cocoa solids), grated
2 tablespoons chilled unsalted butter, cut into small pieces
1 tablespoon chopped parsley
Salt and freshly ground black pepper

FOR THE MARINADE:
1 3/4 cups red wine
2 1/2 cups orange juice
1 bay leaf
1 red chile, seeded and finely chopped
1 garlic clove, crushed
1 carrot, finely chopped
1 celery stalk, finely chopped
1 onion, finely chopped

Put the monkfish cubes in a bowl and pour the red wine and orange juice over them. Add all the remaining marinade ingredients, then cover and let marinate for 1 hour.

Strain the monkfish and vegetables, reserving the marinade. Heat the oil in a heavy, flameproof pan, add the monkfish, and season with salt and pepper. Fry for 2 minutes, then add the vegetables from the marinade and cook for 1 minute. Pour in the marinade and broth, cover with a lid, and simmer for 6–8 minutes, until the monkfish is cooked. Remove the fish and keep warm. Return the sauce to a boil, add the onions, then reduce the heat and simmer until the onions are tender and the sauce has thickened enough to coat the back of a spoon.

Heat a frying pan without any oil, add the bacon strips, and fry for 2–3 minutes, until crisp and golden. Add the mushrooms and fry until golden, then add to the sauce. Remove the sauce from the heat and stir in the grated chocolate, then beat in the butter until smooth. Return the monkfish to the sauce, sprinkle with the parsley, and serve.

mole poblano (turkey in chocolate sauce)

Turkey in chocolate sauce? It might sound outrageous but it is a treasured national dish of Mexico, dating from the seventeenth century, when it was prepared with over a hundred ingredients. Even today, it remains a favorite for weddings, baptisms, and other festive occasions. My version, by the way, is far less complicated but still wonderfully tasty. I like to serve it with white rice and freshly toasted tortillas. You could substitute chicken for the turkey, if you prefer.

SERVES 8–10

1 small turkey, about 9 lbs., cut into small serving pieces
4 garlic cloves (1 sliced, 3 crushed)
2 onions, roughly chopped
1/2 cup vegetable oil
1 cinnamon stick
1/4 teaspoon ground anise
2/3 cup almonds
1/2 cup peanuts
5 oz. dried ancho chiles, cut lengthwise in half and seeded
3 oz. dried pasilla chiles, cut lengthwise in half and seeded
2 oz. dried chipotle chiles, cut lengthwise in half and seeded
2 corn tortillas
14 oz. can of chopped tomatoes
2 oz. best-quality dark chocolate (at least 70% cocoa solids), grated
1 tablespoon sugar
2 tablespoons sesame seeds, toasted, for garnishing
Salt and freshly ground black pepper

Place the turkey pieces in a large pan with the sliced garlic and half the chopped onions. Cover with water and bring to a boil. Poach for up to 1 hour, until the turkey is just tender, then remove from the heat, drain and reserve the broth, and set aside.

For the sauce, heat 2 tablespoons of the oil in a large frying pan, add the turkey pieces, and fry until golden. Remove from the pan and set aside. Add the 3 crushed garlice cloves to the pan along with the remaining onions. Cook for 5–6 minutes, until softened, then add the cinnamon, anise, and nuts, and sauté for another 2–3 minutes.

In a separate pan, heat another tablespoon of the oil and fry the dried chiles over a low heat for 2 minutes, ensuring they do not burn or they will taste bitter. Place in a bowl, cover with hot water, and let soak for 30 minutes. Drain in a colander.

Now place the sweated onions, garlic, and nuts in a blender, add the corn tortillas, tomatoes, and soaked chiles, and blitz to a fine purée. Heat the remaining oil in a large pan, add the purée, and bring to a boil. Reduce the heat and simmer for 5 minutes, then add the chocolate and 2 1/2 cups of the turkey broth. Stir in the sugar and some salt and pepper. Return the turkey pieces to the sauce and reheat gently for 20 minutes. If the sauce is too thick, add a little more broth.

Transfer to a serving bowl, sprinkle with the toasted sesame seeds, and serve.

Paul's Tip If you can't get hold of the dried chiles, replace with one teaspoon dried chili powder

chocolate rosemary custards

SERVES 8

$^2/_3$ cup sweet white wine
$^2/_3$ cup whole milk
$1^1/_4$ cups heavy cream
2 teaspoons chopped rosemary
6 egg yolks
$^1/_4$ cup sugar
5 oz. good-quality milk chocolate, coarsely chopped

Put the wine, milk, cream, and rosemary in a saucepan and bring slowly to a boil. Set side and let infuse for 10 minutes. In a bowl, beat together the egg yolks and sugar until creamy. Strain the milk mixture onto the egg and sugar mixture, beating constantly. Return to the pan and cook, stirring, over a low heat until the mixture has thickened enough to coat the back of the spoon (do not let it boil or it will curdle).

Put the chocolate in a bowl, pour the thickened custard over it, and leave for 2–3 minutes to let the chocolate melt. Stir it gently, so it doesn't become aerated. Pour into 8 small tea cups or ramekins and leave in the fridge overnight. Serve chilled.

no-nonsense chocolate soufflé

The thought of making a soufflé is a frightening one for many cooks—such a complicated procedure and the worry of a collapsed mess at the end. This recipe is made from just four ingredients, plus a little confectioners' sugar for dusting, and is simple in every sense. Try it!

2 tablespoons unsalted butter, plus extra for greasing
Confectioners' sugar for dusting
5 oz. good-quality dark chocolate (at least 40% cocoa solids)
6 eggs, separated
$2^1/_2$ tablespoons sugar

Preheat the oven to 400°F. Generously butter four 1-cup soufflé dishes or ramekins and lightly dust them with confectioners' sugar. Set aside.

Break up the chocolate and put it in a bowl along with the butter. Set the bowl over a pan of gently simmering water and let it melt. (Alternatively you could melt the chocolate and butter in the top of a double boiler or in a microwave.)

Put the egg yolks and $1^1/_2$ tablespoons of the sugar in a large bowl, set over another pan of hot water, and beat with an electric beater until the mixture has thickened and doubled in volume. Remove from the heat. Pour the melted chocolate onto the egg yolks and fold it in.

In a separate clean bowl and with clean beaters, beat the egg whites with the remaining sugar until they form stiff peaks, then fold them carefully into the chocolate mixture with a large metal spoon. Pour the mixture into the prepared soufflé dishes so they are three-quarters full, then place on a baking sheet. Place in the oven to bake for 10–12 minutes, until well risen and beautifully light. Dust with confectioners' sugar and serve immediately.

Paul's Tip At the Lanesborough, vanilla icecream is a particular favorite with chocolate soufflé and I find raspberry sorbet always complements it well, too.

velvet chocolate mousse with mint glass wafers

A new twist on the After Eight, no less! A rich, creamy mousse, sandwiched between the crispest mint wafers imaginable. Chocolate and mint are a great combination. Serve with vanilla custard, if you like.

1 1/2 cups heavy cream
1 1/2 cups whole milk
6 egg yolks
1/2 cup sugar
2 gelatin leaves
13 oz. good-quality dark chocolate (at least 70% cocoa solids), chopped

FOR THE MINT GLASS WAFERS:

2 tablespoons mint leaves
1/3 cup (3/4 cup) unsalted butter
1/3 cup golden syrup
1/4 cup crème de menthe
1 cup sugar
3/4 cup all-purpose flour

Bring the cream and milk to a boil in a saucepan. In a separate bowl, beat together the egg yolks and sugar until light and creamy. Beating constantly, pour in the cream and milk and stir well. Return to the pan and cook, stirring, over low heat, until the mixture has thickened enough to coat the back of the spoon (do not let it boil or it will curdle). Remove from the heat.

Cover the gelatin leaves with cold water and let soak for 5 minutes. Drain well, squeezing out excess water, and add to the custard mixture. Stir well to dissolve the gelatin.

Place the chocolate pieces in a bowl, pour the hot custard over them, and let melt, stirring occasionally. When all the chocolate has melted, strain the mixture through a fine strainer into a bowl. Let cool, then cover with plastic wrap and place in the fridge for at least 4 hours, until set.

To make the wafers, blanch the mint leaves for 10 seconds in a pan of boiling water, then drain well, refresh in iced water, and pat dry. Chop finely and set aside. Put the butter, golden syrup and crème de menthe in a saucepan and heat gently until the butter has melted. Mix the sugar and flour together in a bowl, then pour in the syrup mixture, add the chopped mint and stir well to form a paste. Cover with plastic wrap and leave in the fridge for about 1 hour, until very cold.

Preheat the oven to 350°F. Remove the wafer dough from the fridge and, using the palms of your hands, shape into 12 balls, 1 inch in diameter. Place them well spaced out on 2 cookie sheets lined with baking parchment, and press each one out with your fingers to form a small disc; as they cook they will spread out into thin wafers. Bake for 8–10 minutes, until pale golden, then remove from the oven and let them cool and crisp up. Store in a sealed container until ready to use.

To serve, place one mint wafer on each serving plate, top with a scoop of chocolate mousse, then another cookie, and then another scoop of mousse (you will probably find that there is some mousse left over but it won't hang around for long!). Finally, top with the last wafer.

Paul's Tip You will probably have some of the wafer dough left over. Shape it into balls, as above, and then store in the fridge or freezer, ready to bake.

chocolate and hazelnut polenta

This rich chocolate and cornmeal dessert comes from South America. It has the characteristics of a soufflé but not quite the lightness. It is, however, utterly delicious and very addictive!

SERVES 8

1 lb. good-quality dark chocolate (at least 40% cocoa solids)
1/2 cup Nutella (or other chocolate-hazelnut spread)
1/3 cup (3/4 stick) unsalted butter, plus extra for greasing
1/3 cup quick-cook cornmeal (polenta)
1 1/4 cups whole milk
6 egg yolks
8 egg whites
1/2 cup sugar, plus extra for dusting

FOR SERVING:

Vanilla or hazelnut icecream
Chocolate sauce (see page 180)

Preheat the oven to 400°F. Break up the chocolate and put it in the top of a double boiler or in a bowl set over a pan of gently simmering water. Let melt, then stir in the Nutella.

Meanwhile, melt the butter in a saucepan, stir in the cornmeal, and cook for 2–3 minutes. Stir in the milk, reduce the heat and cook, stirring, over low heat for 5–10 minutes, until thickened. Stir the cooked cornmeal into the chocolate mixture, then beat in the egg yolks one at a time.

Generously butter eight 3-inch ramekins, dust with superfine suga,r and set aside. With an electric beater, beat the egg whites until stiff, adding the sugar gradually. Fold the egg whites into the chocolate cornmeal mixture. Fill the prepared ramekins with the mixture and bake for 20–25 minutes, until the tops begin to split. Serve hot, topped with a good dollop of vanilla or hazelnut icecream and some chocolate sauce.

chocolate and ginger cheesecake

For me, chocolate has always had a great affinity with ginger, and I use them in many combinations. Here is one of my particular favorites.

SERVES 6–8

6 oz. chocolate chip cookies, crushed finely in a food processor
1/4 cup (1/2 stick) unsalted butter, melted
14 oz. good-quality dark chocolate (at least 50% cocoa solids)
2 oz. (1/3-1/2 cup) confectioners' sugar
3 pieces of preserved ginger, finely chopped
2 tablespoons syrup from the ginger jar
1/4 cup dark rum
1 cup fromage frais (if unavailable, use low-fat, sour cream)
1/2 whipping cream, semi-whipped

FOR SERVING:

Whipped cream
Cocoa powder

Oil the inside of an 8-inch removable-bottomed tart pan, line the bottom with waxed paper, and oil again. Mix together the crushed cookies and melted butter, then press the mixture over the bottom of the pan. Place in the fridge to set firm.

Break up the chocolate, put it in the top of a double boiler or in a large bowl and place it over a pan of gently simmering water. Add the confectioners' sugar, ginger, ginger syrup, and rum, and stir until the chocolate has melted and the mixture is smooth and glossy. Remove from the heat and let cool, stirring occasionally.

Beat in the fromage frais, then fold in the semi-whipped cream. Pour into the pan, cover, and place in the fridge for about 3 hours, until set firm. To serve, carefully remove the cheesecake from the pan and cut into wedges. Place on serving plates, top with whipped cream, and dust with cocoa powder.

chocolate-dipped florentines

MAKES 20

9 oz. unsalted butter
1/2 cup sugar
1/4 cup chestnut honey (or other honey)
3 tablespoons liquid glucose (if unavailable, use corn syrup)
3 tablespoons heavy cream
5 oz. (1 cup) candied mixed peel, finely chopped
5 oz. (1 1/3 cups) hazelnuts, finely chopped
1 1/4 cups sliced almonds
1 x 3 1/2 oz. best-quality dark chocolate (at least 70% cocoa solids)

Preheat the oven to 350°F. Line a shallow baking pan, about 8 x 10 inches with baking parchment. Melt the butter in a heavy saucepan, add the sugar, honey, glucose, and cream, and bring to a boil. Boil rapidly until the mixture reaches 230°F on a sugar thermometer. Remove from the heat, stir in the candied peel and nuts, and let stand for 1 minute.

Using a spatula, spread the mixture into the lined baking pan, then place in the oven and bake for about 25 minutes, until golden and caramelized. Remove from the oven and let cool completely. Cut into twenty 2-inch squares.

Break up the chocolate and put it in the top of a double boiler or in a bowl set over a pan of gently simmering water. Stir until melted, then remove from the heat. Dip each florentine into the chocolate, coating just half of it. Place on a wire rack and let them set. Store in an airtight container.

white chocolate and wild blackberry muffins

MAKES 18

3 cups all-purpose flour
1 1/2 cups confectioners' sugar
2 1/2 teaspoons baking powder
A pinch of salt
1 egg
1/3 cup (3/4 stick) unsalted butter, melted
1 cup whole milk
4 oz. wild blackberries (or frozen blackberries)
3 oz. good-quality white chocolate, coarsely chopped

Preheat the oven to 400°F. Sift the flour, sugar, baking powder, and salt into a large bowl. In another bowl, beat the egg until aerated, then gradually beat in the warm melted butter and the milk. Add to the dry ingredients and mix until only just combined (overmixing will make the muffins tougher in texture). Fold in the berries and chocolate pieces, again being careful not to overmix.

Spoon the mixture into 18 well-buttered deep muffin cups, filling them two-thirds full. Bake for about 20 minutes, until well risen and golden brown. To check if they are done, insert a toothpick or skewer in the center; it should come out clean. Cool the muffins in the tin for a few minutes, then turn out onto a wire rack. They are best served warm, although they are good cold, too.

white chocolate and basil profiteroles with hot chocolate sauce

White chocolate and basil make an interesting twist on this much-loved dessert. The beauty of it is that it can be prepared in advance over several days.

SERVES 4–6

FOR THE WHITE CHOCOLATE AND BASIL ICECREAM:

10 basil leaves
1 cup heavy cream
3/4 cup whole milk
7 oz. good-quality white chocolate, broken into small pieces
4 egg yolks
2 tablespoons superfine sugar

FOR THE CHOUX PASTRY:

1 cup minus 2 tablespoons whole milk
1/4 cup (1/2 stick) unsalted butter, chopped
1 1/2 cups sugar
1 cup all-purpose flour
4 eggs
1 egg yolk, beaten with 2 tablespoons milk
2 tablespoons sliced almonds

FOR THE CHOCOLATE SAUCE:

3 1/2 oz. good-quality dark chocolate (at least 40% cocoa solids)
1/2 tablespoon sugar
1/3 cup heavy cream
A small pat of butter

To make the icecream, tear the basil leaves into small pieces, reserving the stalks, and set aside. Put the stalks in a saucepan along with the cream and milk, bring gently to a boil and simmer for 1 minute. Add the white chocolate, stir well, then remove from the heat and let infuse for 10 minutes.

In a bowl, beat together the egg yolks and sugar until creamy. Strain the basil-infused cream onto the egg yolks, beating constantly, then return to the pan and cook, stirring, over low heat, until the mixture thickens (do not let it boil or it will curdle). Remove from the heat and let cool. Stir in the torn basil leaves, pour into an icecream machine and freeze according to the manufacturer's instructions.

Next make the choux pastry dough. Preheat the oven to 400°F. Put the milk, butter, and sugar in a medium pan and bring to a boil. As soon as it reaches a boil, quickly sprinkle in the flour and beat with a wooden spoon until the mixture leaves the sides of the pan clean. Let cool slightly, then beat in the eggs one by one to give a thick, glossy mixture.

Lightly oil a baking sheet and then sprinkle it with a little water so it is slightly damp. Fit a pastry bag with a 1-inch plain nozzle and fill it with the choux pastry dough. Pipe walnut-sized mounds on to the baking sheet at regular intervals, brush with a little of the beaten egg wash, and sprinkle the sliced almonds over them. Place in the oven and bake for 15 minutes, then open the oven door slightly and leave for another 10 minutes so that the profiteroles can dry out. Remove from the oven, pierce each profiterole with a skewer so the steam can escape, then let cool (if you make them in advance, store in a cookie tin).

For the chocolate sauce, place all the ingredients in a pan and bring gently to a boil, then beat until smooth, adding a little boiling water if it is too thick.

To serve, cut each profiterole in half horizontally (allowing about 3 per person), fill with a ball of the icecream and top with the lid. Arrange on serving plates and pour the hot chocolate sauce over and around them—pure indulgence!

Paul's Tip If you don't have an icecream machine, pour the icecream mixture into a bowl and place it in the freezer. After 30 minutes, when it is beginning to set, remove it from the freezer and beat well with an electric beater or immersion blender to disperse any ice crystals, then return it to the freezer. Repeat this 2 or 3 times, then leave until set firm.

index